BEYOND
WESTMINSTER
IN THE CARIBBEAN

BEYOND
WESTMINSTER
IN THE CARIBBEAN

edited by

Brian Meeks

•

Kate Quinn

IAN RANDLE PUBLISHERS

Kingston • Miami

First published in Jamaica, 2018 by
Ian Randle Publishers
16 Herb McKenley Drive
Box 686
Kingston 6
www.ianrandlepublishers.com

© Brian Meeks • Kate Quinn
ISBN: 978-976-637-956-8

National Library of Jamaica Cataloguing-In-Publication Data

Beyond Westminster in the Caribbean / edited by Brian Meeks, Kate
   Quinn.

   p. ; cm
Includes index
ISBN 978-976-637-956-8 (pbk)

1. Caribbean, English-speaking – Politics and government
2. Democracy – Caribbean, English-speaking
3. Representative government and representation – Caribbean,
    English-speaking
I. Meeks, Brian   II. Quinn, Kate

321.8   dc 23

Book and Cover Design by Ian Randle Publishers
Printed and Bound in the United States of America

Contents

List of Tables

Preface
Questioning Westminster

Brian Meeks

The contemporary history of constitutional reform in the Commonwealth Caribbean, at least since the emergence of the first independence constitutions in Jamaica and Trinidad and Tobago in 1962, has been intense and fraught.[1] There is a well-known but little referenced speech,[2] which then Jamaican Premier Norman Manley gave in January 1962 to the House of Representatives detailing the draft features that would become the Jamaica Independence Constitution, Order in Council, 1962. In it is compactly captured, either in the form of positive assertion or defensive opposition, all of the critical debates that surrounded the preparation of that critical document that helped determine not only the framework for Jamaica's political future but by being the first, significantly set the template for the future direction of Caribbean constitutional and, by implication, political history.

Thus, at the very start, Manley's comments are defensive on the speed with which the Constitution was drafted, in which most decisions were taken at the first meeting of the Committee in October 1961 and a final document tabled before the UK Parliament on July 24, 1962 – a mere ten months later. His argument was that the country had been travelling on the road of constitutional reform for some time and legislators at least, were familiar with all its critical requirements and, therefore, there was consensual agreement on almost all points.[3] He continued to commend the involvement of the public (though hardly massive, with 30-odd people making submissions on the first day and only 78 memoranda in all[4]), without reference to the deeply restrictive character of the deliberative process, the exclusion of the press from access to the Committee's discussions and minutes and the absence of any genuinely public deliberation and debate. The critical features of Jamaica's political and legal framework, beginning with the exclusive nature of this drafting, were therefore decided largely *in camera* with profound implications for the future direction of the country's politics.[5]

Many of the other features of that first few hours of rapid deliberation remain in place to this day, including:

1. The absence of an indigenous or autochthonous frame of reference, captured in the notion that Jamaicans had been steeped in Westminster traditions and most egregiously evident in the retention of the British Monarchy as the sovereign, with both legal and symbolic implications for any notion of substantial independence.

2. The conscious decision to go for the powerful, quasi-dictatorial cabinet/prime ministerial form of government and to reject the presidential form. Manley's noteworthy conclusion was that while the US President was not answerable to Parliament, he was subject to tremendous limitations, imposed by the separation of powers and the independence of both legislative and judicial arms, with implications for the smooth governability of the country.[6] In other words, the expediency of the smooth execution of policy was chosen over a path that might have allowed for compromise and consensus-building.

3. The retention of a conservative bi-cameral legislature. The Senate, both in its conception as a nominated upper house which nonetheless can forestall legislation, closely mimicking the House of Lords model, undermined the principle of representative democracy in which the MPs presumably make the law on the people's behalf. The notion in the Jamaican case that the Senate's membership is divided between only two parties – the government majority and the opposition minority – rigidly excluding third parties, locked into place a particular historical political alignment as a permanent legal feature.

4. The clear skewing of both the deliberative process and critical provisions in the interest of elites, such as the manner in which the Bill of Rights was enacted in order to satisfy demands of foreign and local capital that property rights should be deeply entrenched.[7]

5. The parallel entrenching of the first past the post, constituency-based parliamentary electoral system, with its winner takes all provisions, with implications that were already apparent for the division of the populace into sharply divided and hostile 'tribal' factions.

The years subsequent to the 1960s have led to accumulated experiences of the weaknesses and dangers associated with Westminster-centralized power and first-past-the-post exclusivity and have witnessed a series of political and theoretical efforts to address, rethink, and challenge many of these provisions. The questions arising from these debates, many of which are posed in this collection, all remain relevant and among them:

While Westminster in the Caribbean has undoubtedly provided a degree of stability, facilitated regular transitions of power and avoided for the most part the occurrence of military coups when viewed in comparison to the political trajectories of other postcolonial countries and regions,[8] what is the price that has been paid?

How much of that relative stability is to be placed at the doorstep of Westminster and how much is owed to other features of Caribbean society from which the political system has benefited?

What cost has arisen from the avoidance of the weaker executive of the US Presidential system? What, in other words, would a less dictatorial, more consensual, political executive have meant for broadly 'national' projects of development that would have been forced to find ways to compromise with legislatures, bend to the laws of the judiciary, and involve the opposition and hostile social and political sectors in decision-making?

What could a more democratic system of governing look like that went beyond the limited notion of 'representation' to incorporate expansive notions of popular participation, beginning with broad constitutional conventions involving the populations of the diaspora, incorporating radical approaches to opinion gathering and decision-making, including internet participation and crowd-sourcing[9] and addressing radical provisions such as the recall of non-performing representatives and the popular proposal of new legislation?[10]

What would a Bill of Rights, starting not with the entrenching of the will of the elites, but soliciting popular opinion through wide education and popular involvement in its framing look like?

Conversely, what are the limitations of really thoroughgoing rights in societies with deeply conservative values held by large swathes of the population, including, outstandingly, extensive homophobic perspectives and widespread support for capital punishment?

To return to the federal experiment whose breakup led to insular independence in the first instance, what role is there for regional structures, not only or primarily for accumulating small states together for economic or 'critical mass' purposes, but more importantly for checking and balancing corruption and hometown decisions in tiny, insular jurisdictions?

What are the limitations of constitutional change as a means of addressing deep inequality and persistent poverty in the interlinked, globalized world of late capitalism? Is, in other words, the exercise of rethinking, proposing, and reforming constitutions futile, within the context of a socio-political system that leans inevitably towards deepening inequality and global marginalization?

To the last question alone, I suggest an answer: that if the efforts towards constitutional debate and reform move beyond the limiting, elitist framework that was adapted in 1961–62, then they become qualitatively wider platforms and projects that might involve in the future huge, unanticipated sectors of the Caribbean population in genuine debate about not only how one is governed but how one lives. That, I suggest, is neither pointless nor futile, but may be the beginning of a process of education and popular involvement that could lead to not only new and unanticipated ways of governing, but new creative answers to the questions as to what are the purposes of community, what are the benefits of social living and how to make the Caribbean a place worth living in and fighting for in the twenty first century and beyond.

NOTES

1. See, for instance, Selwyn Ryan, *Winner Takes All: The Westminster Experience in the Caribbean* (St Augustine, Trinidad: ISER, 1999) and Simeon McIntosh, *Caribbean Constitutional Reform: Rethinking the West Indian Polity* (Kingston: The Caribbean Law Publishing Company, 2002).

2. See Rex Nettleford, ed. *Manley and the New Jamaica: Selected Speeches and Writings 1938–1968* (Trinidad and Jamaica: Longman Caribbean, 1971), 296–311.

3. See ibid., 298–99.

4. Ibid.

5. See Trevor Munroe, *The Politics of Constitutional Decolonization: Jamaica, 1944–1962* (Kingston: Institute of Social and Economic Research, 1983).

6. See Nettleford, *Manley and the New Jamaica*, 300.

7. See Munroe, *The Politics of Constitutional Decolonization*, 156–62.

8. See Jorge Dominguez, 'The Caribbean Question: Why has Liberal Democracy (Surprisingly) Flourished?' in *Democracy in the Caribbean: Political, Economic and Social Perspectives*, ed. Jorge Dominguez, Robert Pastor and Delisle Worrell (Baltimore: Johns Hopkins University Press, 1993), 1–25.

9. The 2010 attempt to redraft the Icelandic Constitution involving ordinary citizens in both the drafting and election of a constitutional council is a remarkable if flawed attempt to write a constitution from below. Its efforts and failures are worth noting, particularly in the context of small states. See

Giulia Dessi, 'The Icelandic Constitutional Experiment', *Open Democracy* http://www.opendemocracy.net, October 23, 2012.

10. See, for instance, Brian Meeks, *Envisioning Caribbean Futures: Jamaican Perspectives* (Kingston: The University of the West Indies Press, 2007), 108–160.

Acronyms and Abbreviations

ACCP	Assembly of Caribbean Community Parliamentarians
ACP	African, Caribbean and Pacific Group of States
AGM	Annual General Meeting
APNU	A Partnership for National Unity
BRICS	Brazil, Russia, India, China, and South Africa
CARICOM	Caribbean Community
CBI	Caribbean Basin Initiative
CCJ	Caribbean Court of Justice
CEMIU	Customs and Excise Marine Interdiction Unity
CIA	Central Intelligence Agency
CIVETS	Colombia, Indonesia, Vietnam, Egypt, Turkey, and South Africa
CLC	Caribbean Labour Congress
CPEP	Community Empowerment Protection and Enhancement Programme
CRC	Constitutional Reform Commission
CRSC	Constitutional Reform Steering Committee
CSF	Civil Society Forum
CSME	Caribbean Single Market and Economy
DEA	Drug Enforcement Agency
DPP	Director of Public Prosecutions
DLP	Democratic Labour Party
EDF	European Development Fund
EPA	Economic Partnership Agreement
HOG	Heads of Government
IFI	International Financial Institutions
IMF	International Monetary Fund

INDECOM	Independent Commission for Investigations
JCPC	Judicial Committee of the Privy Council
JLP	Jamaica Labour Party
MIST	Mexico, Indonesia, South Korea, and Turkey
MMM	Mixed-member Majoritarian
MMP	Mixed-member Proportional
NNP	New National Party
OAS	Organization of American States
OECS	Organisation of Eastern Caribbean States
OPEC	Organization of the Petroleum Exporting Countries
PNM	People's National Movement
PNP	People's National Party
PUP	People's Unity Party
RTC	Revised Treaty of Chaguaramas
SCL	Strategic Communications Laboratories
TCA	Telecommunications (Amendment) Act
TCCTP	Targeted Conditional Cash Transfer Programme (see gov.tt)
TCN	Transnational Criminal Networks
ToC	Treaty of Chaguaramas
UCL	University College London
UDP	United Democratic Party
ULP	United Labour Party
UNC	United National Congress
URP	Unemployment Relief Programme (see gov.tt)
UWI	University of the West Indies
WFTU	World Federation of Trade Unions
WSF	World Social Forum
WTO	World Trade Organization
YTEPP	Youth Training and Employment Programme Partnership (see ytepp.edu.tt)

1 Introduction:

Beyond Westminster in the Caribbean

Kate Quinn

This book examines the experience of democratic governance in the Commonwealth Caribbean in the last few decades of crisis and change. The need to revisit old questions about the form and, more importantly, substance of Westminster-style democracy in the Caribbean is all the more urgent given the radical shifts in the global environment that have had serious consequences for governance in these vulnerable small states. The late Norman Girvan summed this up most incisively in his reflections on the 'existential threats' that pose 'systemic challenges to the viability of [Caribbean] states as functioning socio-economic-ecological-political systems'. The contemporary Caribbean, Girvan argued, faces 'an overlapping and interconnected series of challenges' deriving from 'acute climate change-related stress' and:

> (a) the acute economic stress arising out of erosion of trade preferences and the failure to develop a new "insertion" into the global economy; (b) fiscal stress due to unsustainable debt burdens and the impact of the global economic crisis; and (c) the seeming incapacity of governments to control the impact of transnational crime....[1]

To these challenges might be added the uncertainties arising from recent changes in the global political environment, including the election of an unpredictable and openly anti-immigration president of the United States (US) in November 2016; and Britain's vote to leave the European Union, the consequences of which may have profound implications for the African, Caribbean and Pacific (ACP) group of states whose primary trade relations are bound up with European treaties now being unpicked by the former colonial powers.

The Brexit referendum and resultant political tremors at the heart of the 'original' Westminster system make a re-examination of models of governance all the more timely. The 52 per cent 'leave' vote on June 23, 2016 catalysed a series of debates touching on the fundamentals of Westminster parliamentary democracy. These debates centred on questions of representative versus participatory democracy, the supremacy of Parliament, the utility and authority of referenda, the role of the judiciary, national sovereignty and the relationship with a supranational and 'unelected' regional entity. All of these subjects can find echoes in recent Caribbean political debate, while Caribbean political leaders may well find sobering lessons in the consequences of elite detachment from marginalised groups now vocally asserting the will of 'the people'.

In recent years, Caribbean governments have faced their own series of challenges that have raised direct questions about the functioning and resilience of the Westminster model in the Caribbean context. Trinidad and Tobago, St Lucia, and Dominica, for example, have all experienced political corruption scandals in recent years, raising familiar questions about democratic accountability, (lack of) parliamentary oversight, clientelism, and the over-reach of prime ministerial authority. The proclamation of the notorious 'Section 34' on the 50th anniversary of Trinidadian independence gave added pungency to this particular scandal: the early proclamation of this section of the Indictable Proceedings Act allowed key party financiers to file petitions to have outstanding charges of fraud and money-laundering levied against them dismissed.[2] In Dominica, opposition demonstrations protesting the dubious dealings of the government in the sale of passports were denounced by the prime minister as an 'attempted coup';[3] the resultant arrests of senior members of the opposition exemplify an alarming process of authoritarian creep within the framework of Westminster democracy. In Guyana, the constitutional crisis resulting from the suspension of Parliament in November 2014, ultimately led to an historic defeat of the incumbent regime, bringing to an end 23 consecutive years of one-party rule. The defeated party's initial refusal to accept the election results and boycott of the swearing-in ceremony of new President David Granger, however, suggests that Guyana's 'democratic contradiction' is far from being resolved.[4] And in Grenada, a referendum in November 2016 produced an overwhelming 'no' vote to 'seven pieces of legislation that would have reformed the Constitution the island received when it attained political independence from Britain 42 years ago', including proposals to replace the Privy Council with the Caribbean Court of Justice (CCJ) as the final court of appeal, the introduction of term limits for the prime minister, fixed dates for elections, and the expansion of individual rights and freedoms, including protections relating to gender equality and the rights of the child.[5] The electorate's rejection of the proposed amendments prompts critical questions about popular engagement with the reform agenda and whether there is something in the Westminster system itself that has militated against attempts to reform it.

The above examples provide mixed lessons on the performance and quality of Westminster democracy in the contemporary Caribbean. On the one hand, the examples of alleged corruption in Trinidad and Tobago and Dominica suggest a decomposition of democracy within the framework of Westminster rule; on the other, the role played by civil society in holding both administrations to account may denote a positive adherence to, and assertion of, fundamental democratic norms. In Guyana, the crisis of 2014 holds lessons in both the abuse of constitutional powers, and in the capacity of the electoral system to throw out administrations perceived to be engaged in such abuse. And in Grenada, the defeat of the constitutional amendments might speak to the resilience of the Westminster model, or to its stagnation and inability to reform. Such tensions and contradictions in the form and practice of Westminster rule are the subject of analysis in this volume. Can the Westminster model survive and thrive in the contemporary Caribbean, or is it time to move beyond Westminster?

Looking beyond Westminster in the Caribbean

This book is the product of two conferences on the history, legacies, and contemporary realities of the experience of Westminster-style governance in the Commonwealth Caribbean. Held at University College London (UCL) and in Kingston at the University of the West Indies, Mona (UWI),[6] the conferences responded to critical questions about the performance and efficacy of the Westminster model in the Caribbean context. In Jamaica, the discussion centred on the challenges of governance in the twenty-first century, a period in which the capacity to govern – and indeed the very sovereignty of the state – has been considerably weakened by the forces of globazsation. As many of the contributors to this book emphasize, the conditions in which democracy is practised in the contemporary Caribbean have fundamentally altered since the period of state-led development that followed independence. The end of the Cold War, the erosion of preferential trade arrangements, the collapse of previously protected staple industries, and the ideological and economic imperatives of neoliberalism have established a new environment in which the size, role, autonomy, and authority of the state have been diminished, reducing the capacity of national governments to pursue local priorities.[7] This qualitative shift requires a new analysis of the functioning of Westminster democracy in the Caribbean, modifying the conclusions of earlier scholarship on the Westminster model that spoke largely to the concerns of a different epoch in Caribbean political development.[8]

This book, then, provides an expanded and updated analysis of the experience of Westminster governance in the post-Cold War Commonwealth Caribbean, adding to the new body of scholarship on this theme represented in recent works by (among others) David Hinds (2008), Matthew Bishop (2010), Cynthia Barrow-Giles (2011), and Paul Sutton (2013); and complementing research initiatives such as the Fifty/Fifty Project based at the University of the West Indies.[9] The volume presented here brings together contributions by distinguished scholars of Caribbean politics, several of whom have played active roles in national and regional processes of political reform, and by prominent serving politicians (including one sitting prime minister, one former prime minister, and one leader of the opposition and former cabinet minister), all of whom have experienced the challenges of Westminster governance from the frontline. Together, these contributions offer reflections on (a) the weaknesses of the Westminster model, particularly in relation to the new global and regional challenges of the last few decades; (b) the persistence of Westminster, its rootedness in the region and the apparent absence of a popular will to change; and (c) proposals to move beyond Westminster, whether through incremental reform, or through a radical abandonment of the system as a whole. If, as the contributors agree, Westminster in the Caribbean is ailing, what might be the cure? Is moving beyond Westminster either achievable or desirable?

Westminster Deficient

Regardless of their position on the political spectrum, all the contributors here agree that the existing political system is flawed. With regards to the formal institutions and structures of democratic rule, there is a broad consensus on the weaknesses of the Westminster system in the Commonwealth Caribbean context, including the distorting effects of the first-past-the-post electoral system; the divisiveness of partisan politics and 'winner takes all'; the excessive powers of the prime minister; dominance of the executive over the legislature; the failure to promote accountability and counter the entrenchment of corruption in public life; and the absence of mechanisms to encourage meaningful participation in governance by the ordinary citizen beyond the act of entering a mark on the ballot paper once every five years.[10] There is consensus, too, on the need to enhance the quality of democracy experienced by the citizenry as a whole, and to make good on delivering the basic rights and freedoms that constitutions are meant to enshrine. Looking back on a long political career in Jamaica, former Prime Minister Bruce Golding (chapter six) laments the failure of postcolonial Westminster governance to secure 'basic human rights for the ordinary citizen', a sentiment echoed in the contribution by his opposition counterpart, Peter Phillips, who queries 'the extent to which constitutionally guaranteed rights [have] actually [been] enjoyed by the populace' (chapter five). Though neither is likely to agree with Percy C. Hintzen's radical rejection of the Westminster system (chapter ten), his assertion that the quality of governance must be measured by its effects on the governed finds resonance across the contributions, despite their political differences.

The diminishing power of national governments is a concern raised across the collection. Hintzen, Tennyson S.D. Joseph, and Clifford E. Griffin all emphasize changes in the global environment and the ability of powerful international actors to dictate the terms of governance in the Caribbean. For Hintzen, the role of postcolonial governments in the Caribbean has been fundamentally shaped (and limited) by the 'networks of neo-colonial and imperialist relations' in which they are inscribed. Responding to the demands of 'powerful global interests' that have reduced the practice of governance 'almost exclusively to the pursuit of growth in production, consumption, and accumulation', Caribbean governments have been severely constrained in their capacity to consolidate and expand 'substantive freedoms' and the 'conditions for genuine development', which, for Hintzen, are the benchmarks of a genuinely achieved democracy. Hintzen's concerns are echoed in the contribution by Joseph, who notes that '[critical] decisions impacting the lives of Caribbean people are now being made more and more in the IMF, World Bank, and the G20, rather than in domestic cabinet rooms'; and in the contribution by Griffin, who asserts that the 'hardships inflicted by neoliberal reforms have weakened the state and limited its ability to pursue national development alongside democracy'. All three raise critical questions about the determining force of international interests, the erosion of state capacity, and the relationship between democracy and development. While Joseph emphasizes the role of powerful international financial institutions, Griffin highlights the nefarious impact of illegal actors, arguing that weakened Caribbean states have been peculiarly vulnerable to 'state capture' by transnational crime networks (TNCs), with devastating implications for democracy. Taking examples from Jamaica and Trinidad and Tobago, Griffin argues that '[perhaps] no other complex phenomenon...threatens to undermine the two-generation old democratic political system in the Caribbean than TNC-related armed violence'. Whether the Westminster system is 'modified or jettisoned', he concludes, is immaterial in a context where 'companies, institutions or powerful individuals' can 'shape a country's policy, legal environment and economy to their own interests'.

The question of where real power is located also informs the analyses presented by Derek O'Brien and Patsy Lewis, whose chapters explore how the Westminster system and its governance outcomes are affected by the 'dynamic interface between regional and national politics'. There is growing consensus among scholars sympathetic to the regional project that the major challenges facing the Caribbean – including transnational crime, environmental vulnerability, negative growth rates, increased debt burdens, and high levels of unemployment in the region – can only be effectively tackled by a coordinated regional response.[11] At the same time, however, it is widely acknowledged that progress on regional integration has been painfully slow. The contribution by Lewis revisits the question of the Caribbean Community's (CARICOM's) 'implementation deficit', providing a novel analysis of how central features of the Westminster model have served to inhibit the regional integration project. Expanding scholarship on the Westminster model, which tends to confine its analysis to the national level, Lewis shows how the divisive effects of the first-past-the-post system and the predominance of the prime minister are carried over into the regional domain, with negative implications for regional integration. Calling for a transformed and democratized regional decision-making process that would give more space to opposition and civil society voices, Lewis proposes that 'any progress towards a new form of regional governance...is contingent on national constitutional change or a regional structure that is able to overcome the effects of partisan politics'.

The chapter by Derek O'Brien, by contrast, emphasizes not the weaknesses but the growing strengths of regional institutions relative to the powers of national Parliaments. Analyses of the Westminster model in the Caribbean universally emphasize the weakness of the legislative branch of government, most often attributing this to the dominance of the executive and the lack of separation between the two branches in a small state context. Little attention has been paid to the judicial branch of government and the role that national and supra-national judiciaries might play in the democratic process – not only as a check and balance on executive power, but as active agents shaping such democratic fundamentals as the interpretation of national constitutions, the definition and enforcement of citizenship rights, and access to a broad range of rights and freedoms. As O'Brien's chapter shows, tensions between national law and CARICOM law raise important questions about the sovereignty and supremacy of Parliament assumed by the Westminster model. Analysing recent rulings by the CCJ on matters relating to constitutional reform, O'Brien observes 'a significant encroachment by the courts on Parliament's constitutional sphere', with the CCJ making 'remarkable in-roads into the law-making powers of Commonwealth Caribbean Parliaments'. Efforts to deepen the regional integration project, he argues, have significant implications for the authority of national Parliaments, whose laws can be effectively trumped by decisions taken at regional level by CARICOM Heads of Government. The unintended consequence of such a shift, O'Brien suggests, may be a further diminution of the status and prestige of Parliaments, and, by extension, of the democratic process.

Beyond Westminster: Reform

Constitutional arrangements in the contemporary Commonwealth Caribbean display a remarkable continuity with the institutional structures established at independence. In a 2011 report on constitutional reform prepared for the Conflict Prevention and Peace Forum, the authors note that:

> The region has produced a total of sixteen new constitutions with Guyana and Trinidad and Tobago the only countries no longer operating under their independence constitutions. Including amendments, just four countries account for approximately seventy percent of all constitutional events (amendments or replacements) since 1962: Barbados, Guyana, Jamaica, and Trinidad and Tobago.[12]

While the period since the 1990s has witnessed 'a flurry of rhetoric and constitutional reform efforts in virtually every Caribbean country',[13] actual constitutional change, with some significant exceptions, has been limited and piecemeal. Further, several attempts at constitutional reform have been defeated by a popular vote, including, most recently, in Grenada, where seven bills covering various amendments were resoundingly defeated in the referendum of November 2016. Given that by and large the 'fundamental institutional structures [laid down at independence] remain unchanged',[14] it is difficult to assert that the region has moved much 'beyond Westminster', despite the considerable efforts of those committed to change.

Several chapters in this collection address the recent efforts at constitutional reform, and offer reflections on the slow pace of change. These reflections provide an invaluable insider perspective on the politics and mechanics of reform by persons intimately involved in attempts to modify, if not radically overhaul, the Westminster model in the Caribbean: Prime Minister Ralph Gonsalves, who details his government's attempt to push through an extensive package of constitutional reforms in St Vincent and the Grenadines between 2000 and 2009; former Prime Minister Bruce Golding and current Leader of the Opposition Peter Phillips, who grappled with Jamaica's constitutional review processes of the 1990s and 2000s from opposite sides of the parliamentary bench; and Cynthia Barrow-Giles, who served on St Lucia's Constitutional Reform Commission (CRC) from 2005 to 2011. Despite the rejection of recommended reforms (in the case of St Vincent and the Grenadines) or their minimal or delayed adoption (Jamaica, St Lucia), reflections on the process and content of previous CRCs offer valuable lessons for legislators engaged in present-day constitutional debates.

Cynthia Barrow-Giles provides an overview of various CRCs in the region over the last 20 years, focusing in particular on three areas of reform that could address longstanding critiques of the Westminster model: the electoral system and how to overcome the 'representational distortion' produced by the first-past-the-post method of election; the functioning of Parliament and how to reform its relationship with (a) the executive and (b) its constituents, to enhance democracy and accountability; and the case for and against introducing a system of fixed parliamentary terms. While acknowledging that CRCs 'do not generally recommend departure from Westminster', Barrow-Giles takes the view that there is 'an urgent case for constitutional reform in the Commonwealth Caribbean' if greater democracy and representation are to be achieved. The concrete measures she suggests – for example, replacing first-past-the-post with a 'mixed member system that combines plurality and proportionality' – do not seek to jettison the fundamental institutions of Westminster but rather to temper its negative elements 'while retaining its good features'. This is a case, in other words, for 'Westminster further modified', in keeping with the historical trajectory of post-independence constitutional reform in the region that has 'typically occurred in the form of amendments to existing constitutions rather than wholesale replacement of texts'.[15]

The chapter by Ralph Gonsalves offers first-hand analysis of one of the most extensive exercises in democratic reform to have taken place in the region in recent decades. By contrast with the formulation of the independence constitutions – negotiated in London by representatives of the incumbent and opposition political parties with little to no public input – post-independence efforts at constitutional amendment have made conscious efforts to engage 'the people' in whose name the constitutions are proclaimed. In St Vincent and the Grenadines, the United Labour Party (ULP) government engaged in 'extensive public consultations' on the proposed package of reforms, while ensuring that the Constitutional Reform Commission was populated not only by representatives of the government and opposition but also by members of civil society and the diaspora. Again, in contrast to the independence constitutions, which in their original form do not mention 'the people' at all, St Vincent and the Grenadines' proposed constitution codified in its opening preamble 'the assertion of the people as sovereign and as the true holders of power'.

Analysing the extensive suite of reforms that were put to the vote in St Vincent's 2009 referendum, it is possible to observe what a 'modified' variant of Westminster – borne out of and responsive to the particular concerns of the Caribbean – might look like. This includes a range of 'technical' measures dealing with such issues as the electoral system, election machinery and oversight, the responsibilities of parliamentary representatives, limitations on prime ministerial powers, integrity mechanisms, the creation of service commissions, delineation of the role of the attorney general, and so on. Among these structural/institutional provisions, was an innovative proposal to allow for 'the active participation of civil society invitees in the National Assembly' (clause 78), addressing, to a limited extent, the familiar complaint that political institutions have been for too long detached from the people they are meant to represent. The proposals also make some reference to social and economic rights which have been weakly represented in post-independence constitutions, including, for example, enshrining 'the striving for sustainable economic development and full employment' in the 'Guiding Principles of State Policy' that underpinned the proposed constitution. The St Vincent and the Grenadines constitution also represented a considered attempt to confront the 'colonial anachronism' that still overhangs the majority of Commonwealth Caribbean states: the continued retention of the British monarch as the symbolic head of state. Recognising the profound psychological impact of this colonial device, the draft St Vincent constitution framed the bid to terminate the relationship with the British Queen (and Privy Council) as 'an act of historical reclamation...proclaiming the authenticity and legitimacy of our Caribbean civilisation'.

It is important to note, however, that such claims of conformity to 'authentic' Caribbean values can also serve to legitimize such provisions as the legalisation of the death penalty, the definition of marriage as limited to 'persons biologically male at birth and biologically female at birth', and the absence of protections from discrimination on grounds of sexuality, as in the St Vincent proposals outlined by Prime Minister Gonsalves. The recent case of *Caleb Orozco v the Attorney General of Belize* (2016) may herald some changes with regards to the latter (the Belize Supreme Court ruling that the criminalization of homosexual intercourse contravenes basic constitutional rights),[16] but such a position is far from enjoying majority support in the region. In remaking Caribbean constitutions, then, the fundamental principles of democracy are at stake: on the one hand, guaranteeing the expression of the popular will of the majority; on the other, protecting the rights of the minority against that majority will.

Despite almost a decade of preparation, consultation and public debate, the St Vincent and the Grenadines constitutional proposals were defeated by a majority of 55 per cent in a referendum in November 2009. The recent rejection of the Grenadian reforms in the November 2016 referendum appears to confirm the historical pattern. Several explanations are offered to account for this cautious affirmation of the status quo. Both Golding and Phillips (with reference to Jamaica's reforms) point to the lack of popular demand for reform and the issue of public disengagement from elite-led processes of constitutional reform. Historical attachment to the Westminster model in the context of '250 years of colonial tutelage', according to Gonsalves, also goes some way to explaining the pattern of public votes, and the caution of policymakers whose proposals typically seek to modify rather than discard the existing model. As Barrow-Giles explains, in the case of St Lucia, members of the CRC concluded that they could not 'divorce [the] constitution from the political culture in which it is immersed', nor simply replace 'one foreign culture's constitution for another'. Available alternatives – be that the US model of executive presidency, or other Commonwealth models of proportional representation – were acknowledged to bring their own problems, with Westminster 'stability' preferred to the potential for instability and deadlock that might come with the translation of other forms to the partisan Caribbean context.[17] This stability – reflected in the region's basic fidelity to the original independence constitutions – has indeed been interpreted by some as 'an indicator of [the Westminster model's] institutional success'.[18]

As the chapters in this volume illustrate, two features of the Westminster system itself have played a significant part in preventing its reform. First, the much-noted partisanship of Caribbean politics (as highlighted by Gonsalves, Barrow-Giles, Lewis, Phillips and Golding) has posed a significant obstacle to constitutional reform, despite some real efforts to generate bipartisan consensus. Too often, issues of national import (constitutional change, regional integration and so on) become prey to sectional politics, fracturing on the rocks of partisan allegiance. Simply put, if one party actively supports and is closely associated with a reform agenda, the other party will oppose it, as turned out to be the case in St Vincent, where the 'no' campaign 'was conducted from a narrow, partisan political perspective' (Gonsalves). Secondly, the sovereignty of Parliament under the Westminster system makes politicians the 'gatekeepers to constitutional change'.[19] Hence:

> The very process of constitutional reform...reduces the likelihood of substantive change to the Westminster system...As with the adoption of the parliamentary system in the first place, sitting legislators are unlikely to propose or accept institutional changes that could threaten their position.[20]

Taking this argument further, Tennyson Joseph suggests that political elites have, in fact, deliberately used 'the formal mechanisms of constitutional change to resist the radical reform of the Westminster system'. Viewing CRCs as 'government directed mechanisms', Joseph contends that 'much of the region's conformity to Westminster can be explained by the deliberate mismanagement of the process of constitutional reform by regional elites who have resisted radical options'. So long as the state serves as a 'facilitator of international capital', he argues, exercises in constitutional reform will remain merely '"technical"... rationalised on the need to "modernise" the governance framework'. In this context, 'demands for transformation' have been severely constrained.

Beyond Westminster: The Quest for a New Democracy

Reflecting on the future of Caribbean regional integration, Patsy Lewis asks 'what a new regional democratic process should look like' and concludes that 'this might require the emergence of a political form, new and uniquely developed to suit the specific requirements of the region'. This concern with the renovation of democracy and grappling towards the realization of innovative, inclusive and locally appropriate forms of governance is expressed, in varying degrees, across the contributions to this collection. Moving beyond the formal, institutional dimensions of governance, the chapters by Tennyson Joseph, Clifford Griffin and Percy Hintzen all explicitly or implicitly make the case for a broader definition of democracy that incorporates 'meaningful access to economic and social goods' (Griffin) and the achievement and extension of 'economic opportunities, political liberties, social powers and the enabling conditions of good health, basic education [and]...the expansion of human capabilities' (Hintzen, citing Sen).

But where might the impetus for such a reimagined democracy come from and what shape would it take? For Joseph, the economic crisis faced by the Caribbean since the global downturn of 2008 marked a historical turning point that heralds 'the collapse of the postcolonial order' and presents an opportunity for radical change. This collapse, he argues, provides the 'basis upon which a more radical overhaul of Westminster will be possible' as the abandonment of the social contract between citizens and the state brings the legitimacy of the model into question. Though he does not delineate what might replace the Westminster system, he anticipates that the crisis will provide an opening in which 'voices linking demands for constitutional change with specific economic demands' can lay the grounds for a 'deeper transformation'. At the very least, he contends, the current crisis suggests 'the beginning...of a process in which the historical acceptance of the Westminster system as given and natural might be coming to an end'. For Hintzen, who proposes a radical abandonment of Westminster as the 'instrumentality...[that] has systematically limited, constrained, and/or foreclosed the imperatives of freedom and conditions for the realization of true development', opportunities for change may lie in realignments of global power (South–South relations and the relative decline of the West) and in 'the emergence of counter-hegemonic transnational networks' operating outside the formal spaces of governance. Examining transnational phenomena such as women's movements, indigenous movements and informal entrepreneurship, Hintzen suggests that these 'novel articulations of social power' may open up spaces for alternative, subaltern visions of sovereignty through which more meaningful realizations of democracy and development in the Caribbean might be achieved.

Westminster Persistent

Whether the above renovation of Westminster Caribbean democracy can be achieved – be that through reform or through root and branch transformation – will depend on a number of factors, not least the constraints and opportunities presented by the shifting global environment, the political will (or lack of) to drive through necessary reforms, and the extent of public mobilization behind any initiatives for change. What is undeniable, however, is that there remains considerable attachment to the Westminster model, despite the well-rehearsed critiques of its shortcomings. This attachment is most explicitly and positively expressed in the chapters by the serving politicians, whose analysis draws on decades of experience of the workings of the model from within the belly of the beast. Despite their party political differences, there is significant common ground in the chapters by Golding and Phillips, perhaps in itself indicative of the strength and persistence of the shared political culture in which several generations of post-independence politicians and voters have been baptised. Both underline the historical rootedness of the model, the extent to which it has acquired 'indigenous' standing in the region, and the absence, at the transition to independence, and in the present day, of a popularly articulated alternative. As Golding notes (citing Barnet), the Westminster model in the Caribbean was:

> the product of three centuries of historical development and a deliberate decision to continue the pattern of a constitutional system which had gradually evolved and in the operation of which the country had acquired considerable experience.

Or as Phillips asserts:

> We should...acknowledge that the basic institutional structure of the so-called "Westminster System" has deep organic roots in [the region's] history...[its] basic institutional structures are well understood and it has functioned well as a system in preserving basic democratic rights and freedoms. Not perfectly, but well.

In this account, the implantation and evolution of a transplanted colonial political system is conscripted into a narrative of Caribbean liberation. We should not forget, Phillips asserts, that '[the] population has over hundreds of years fought battles to be included in its ambit'; 'the quest for expanded rights of citizenship and social development...was to be a demand for inclusion within the representative politics of the day'.

Phillips's assertion that 'there has never been any sustained popular demand for substantial changes to the Westminster model' (a view echoed throughout the collection) is largely accurate, but occludes two important considerations: the existence of historical examples of attempts to enact alternative models of political organization ('people's parliaments', village, workplace and parish assemblies, experiments in shared leadership);[21] and explanations for why such alternatives have largely failed to gain popular traction. The reason for the latter must partially lie in the external and internal limitations that have been placed on any radical attempt to deviate from the liberal democratic Westminster norm and its assumed economic corollary, capitalism. It must also encompass the careful delineation of 'politics' as the sole domain of 'politicians', and resulting public disengagement. So where might demands for alternative models of governance emerge from in the present day? Is there anyone articulating such alternatives outside of narrow academic or policy circles? And can and should attachment to the Westminster model be abandoned? Whether we attribute it to hegemony or to the 'intrinsic legitimacy [of the model] throughout the region',[22] the apparent fidelity to Westminster is something that both supporters of reform and those who seek a more revolutionary alternative will have to confront if any transformation is to be achieved.

NOTES

1.   Norman Girvan, 'Are Caribbean Countries Facing Existential Threats?' http://www.normangirvan.info/wp-content/uploads/2010/11/existential-threats.pdf (accessed April 18, 2017).

2.   The Indictable Proceedings Act passed in 2011. Section 34 of the Act granted certain categories of accused persons 'the right to apply to a judge to dismiss criminal proceedings against them if ten years had passed since the crime was [alleged] to have happened and a trial had still not begun'. Days after the proclamation of section 34, businessmen and known United National Congress party donors, Ishwar Galbaransingh and Steve Ferguson, 'filed requests with the High Court to have their corruption charges dismissed'. As a result of intense public pressure and accusations of a government 'conspiracy to manipulate the Constitution to benefit two of its financiers',

section 34 was 'repealed with retroactive effect' in September 2012. Tremaine Warner, 'Civil Society Activism and Democratic Accountability in Trinidad and Tobago: The Case of Section 34' (unpublished BA thesis, University College London, 2017).

3. 'Opposition leader says the arrests of Dominicans over a fictitious coup are irrational and unconstitutional', *QTV News*, March 9, 2017, http://www. q95da.com/news/opposition-leader-says-arrests-of-dominicans-over-a-fictitious-coup-are-irrational-and-unconstitutional (accessed April 18, 2017). Demonstrations in Dominica in February and March 2017 responded to a number of issues, including the arrest of senior members of the opposition United Workers Party and Freedom Party; questions over the misuse of public monies relating to the Citizenship by Investment Programme; and the issuing of a diplomatic passport to an Iranian national charged with money laundering and the evasion of international sanctions.

4. K. Quinn, 'Colonial Legacies and Post-colonial Conflicts in Guyana', in *Postcolonial Trajectories in the Caribbean: The Three Guianas*, ed. R. Hoefte et al. (London and New York: Routledge, 2017), 10, 28. Guyana's 'democratic contradiction' refers to the fact that democratic elections have led to one-party dominance and political polarization based on ethnic voting patterns. Though the May 2015 elections brought in a new governing coalition, this was only by a slim majority. The elections were still characterized by traditional ethnic voting patterns and intense party political rivalry.

5. '"No" vote dominates in Grenada's constitutional reform referendum', *CARICOM Today*, November 25, 2016, http://today.caricom.org/2016/11/25/ no-vote-dominates-in-grenadas-constitutional-reform-referendum/ (accessed April 18, 2017).

6. The London conference was held at the Institute of the Americas, UCL, September 19–20, 2013, and the Jamaica conference was held at the University of the West Indies, Mona, September 11–12, 2014. The conferences and research network were funded an International Research Networks grant awarded by the Arts and Humanities Research Council (AHRC) [AH/ J00488X/1]. The conferences were co-organized by the editors of this volume.

7. See, for example, Hintzen, Joseph and Griffin in this volume.

8. See, for example, the essays in *Democracy in the Caribbean: Political, Economic and Social Perspectives*, ed. J. Domínguez et al. (Baltimore: The Johns Hopkins University Press, 1993) especially the chapters by Jorge Domínguez: 'The Caribbean Question: Why Has Liberal Democracy (Surprisingly) Flourished', 1–25; and Anthony Payne, 'Westminster Adapted: The Political Order of the Commonwealth Caribbean', 57–73.

9. See, for example, David Hinds, 'Beyond Formal Democracy: The Discourse on Democracy and Governance in the Anglophone Caribbean', *Commonwealth and Comparative Politics* 46, no.3 (2008): 388–406; Matthew Bishop, 'Slaying the "Westmonster" in the Caribbean? Constitutional Reform in St Vincent

and the Grenadines', *British Journal of Politics and International Relations* (2010): 1–18; Cynthia Barrow-Giles, 'Democracy at Work: A Comparative Study of the Caribbean State', *The Round Table* 100, no. 414 (2011): 285–302; and Paul Sutton, 'Westminster Challenged, Westminster Confirmed: Which Way Caribbean Constitutional Reform?' *Journal of Eastern Caribbean States* 38, nos. 1/2 (2013): 63–79. The 50/50 project reflecting on the last 50 years of independence in the Anglophone Caribbean and assessing prospects for the next 50 years was launched by the Sir Arthur Lewis Institute of Social and Economic Studies (SALISES) at the University of the West Indies in 2012.

10. The chapter by Cynthia Barrow-Giles in this volume addresses these deficiencies in depth, focusing in particular on the 'institutional practices' of the representative system and their impact on good governance.

11. 'Caribbean Regional Integration: A Report by the UWI Institute of International Relations', April 2011, 5. http://www.normangirvan.info/wp-content/uploads/2011/06/iir-regional-integration-report-final.pdf (accessed April 28, 2017).

12. Zachary Elkins and Tom Ginsberg, 'Constitutional Reform in the English-Speaking Caribbean: Challenges and Responses', a report prepared for the Conflict Prevention and Peace Forum, January 2011, 14. http://comparativeconstitutionsproject.org/files/CDG_Constitutional%20Reform%20in%20the%20English%20Speaking%20Caribbean_CPPF%20Briefing%20Paper_January%202011_f.pdf?6c8912 (accessed April 28, 2017).

13. Ibid., 15.

14. Ibid.

15. Ibid., 3.

16. See Supreme Court of Belize AD 2016, Claim no. 668 of 2010 in the Matter of the Constitution of Belize and in the Matter of the Alleged Unconstitutionality of Section 53 of the Criminal Code. http://www.humandignitytrust.org/uploaded/Library/Case_Law/Judgment-Orozco-v-The-Attorney-General-of-Belize.pdf. The ruling (p. 36) stated that 'section 53 of the Belize Criminal Code, Chapter 101 contravenes sections 3, 6, 12 and 16 of the Belize Constitution to the extent that it applies to carnal intercourse against the order of nature between persons'.

17. See, for example, the chapter by Bruce Golding in this volume. He asserts that he changed his mind on the unsuitability of the Westminster model for the Caribbean. Previously supporting a US-style system with a directly elected president and effective separation of powers, he subsequently came to the conclusion that such a system could create deadlock in the Caribbean context.

18. Elkins and Ginsberg, 'Constitutional Reform in the English-Speaking Caribbean', 17.

19. Ibid., 10.

20. Ibid. See also Cynthia Barrow-Giles in this volume, who states that just as turkeys do not vote for Christmas, so politicians are 'not likely to support a system that may threaten their potential standing'.

21. I refer here to the model of 'people's parliaments' developed by the National Joint Action Committee (NJAC) in Trinidad and Tobago in the 1970s, the experiment in 'revolutionary democracy' enacted under the Grenada Revolution, 1979–83, and attempts to democratise party political structures through a proposal for shared leadership by the United Labour Front in Trinidad in the mid-1970s.

22. A. Maingot cited in the chapter by Cynthia Barrow-Giles in this volume.

2 Good Governance or Penance:
Enhancing Westminster in the Caribbean

Cynthia Barrow-Giles

Introduction

In modern societies, democracy is achieved not by the direct rule of the people but through a representative system in which it is anticipated that the people will have the final say. It is expected that the system will be defined by the popular control over the political processes as well as political equality in the exercise of that control. In representative democracies like Westminster parliamentary systems, representatives acting on behalf of the citizenry take decisions on behalf of the society. In effect, democracy is achieved via the control of the citizens over their representatives. So that the extent to which that control is achieved and the equality of the control exercised by citizens are both crucial elements of representative democracy. For the most part, electoral systems are critical determinants of the exercise of such control and the exercise of power. The second component of democracy is the accountability of governmental institutions and public officials to the electorate both directly and indirectly through Parliament and other oversight mechanisms, such as the judiciary.

Within that context of what democracy ought to embody, I shall not endeavour to deal with all the myriad problems confronting Westminster in the Caribbean and their implication for the fulfilment of democracy. Rather, I narrowly focus on what is seen as three institutional practices that can minimize participation and control of critical decision-making, limit the overall quality of representation and frustrate consensual decision-making and lead to abuse of incumbency. Firstly, the chapter focuses on the overall performance of the electoral system in the region, arguing that in its present form the model certainly does little to enhance representation and thus good governance. Secondly, the chapter looks at parliamentarism and its intrinsic value or lack thereof to the region given its tendency to restrain parliamentarians in a context where perhaps greater cooperation is required. Finally, I consider the value of a fixed term of office in a context where variability and flexibility have been emphasized. Much of the discussions centres on the reports of Constitution Reform Commissions which have considered how governance can be improved regionally.

Framing Reform for the Commonwealth Caribbean

Nearly two decades ago in a relatively little known journal produced by the University of Guyana, Harold A. Lutchman published an article entitled 'The Westminster System in the Commonwealth Caribbean: Some Issues and Problems'. The many issues which he reflected upon in 1995 continue to characterize the region and have proven to be so culturally acceptable that some 20 years later, in 2014, we have been unable or unwilling to transcend them. While Lutchman conceded that the states of the Commonwealth Caribbean have enjoyed apparent efficiency and are generally numbered among the most successful in achieving satisfactory results, nonetheless, according to him the framers of the Constitutions had clearly not anticipated a number of problems which had manifested themselves shortly after independence.[1] Notwithstanding these unanticipated difficulties of Westminster in the Caribbean, the model has enjoyed widespread support which has allowed several Commonwealth Caribbean States to survive sudden and sometimes dramatic changes.[2] Lutchman, however, concluded that '...elements of the Westminster system have come under critical scrutiny regarding their suitability...' for the region.[3] Echoing these sentiments, Anthony Maingot also asserts that while Westminster is certainly valued, its validity for the region can be questioned.[4] Nearly ten years later, in 2003, Prime Minister of St Vincent and the Grenadines, Ralph Gonsalves, pointed to the travails of Westminster parliamentary democracy in the Caribbean and reminded us of its many limitations.[5] These included, an externally located Head of State; an insufficiently strong enforcement of the protective provisions regarding individuals' rights and freedoms; a first-past-the post electoral system, which according to him does not permit a sufficiently fair and democratic representation of voters' preferences; the absence of any or proper mechanisms for voters to bring their elected representatives to account during their term in office; the highly inadequate and ineffective control that the legislature exercises over the executive; the excessive powers of the prime minister in both the constitutional and political apparatuses; the lack of an appropriate mechanism for voters and non-governmental organizations to routinely and consistently participate in the governance of the country, the unacceptable interference of the executive into the practical workings of the judiciary, and the absence or inadequacy of the constitutional provisions governing or regulating the integrity of members of the legislature and other public officials. Gonsalves further notes that these weaknesses can be remedied by a package of reasonable constitutional arrangements which rest on strengthening individual rights and freedoms, the deepening and decentralization of political democracy, the strengthening of representative democracy, accountable and effective government, and the independence of the judiciary.

So that whereas post-independence Caribbean democracies can be deemed successful in a formal sense, there are a number of institutional issues and political developments that have clouded the seeming success of these democracies. Popular involvement in politics is evident in the area of elections as indeed in the acceptance of the outcome of elections by the citizenry. Yet, outside of a few Commonwealth Caribbean countries such as Jamaica, Trinidad and Tobago, the Commonwealth of the Bahamas, and St Kitts and Nevis, local government is not an arena where citizens are involved. Further, the dangers evident in the operation of Westminster in the Caribbean are stark especially given the recent increasing tendency of prime ministers to prorogue Parliament when faced with the possibility of a successful no-confidence motion. Thus, in Guyana, with the government facing challenges from a majority combined opposition and unable to compromise, President Donald Ramotar prorogued Parliament for six months on November 10, 2014.[6] In his address to the nation, President Ramotar stated that his decision was motivated by what he described as 'political gamesmanship' on the part of the political opposition.[7] Defending his decision on the grounds that the opposition wanted to:

> ...disrupt Government's business by forcing a debate on their No Confidence Motion, I resolved to respond immediately by exercising my Constitutional options to either Prorogue or Dissolve Parliament paving the way for holding of general elections. Consistent with my earlier position and in accordance with powers conferred on me by Article 70 (1) of the Constitution of the Republic of Guyana, I earlier today issued a Proclamation proroguing the 10th Parliament.[8]

That decision was described by the main opposition grouping, A Partnership for National Unity (APNU) as 'the darkest day for democracy in Guyana'.[9]

Just two years earlier in 2012, Prime Minister Tillman Thomas of Grenada, prorogued the Parliament to forestall a no confidence motion in him, following the development of schisms within his party. Outspoken former Grenada attorney general Jimmy Bristol in addressing the issue of the avoidance of the no confidence motion by governments and prime ministers pointed to abuse of the system and condemned all three administrations. According to him:

> Amazing similarities, and amazing how...our leaders in the Caribbean could talk on one hand about trying to further justice by... abolishing the Privy Council...and yet abuse our constitutions as these three countries have done.[10]

Electoral Triumphalism as a Critical Governance Issue: The Political Effects of Westminster Elections

In his musings on citizenship and parliamentary politics in the English Speaking Caribbean, Anthony Maingot conceded that:

> ...there is wide recognition of the importance of political parties and the electoral process in the West Indies. And not without reason, for despite its many failings... West Indian political systems have provided these societies with regular, usually honest, and basically reliable mechanisms for elite recruitment and circulation.[11]

Given the number of individuals who have urged a change in the present political system, it is highly debatable that the main political issue is with the institutions of elections. Nonetheless, Maingot argued that much of the discontent with constitutionalism in the West Indies stems from deficiencies in the electoral system, not in the nature of parliamentarianism or political pluralism proper.[12] These deficiencies, he contended, can lead to the erosion of the Westminster parliamentary system despite its intrinsic legitimacy throughout the region.[13]

The first-past-the-post or plurality system of elections in the region is rooted in single-member districts. A second major feature of these parliamentary democracies is the domination of the political process by two major political parties. The latter is one of the most remarkable features of Commonwealth Caribbean politics, for when compared to political democracies in other parts of the developing world, only two and essentially the same two parties have controlled elections and thus governments in most states for an extensive period of time. This is particularly true for

Barbados and Jamaica. Third-party challenges have only rarely disrupted the system in some countries as they did in Dominica in 1990 and 1995. Here, the challenge posed by the Dominica United Workers Party in the 1990s led to what appears to be an enduring organization which has replaced the Dominica Freedom Party as the second major political organization.

Further, Westminster in the Caribbean is also defined by majoritarian politics. A review of election results in several Commonwealth Caribbean States would show the frequency with which one party has dominated the electoral landscape and or parliament. This has occurred for two reasons. The first relates to the ability of the party to win the geographic race in every constituency or an overwhelming majority of these constituencies leading to the domination of Parliament by one party. In that regard in both St Vincent and the Grenadines in 1989, and Grenada in 1999 and 2013, one party enjoyed a clean sweep thereby totally excluding any opposition from parliament. Secondly, as in the case of Jamaica and Trinidad and Tobago in 1983 and 1971 respectively, the effective boycott of the elections by opposition groups, also resulted in a single party hegemony in parliament. Table 2.1 shows quite clearly the frequency with which opposition voices are either silenced or marginalized across the region with the tendency to be accentuated in Antigua and Barbuda that has witnessed such domination in five of seven general elections held in that country since independence in 1981. Jamaica, too, has frequently experienced this phenomenon. Quite apart from the unusual circumstances that led to the PNP boycott of the 1983 elections, Jamaica has witnessed this development at least six times since independence with 1993 manifesting the greatest electoral gulf between the two protagonists.

Though the outcome of a number of general elections in the Caribbean between 2005 and 2010 has shown a tendency for the electorate to restrict ruling political parties to a single term, as table 2.1 shows, the feature of one-party-dominance has continued. Cynthia Barrow-Giles and Tennyson Joseph argued that such dominance presents a distorted view of the nature of political support and leads to a questioning of the efficacy of the electoral system in place.[14] At a minimum level, the phenomenon of the one-party monopoly poses problems for the quality of Caribbean democracies. In the case of St Vincent and the Grenadines following the landslide victory of the National Democratic Party led by James Mitchell, opposition party leader Vincent Beache complained that:

Essentially, the government is operating more by executive decree, rather than through the legislature. Of course, in small parliaments, like ours, it is not really possible to have a proper separation of powers. In practice, the executive is the legislature in the sense that because they are in a majority, they can put anything through the House. Even so, at least you can debate it there and the public can hear it. But what the government is doing is using subsidiary rather than substantive legislation in a lot of areas.[15]

TABLE 2.1: One-Party Monopoly Phenomenon in the Commonwealth Caribbean 1960–2014 (Post Independence Elections in Relevant Countries)

Country	Year of Election	Party	No of Seats	% Vote	Year of Election	Party	No of Seats	% Vote
Antigua and Barbuda	1984	ALP	16	67.9	2004	ALP	4	41.72
		IND	1	7.2		UPP	12	55.24
	1989	ALP	15	63.8	2014	ALP	14	56.45
		Others	2	35.3		UPP	3	41.95
	1999	ALP	12	52.57				
		UPP	4	44.15				
The Bahamas	1997	PLP	5	41.90	2012	PLP	29	48.62
		FNM	35	57.70		FNM	9	42.09
	2002	PLP	29	51.78				
		FNM	7	40.87				
Barbados	1997	BLP	26	64.87				
		DLP	2	35.09				
Belize	1998	PUP	26	59.29	2008	PUP	6	40.72
		UDP	3	39.15		UDP	25	56.61
	2003	PUP	22	52.75				
		UDP	7	45.22				
Dominica	1980	DFP	17	51.3	2009	DFP	0	2.40
		Others	1	28.1		DLP	18	61.21
		IND	2	3.8		UWP	3	34.85
	1985	DFP	15	56.7				
		DLP	5	39.1				
		Others	1	1.9				
Grenada	1984	GULP	1	36.1	2013	NDC	0	40.69
		NNP	14	58.4		NNP	15	58.82
	1999	NDC	0	25.08				
		NNP	15	62.47				

Country	Year of Election	Party	No of Seats	% Vote	Year of Election	Party	No of Seats	% Vote
Jamaica	1976	JLP	13	43.2	1993	JLP	8	39.37
		PNP	47	56.8		PNP	52	60.03
	1980	JLP	51	58.9	1997	JLP	10	38.88
		PNP	9	41.0		PNP	50	56.19
	1983	JLP	60	-	2011	JLP	21	53.28
		PNP	-	-		PNP	42	46.61
	1989	JLP	15	43.3				
		PNP	45	56.6				
St Lucia	1982	SLP	2	16.7	2001	SLP	14	54.49
		UWP	14	56.2		UWP	3	36.86
		PLP	1	27.1				
	1997	SLP	16	60.04				
		UWP	1	35.80				
St Vincent and the Grenadines	1989	SVLP	0	30.3	2001	ULP	12	56.49
		NDP	15	66.3		NDP	3	40.91
	1994	SVLP	2	26.0				
		NDP	12	54.62				
		Others	1	18.38				
Trinidad and Tobago	1971	PNM	36					
	1986	PNM	3	32.1				
		NAR	33	66.3				

Compiled from general election reports

The first-past-the-post system merely requires that the winning candidate capture a plurality and not a majority of the vote in a constituency and therefore a slight edge at the poll by one party can result in substantial or a large majority of parliamentary seats. Consequently, although electoral landslides are not uncommon as table 1 shows, and the partisan division of the vote fluctuated significantly over the period under consideration, the winning political party rarely captured more than 60 per cent of the two-party vote. The loser rarely lost with less than 40 per cent. For much of the period under consideration, the national Parliament has been dominated by a party with a majority in the House of Assembly which was considerably greater than its popular support. Representational distortion has also resulted in situations where a party may be able to win the government (the absolute majority of seats) while finishing second in popular vote thereby creating an artificial majority. Simply put, it is not impossible for a party to win the government on a substantially less than the majority vote.

Yet, despite the fact that it appears that party competition is not unduly uncompetitive; given the electoral system in place, losing political parties are sometimes totally excluded or at best are marginally represented.

This has had unintended constitutional consequences. As Lutchman noted, in the more extreme case of the virtual absence of a political opposition in parliament, the constitutional requirement that there should be a leader of the opposition with clearly defined roles cannot be actualized and consequently can expose the government to constitutional challenges as the cases of St Vincent and the Grenadines and Grenada confirm.[16] This exclusion has led to a situation where not only are opposition political voices stifled, but the composition of the Senate has been impacted, as only one party can be represented in this nominated chamber. The exception to this is where the governor general or president has the power to appoint independent senators thereby providing the opportunity for dissent and critical input into the political system to continue in the absence of the formal presence of the political opposition.

The Way Forward

Clearly, the issue that arises is the extent to which the votes of all electors carry equal weight, and the manner in which the vote informs the composition of parliament. It is quite possible that a political party may be able to poll a significant number of votes nationally but is unable to win a majority in any single seat and consequently is not represented in parliament. In that regard, Peter Jamadar noted that:

> The most serious and fundamental defect in the First Past The Post system is that it regularly and repeatedly fails to create a Parliament in which the image of the feelings of the nation are truly reflected. There is the general tendency to exaggerate the representativeness of the largest party and to reduce that of the smaller ones.[17]

However, regionally there is strong support for the plurality electoral system, yet its retention poses serious problems for representation. One of the primary reasons for this attachment to the model is its ability to produce a close relationship between parliamentarians and residents of the geographic district they represent. Quite apart from the opportunities provided to constituents to seek assistance from their directly elected representatives, the direct election of their representative also provides them with the ability to hold their parliamentary and constituency representatives accountable for their actions during the parliamentary term.

Moreover, the system has also invariably produced strong governments, although some jurisdictions, namely Trinidad and Tobago, and St Kitts/ Nevis have also experienced balanced parliaments. In others, for example St Lucia in 1987, Belize in 1989, and Barbados 2013, the result of the general elections led to a government operating under a slim victory which has consequences for governmental stability. In the case of St Lucia, one opposition member of Parliament crossed the floor to strengthen the John Compton-led United Workers Party government, which had secured nine of the 17 parliamentary seats. Having secured 15 of the 28 parliamentary seats in the 1989 elections in Belize, the People's United Party (PUP), succeeded in enticing a member of the United Democratic Party (UDP) to cross the floor, increasing its slim majority to three. Following the February 2013 general elections in Barbados, the Democratic Labour Party (DLP) retained control of the government with a slim margin of two seats.

Since the late '90s, several constitutional reform commissions have considered the efficacy of the model and although the majority of them have lamented on its limitations and wrestled with the possibility of replacing the electoral system, nevertheless, they have nearly all failed to recommend meaningful if any change. In that regard, the 1998 Constitutional Commission which was appointed by the government of St Kitts and Nevis under the chairmanship of Sir Fred Phillips was charged with the responsibility to review the constitution and to make recommendations in relation to 'expedient' reform said little on the issue. In the context of the call for secession of Nevis, it is clear that the Commission would have devoted considerable attention to the nature of the relationship between the two islands.[18] The four-volume report, therefore, devoted much of its time to the constitutional structure and the nature of the relationship between St Kitts and Nevis. Indeed, more than one volume of the report was spent on the controversial issue of secession, with other major issues being republicanism, the executive branch of government and the qualifications of parliamentarians, which have all been topical constitutional issues throughout the region. What was absent from the document was any discussion on the electoral system. The Commission accepted that the manner in which the senators were selected to serve in the unicameral chamber was unsatisfactory, as it created lopsidedness and rendered Parliament largely ineffective. The Commission's response to this was to recommend the appointment of independent senators by the Head of State. The Commission argued that this would lead to greater effectiveness and accountability of the executive to the Parliament as it would change the traditional relegation of Parliament which in their view had become a 'charade and a rubber stamp'. Parliament, they surmised, would be increasingly characterized by deliberation and scrutiny of parliamentary business.'[19] As noteworthy as this recommendation was, unfortunately, nowhere in the four-volume report was there any systematic discussion on the electoral system. The logical conclusion to be derived, is that the Commission accepted the usefulness of the system.

In 2003, the St Vincent and the Grenadines 25-member Constitutional Review Commission, which was charged with the responsibility for conducting 'a root-and-branch' review of the Constitution, offered some valuable insights into the position of the Commission on the electoral system. Among the many issues confronted by the Commission were the limitations of the plurality majoritarian system for the country. Its response was perhaps one of the most innovative recommendations setting it apart from earlier reform commissions. In the Commission's assessment, the legislative branch of government should be wholly elected on the basis of the traditional first-past-the-post electoral system and a system of proportional representation based on a party list of candidates. The Commission argued that this mixed-method approach would provide for a greater representativeness of the people while making it impossible for a one-party Parliament to be elected as had been the case in 1989. The Commission also rejected the current constitutional requirement for the appointment of the senate. In its view, the new model would be fairer and more representative while avoiding a situation of a multiplicity of political parties and thus weakened government, should the plurality system be wholly replaced.

In its rather emphatic statement the Commission noted that though proportional representation could deepen representative democracy it was not:

> ...prepared at this point in time to recommend such a system. The examples of the few Caribbean countries which have implemented such system do not suggest additional democratic dividends to be derived from a mixed system. Further the Commission is careful not to superimpose on the Westminster system, principles which may work well in large pluralistic systems, but are ill-at-ease in micro-states.[20]

The Commission noted further that:

> There is a particular political synergy which develops between a constituency and its directly elected representatives which not only

provides the elected person with legitimacy, but is sometimes also essential to the working of government policy and administration.[21]

The 2000 Constitution Reform Report of Belize also showed some concerns as well, particularly with regards to the method of appointment of the senate but failed to recommend any changes in relation to the method of appointment of the House of Assembly. It, therefore, only proposed limited reforms in relation to the manner in which senators would be selected. Accordingly, the Commission recommended that 12 of the 13 senators should be appointed by the governor general based on the proportion of the popular vote received by political parties in national elections.[22]

In contrast to its absence in the recommendations of the report on constitutional reform in St Kitts-Nevis, the Bahamas and Belize, and very similar to the process in St Vincent and the Grenadines, the St Lucia Constitution Reform Commission paid tremendous attention to the impact of the electoral system on the body politic of the country. A reading of the 2011 report of the St Lucia Constitutional Reform Commission shows that while the commission considered the introduction of proportionality it was nevertheless:

> ...troubled by the possibility that, given the historical closeness in the national vote, support of the two dominant political parties in the country, its adoption as the institutional system for Saint Lucia could lead to deadlock in the Parliament, create excessive control by party bosses, and had the potential to create instability. Therefore the Commission reasoned that the post-election bargaining and horse trading which takes place under the Proportional Representation system (PR) would be avoided by the retention of the status quo.[23]

Whereas the commission in St Vincent and the Grenadines was prepared to entertain alternative electoral formulae, the St Lucia Constitution Reform Commission showed great timidity and a lack of creativity in relation to its endorsement of the majoritarian plurality system. It certainly did not examine the possibility of a mixed system and instead satisfied itself that stability of government, not representativeness, was paramount.

One of the major fears of the PR as a system revolves around the method of indirectly electing parliamentary representatives through a party list system. It is generally felt that this electoral method would serve to undermine the capacity of voters to hold their representatives to account, while simultaneously exposing the political system to instability. Such instability, it is further argued, can either stem from third party or multi-partyism which can lead to the possibility of divided government in both arithmetic and behavioural senses.[24] Yet, despite its successes in frequently producing strong governments, as a system of representation the plurality system is unsatisfactory. And while in some quarters, there is growing disquiet about the distortions produced by the system, outside of Guyana, St Vincent and the Grenadines and in Trinidad and Tobago under the administration of Prime Minister Kamala Persad-Bissessar which considered electoral reform, and Grenada, no other Caribbean country has considered any radical modification to the system. Indeed, in the case of Grenada, the government of Keith Mitchell presented seven bills to the electorate in a November 2016 referendum. Three of these bills, namely Bill 7 – term of Office of the Prime Minister; Bill 4 – Fixed date for elections; and Bill 2 – Elections and Boundaries Commission, related to matters concerning the electoral environment. Notwithstanding long-standing concerns germane to these critical issues, the result of the November 24 referendum was a major defeat for proponents of constitutional reform generally and electoral reform specifically as all seven bills were defeated.[25] However, to improve the representativeness of the model and to provide fairly for each party's share of the vote and taking into consideration the overwhelming support for the plurality system, the reform process must continue to centre the model while providing for alternative means for enhancing the quality of democracy.

While proportional representation has been rejected on a number of grounds, it does provide for a level of fairness and would reduce the historical tendency towards distortions and exclusions. For as Stuart Weir and David Beetham contended:

> Put simply, it holds that parties are the principal agents of political choice; that the votes of all electors should count for the same, *regardless of the party they have voted for;* and that the political parties should therefore be allocated seats in an elected assembly in proportion to the number of votes they have obtained in an election. This concept does not necessarily rule out geographical considerations, but it does mean that they cannot be made exclusive.[26]

Electoral reform must also be viewed in the context of wider systemic reform of the political model. The reports of the constitutional reform commissions are also instructive, in this regard, as they do not generally recommend a departure from Westminster. Indeed only in the case of St Lucia was there a recommendation for the adoption of a hybrid political form.

Consequently, it is clear that the attachment to Westminster parliamentary arrangements runs deep. Intuitively, we also understand that 'turkeys do not vote for Christmas' and therefore we must be concerned with the likelihood that persons who benefit from a set of institutions would be likely to support a system that may threaten their political standing. As a result, any tampering with the electoral system must ensure its conformity with the principles of Westminster, especially with regards to the ability of the government to preside in a decisive manner over Parliament. Indeed, Selwyn Ryan in *Winner Takes All* in commenting on the opposition party's view on the 1989 Parliament in St Vincent and the Grenadines and the plausibility of politicians supporting action which may hamper their electoral standing argued that:

> Like other politicians who are defeated by the quirks of the Westminster type elections, Beache was of the view that some sort of proportional representation was called for. The problem, however, was that ruling politicians did not want to change the system when it was working in their favour. The opposition, for its part, also tended to lose interest when it came to power. Given this, nothing ever happened.[27]

It is partly for that reason and given the expressed reservations with respect to proportional representation, that it is proposed that a system which combines both plurality and proportionality be adopted regionally. This would not only achieve the desired end of ensuring that the votes of all electors counting for the same, *regardless of the party they have voted for* and fairer representation of parties, but it would also limit the need for constitutional challenges which have and can occasion landslide victories. In furtherance of the democratic ideal, the electoral system ought not to reduce or increase the impact of the individual vote in forming a government or a representative institution. The region would thus be better served in terms of the democratic ideal by adopting a hybrid mixed member system similar to that practised in many European countries where the attractiveness of the plurality system is maintained while providing for additional members to be elected. This would enhance the representativeness of parliament.[28]

Matthew Soberg Shugart and Martin P. Wattenberg described the mixed-member systems as a variant of a multiple-tier system of voting with the specific requirement that one tier must entail allocation of seats nominally whereas the other must entail allocation of seats by lists. Under nominal voting, voters cast votes for candidates by name and seats are allocated to individual candidates on the basis of the votes they receive. The method employed under the plurality first-past-the-post-system can, therefore, be described as a nominal method of voting. In contrast to nominal voting, the list votes combine the votes among multiple candidates nominated on a list submitted prior to the election by a political party. This is typically used in systems employing proportional representation. Countries employing this hybrid electoral system, therefore, usually permit eligible voters the option of voting twice (one in each tier).[29]

A review of the proposed mixed member system suggests that most of these systems tend to be skewed towards either majoritarian or proportional in their overall effect on representation in the national parliament. Soberg Shugart and Wattenburg identified two broad typologies of the mixed member system, which they refer to as mixed-member majoritarian (MMM) and mixed-member proportional (MMP).[30] According to them, the distinction between the two typologies is the 'the presence or absence of a linkage between tiers'.[31] In that regard, linkage between the two tiers is likely to eliminate or significantly alter the majoritarian bonus afforded the winning party which would normally take place under the MMP system. On the other hand, delinking the two tiers of voting, under the MMM system maintains the typical majoritarian boost received by a large party in the nominal tier of voting.[32]

Proponents of this model argue that the mixed-member system offers the best of both worlds, that is, the direct accountability of members to the constituencies in which they are elected, and the proportional representation of diverse partisan preferences that increases the quality of democratic representation and equality. As Soberg Shugart and Wattenberg reasoned, '...the key point is that such systems allow nations to tailor their electoral systems so as to potentially have their cake and eat it too.'[33]

Regionally, outside of Jamaica, Guyana and possibly Trinidad and Tobago which have 60, 65, and 41 elected members of parliament, the elected legislative branch of government, is normally viewed as too small to be able to effectively hold government to account. This is partly rooted in the tendency of the electoral model to confer large majorities on the winning political parties which are inclined to select almost all its members to the executive branch. Thus, in a context where Westminster politics demands strong party discipline and collective responsibility, it is virtually impossible to have the level of scrutiny, deliberation and accountability that is normally presumed under systems of government defined by the near total or total separation of the legislative and executive branches of government. Adopting a hybrid electoral system would, therefore, provide for an enlarged Parliament which can lend itself to a more effective legislative branch of government that would be better capable of scrutinizing governmental activity. Secondly, we can concede that given the requirement of party cohesion, as long as party discipline is maintained, there is little incentive for a government to cooperate, with the opposition. However, at a minimum the adoption of the system would certainly remove the tendency towards lopsided parliaments and its attendant consequences in the region. This was clearly the thinking behind the 2006 recommendations of the Grenada constitution reform process. In its report, the commission recommended that members of Parliament should be partly elected on the basis of first-past-the post system and on the basis of the percentage of votes each political party has received in the general elections. In the view of the Commission, this would ensure that the opposition would never be excluded from parliament. While the political circumstance of 1999 clearly motivated the commissioners, ironically the opposition was again excluded from Parliament in the wake of the 2013 general elections.[34]

Beyond Electoral Democracy: Reforming Parliament

Much has been said by academics and politicians about the nature of parliamentary democracy, and while I will not list or discuss all the valid issues raised, it bears repeating that there is a strong connection between the electoral system and the nature of Parliament under Westminster arrangements. Indeed, as argued above, the unfortunate effect of the plurality system of voting can lead to the relegation of Parliament to a 'charade and a rubber stamp'. Therefore, how to democratize Parliament and to enable the accountability of the executive to the Parliament remains a critical issue in Caribbean governance.

For obvious reasons, I take my reference point from the recommendations of the Constitution Reform Commission of St Lucia which as Paul Sutton notes, though extremely long in the making, is a reflection of the '...thoroughness of the report and the intensive and extensive process of research, public information and public consultation it involved....'[35] The long-standing frustrations with the functioning of parliaments under Westminster and the subordinate role of the legislative branch of government to the executive branch demanded some attention to this issue. Indeed, this was one of the most consistent issues raised in the consultation process. In that regard, in keeping with the reports of other constitutional reform commissions, four primary criticisms were levelled at the political model. The first criticism was that the system lacked checks and balances; the second related to the nature and composition of the parliament; the third pointed to the often repeated view that the prime minster had too much power while a fourth pointed to the inadequacy of constituency representation.

In proposing the mixed system of elections above, I argued that compromise is warranted and in like vein, the commission needed to reconcile the expressed concerns with the alleged autocratic nature of Westminster system and the lack of effective representation with the need to maintain stability. The Commission, therefore, argued that its flagship proposal of the hybrid system of government was not a reflection of its lack of support for the presidential form or the rejection of the many well stated frustrations with the Westminster system of governance. Instead, it was a reflection of the deeply held view by a majority of members of the Commission that it may not be politically practical to '...push our Constitution, in new and novel directions, to make it more effective, and meet our people's needs.'[36]

In keeping with the Commission's rejection of the proportional representation electoral system on the ground that the potential for instability was too great, the commission argued that its objective was to '...preserve the stability of strong central government that is a defining feature of the British model...' while simultaneously ensuring that the requisite checks and balances that are so attractive in its political alternative were embraced.[37] The Commission thus argued that the American system carried with it too many dangers, not least among which was potential for deadlock in a system where, potentially, the directly elected president could come from a party, different to those who formed the majority in the Legislature.[38] The report therefore states that:

> ...we rejected the all or nothing approach, which would have caused us to simply substitute one foreign culture's constitution for another, as if the process of constitution-making was a straightforward task of swapping meat for fish. At all times throughout our process, the Commission remained mindful that we could not divorce our Constitution from the political culture in which it was immersed.

> Our solutions therefore had to recognise the need to balance the demand for accountability, against the realities of party politics in small island

states. The status quo was unacceptable, but no less so than imposing a totally alien system on our people.[39]

Thus, in what Paul Sutton describes as the unsurprising call for substantive change, the Commission recommended several noteworthy adaptations which considered many of the criticisms levelled at the existing political model. First and foremost, the commission argued that in the context of the fusion of power, the small size of the national Parliament and the absence of functioning parliamentary committees which is possible in larger sized parliaments there was an urgent need to implement some form of separation of powers. While this can clearly be offered by the adoption of the presidential political form, the fear of gridlock influenced the commission's rejection of this alternative. In what constitutes a major point of departure from other reports, the commission borrowed from the French semi presidential political form, recommending that parliamentary scrutiny could be best achieved under circumstances where elected parliamentarians with the exception of the prime minister and his deputy would be separated from the cabinet of ministers. This would free parliamentarians from their triple function as legislators, executives, and constituency representatives and restrict them to the dual function of legislators and constituency representatives. Accordingly, the proposed model would provide for the more effective parliamentary committees and enforce a real separation between the legislature and the executive, thereby ensuring greater checks and balances against the exercise of excessive power. In combination with the increased number of parliamentarians suggested by the adoption of the mixed majoritarian method discussed above, the end result would be that Parliament would no longer be dominated by the executive since members of the executive branch would now be prevented from being members of the legislative branch.

The Case for Fixed Terms: What Do the Constitutional Reform Commissions Say?

Another constitutional provision that has often been flagged for reform is the power of election timing. Generally speaking, there are two broad types of term of office, the rigid fixed term, of which the US and Norway are good examples, and the flexible system which is typically practised in Westminster systems such as the UK, Australia, New Zealand, and the Commonwealth Caribbean where the prime minister has the constitutional right to call an election at any point before the expiration of a maximum term. However, there are several countries that practise a semi-fixed arrangement under which a fixed term is the custom but there are constitutional provisions that provide for an early dissolution of Parliament. This is used in countries such as Germany and Sweden. A semi-fixed arrangement therefore reduces the level of flexibility and control that normally exists under Westminster-type constitutional arrangements.

In 1819, Simón Bolívar in his famous discourse at the Congress of Angostura argued that unlimited terms in office was antithetical to democracy.[40] According to him:

> The continuation of the authority in the same individual has frequently been the end of democratic governments. Repeated elections are essentials in popular systems, because nothing is more dangerous than to leave for a long term the same citizen in power. The people get used to obey him, and he gets used to command them; from where usurpation and tyranny is originated…Our citizens must fear with more than enough justice that the same Official, who has governed them for a long time, could perpetually command them.[41]

Although fixed dates are normal institutional practices in presidential models, this is not the case in parliamentary systems. The constitutional discretion that prime ministers have to control the timing of elections has been the subject of some scholarly attention regionally. Generally, the focus has been on prime ministers' unilateral power to determine the dates of elections and whether this power should be stripped from the office. Several scholars have contended that prime ministers have used this power to call elections during periods that were most conducive to their party's re-election or to improve their election standing. Such was the case in St Lucia when in April 1987 Prime Minister John Compton called elections twice in a bid to improve his parliamentary majority. For sure, the possibility of a vote of no confidence is a constant threat in Westminster and especially so under circumstances where the government has a slim working majority. The constitutional provision of the early dissolution of Parliament is one of the conventions which permit the government the opportunity to compensate for this possibility. It is, therefore, argued that government and the prime minister must retain the right to request the dissolution of Parliament under such circumstances.

In addition, we are often warned that fixing the dates for elections in the context of a parliamentary type system of government is either inappropriate or dangerous. The rationale for this argument is that if the life of the Parliament is fixed, it would then create a serious problem if a government loses the legitimacy to govern, or if, due to discord within the cabinet or a majority in parliament, it became necessary to change the government to restore order. In other words, under circumstances where the date for elections was fixed, a problem could arise where a government needed to return to the polls earlier than the typical five-year period. One of the strengths of the parliamentary system is the flexibility it allows to end the life of Parliament earlier, where circumstances emerge which warrant such action, so that the imposition of a fixed term of office could potentially result not only in governmental crisis but also instability. So that far from improving the quality of democracy, fixed terms are viewed as having the potential to undermine democracy. Those opposed to fixed elections, therefore, contend that fixed terms are retrograde as they constitute a democratic drawback, even more so under conditions where there is the potential for realignments or power shifts occurring in Parliament.[42]

Notwithstanding these concerns, several countries, including Canada, have adopted similar reforms and the UK – the mother of all parliaments – has embraced this as well. Shortly after British Prime Minister Gordon Brown assumed office, a proposal was made that a convention be adopted, in which the dissolution of Parliament by the prime minister should follow a parliamentary resolution. More recently, Prime Minister David Cameron opted for fixed-term Parliaments, barring a 55 per cent majority vote calling for dissolution before the five-year anniversary that led to the adoption of legislation setting an election every five years starting on May 7, 2015. In making the case for the fixed term of office for all parliamentarians, Deputy Prime Minister Nick Clegg pointed primarily to the overwhelming control exerted by prime ministers in the system. Clegg thus contended that:

> We are seeking to remove from the executive and the Prime Minister of the day the ability to play politics with the timing of the election. That is the basic motive of this. Governments have been distorted, paralysed, hobbled and handicapped over and over again by the capricious manner in which Prime Ministers have played cat and mouse with the British people and with the legislature about when elections should be held. ... That is debilitating to good government; it destroys good government. It is humiliating to the legislature and the Parliament. It makes a complete mockery of the relationship between the legislature and the executive.[43]

Under the Fixed-term Parliaments Bill, not only is the prime minister's power to choose when to request a dissolution of Parliament removed but the Bill also included a provision for an election to be held before the fixed date. Britain has, therefore, opted for a semi-fixed arrangement which will not only reduce the level of flexibility which currently exists but will also limit the control of election timing by a single individual and or party.[44] In the view of the Parliamentary Committee on fixed term parliaments:

> Introducing fixed terms would create consistency with international experience. Democratic Audit argued that fixed-term Parliaments of some kind are a democratic norm. Three quarters of the 41 democracies analysed in a 2005 study were found to have fixed terms. Their introduction would also bring Westminster into line with practice in the devolved legislatures.[45]

As Nick Clegg observed 'there are circumstances in which the desire for a general election, to press the reset button, is so great that something needs to happen.'[46] The British semi-fixed term limit model, therefore, makes allowance for an early parliamentary general election to take place under two circumstances. In the first instance, where at least two thirds of the members of Parliament vote in favour of a motion to that effect and, secondly, following the successful passing of a motion of no confidence in the government. These two provisions would certainly go a long way to quiet the unease among opponents of fixed terms.

Where the Commonwealth Caribbean is concerned, a review of some of the more recent reports of constitutional reform commissions suggest that for the most part there was not much of an appetite for reforming Westminster in that direction. However, the constitution reform commission of St Lucia strongly supported the provision of a constitutional amendment on fixed dates of election. A reading of the 2011 report shows that the commission favoured a semi-fixed term similar to that proposed for Britain. In that regard, the Commission acknowledged the necessity of having a safety value and consequently recommended that a successful no confidence motion would automatically trigger a dissolution of the Parliament of St Lucia.[47] Recommendations in St Vincent and the Grenadines also mirrored that of St Lucia. Under the draft constitution submitted to parliament, the commission recommended that Parliament can only be dissolved and elections called upon the expiration of four years and nine months from the first sitting of Parliament after the previous dissolution, thus effectively curtailing the ability of the prime minister to determine the election timing.[48]

In contrast, the Political Reform Commission of Belize and the Constitutional Reform Commission of the Bahamas appeared to have rejected the adoption of a fixed term of office. In Belize beyond stating that fixed terms were incompatible with parliamentary systems of governments, the Belize Political Reform Commission offered no explanation for its decision.[49] Thus, the commission failed to use the opportunity provided to chart a course towards more enhanced governance in the country. Similarly, in the Bahamas, a surface initial reading of the report appears to suggest that there was absolutely no support for the adoption of fixed terms of office, although the commission expressed concerns about the ability of the prime minister to call a snap election. Interestingly, while therefore explicitly showing great disdain for a fixed term of office the commission recommended that the prime minister should be constitutionally required to give at least nine months' notice of his/her intention to call general elections. The report further recommended that the prime minister's ability to call for a dissolution of the House be limited to specific situations and the normal end-of-term dissolution. This, in the commission's view, would address the problem of unfairness in calling 'snap' elections. This is rather curious as such a recommendation is tantamount to accepting the value of a semi-fixed method. The logical explanation for this failure to grasp that it was essentially promoting some model of fixed term of office, is the commission's spontaneous rejection and abhorrence of the fixed term of office as practised in presidential political forms such as the US.

One other recent constitution reform exercise is worthy of mention in this regard. In February 2014, Francis Alexis collected and combined all recommendations from all the constitutional reform commissions of Grenada on behalf of the Grenada Constitution Reform Advisory Committee. Among several noteworthy recommendations, the combined report quotes the 2006 Constitution Commission recommendation that the prime minister should be stripped of the power to call a snap election.[50] In keeping with the general tendency to respect the no confidence motion, the 2006 report also recommended that a specific date for the holding of general elections should be enshrined in the Constitution.[51] In combination, these recommendations were viewed as having the capacity to lead to the 'enhancement of deliberative democracy and of the maturing of democratic governance in Grenada.'[52]

We can thus conclude, that despite some reservations related to the potential for fixed terms of office undermining the functioning of the parliamentary political form, which constitutional reform commissions appear to overwhelmingly favour, there is a general tendency to support some form of fixed term of office. Such support whether explicit or indirect stems primarily from a desire to curb what is viewed to be the excessive powers of the prime minister, and is not driven by any philosophically deep commitment to fixed terms.

Conclusion

Contemporary events, developments, and activities suggest that the case for urgent constitutional reform in the Commonwealth Caribbean cannot be disputed, and several elements of West Indian constitutions are easy targets for criticisms. None are more so than the electoral system; the overwhelming dominance of the prime minister especially with regards to his control of the timing of elections and the nature of the relationship of Parliament to the executive branch. It is certainly regrettable that the national support of political parties is not necessarily translated into accurate and acceptable levels of political representation. Yet as I have shown, the system does have its virtues, and there is a clear attachment to the current system when compared to its alternative. The question I have attempted to address is how best to reform the system to breed greater democracy and representation while retaining its good features and overcoming its more distasteful elements. Secondly, lopsided parliaments and executive dominance of the Parliament do not make for a vibrant democracy. However, while many have enthusiastically heralded the virtues of presidentialism with its strong emphasis on the separation of powers, nonetheless the value of the fusion of power under Westminster is often seen as a virtue permitting strong and stable governments. The proposal of the hybrid political form with semi-fixed terms of office would result in greater checks and balances, reduced manipulation of the election timing, enhance the power of the legislature and achieve greater accountability of the executive. These three proposals discussed above, while not providing a solution to the many problems of Westminster, can in combination certainly reduce the probability of continuing malaise in our system of governance.

NOTES

1. Harold A. Lutchman, 'The Westminster System in the Commonwealth Caribbean: Some Issues and Problems', *Transition*, no. 24 (1995): 1–26.
2. Ibid., 1.
3. Ibid.

4. Anthony Maingot, 'Citizenship and Parliamentary Politics in the English Speaking Caribbean', in *Dual Legacies in the Contemporary Caribbean: Continuing Aspects of British and French Dominion*, ed. Paul Sutton, 120–40 (London: Frank Cass and Co. Ltd., 1986), 125–26.

5. Dr The Honourable Ralph E. Gonsalves, 'Good Governance and Constitution Reform in St Vincent and the Grenadines', feature address delivered at the formal launching of the Constitutional Review Commission at the House of Assembly Building, Kingstown, St Vincent and the Grenadines, Monday, February 10, 2003, Office of the Prime Minister.

6. See Denis Scott Chabrol, 'Updated: President Suspends Parliament', November 10, 2014, *Caribbean News Desk*. Retrieved from http://www.caribnewsdesk.com/news/8915-president-prepares-to-officially-announce-suspension-of-parliament-met-with-gecom-chairman. Had the president not prorogued Parliament, the life of the Parliament, which is constitutionally due to end in December 2016, would have come to an end perhaps as the combined opposition indicated that they would bring down the government in a no confidence motion. The no confidence motion to end the life of Parliament was filed over unauthorized expenditure of some US$21M that was rejected in the 2014 budget; the finance minister responded that he was authorised by the court to spend the money. The opposition filed criminal charges against the finance minister for spending the money; the police threw out the request as frivolous as no crime was committed. The opposition sent the finance minister to the Parliament's Privileges Committee (PC) that has not met as yet. In addition, there are concerns that local government elections have not taken place since 1994.

7. Chabrol, 'Updated: President Suspends Parliament.'

8. Ibid.

9. See also, *Caribbean 360*, 'APNU Calls Decision to Suspend Parliament a "Dark Day,"' November 11, 2014.Retrieved from http://www.caribbean360.com/news/apnu-calls-decision-to-suspend-parliament-a-dark-day#ixzz3JofBI3Io

10. Toni Frederick. 'No Confidence Crises Makes Mockery of Caribbean of Democratic System, Says Former Caribbean Lawmakers', *Real FM Grenada*, November 18, 2014. Retrieved from http://www.realfmgrenada.com/regional-news/no-confidence-crises-make-mockery-of-democratic-system-say-former-caribbean-lawmakers/.

11. Maingot, 'Citizenship and Parliamentary Politics', 125–26.

12. Ibid., 120–40.

13. Ibid., 126.

14. Cynthia Barrow-Giles and Tennyson S.D. Joseph, *General Elections and Voting in the English-Speaking Caribbean 1992–2005* (Kingston: Ian Randle Publishers, 2006), 7.

15. See Selwyn Ryan, *Winner Takes All: The Westminster Experience in the Caribbean* (St Augustine: ISER, 1999), 126.

16. Lutchman, 'The Westminster System in the Commonwealth Caribbean', 7.
17. See Peter A. Jamadar, *The Mechanics of Democracy: Proportional Representation vs First Past the Post* (Port of Spain: Inprint Ltd. 1989), 16.
18. Volume III and IV Report of *A Constitutional Commission appointed by His Excellency the Governor General of Saint Kitts and Nevis*, July 1998, 13.
19. The St Lucia Constitution Reform Commission Report 2011, 142.
20. Report of the Constitutional Commission into a Review of The Bahamas Constitution. 2013, 159, http://www.thebahamasweekly.com/uploads/13/Constitution_Commission_Report_2013_8JULY2013.pdf.
21. Ibid.
22. The Final Report of the Political Reform Commission, January 2000, http://ambergriscaye.com/pages/town/FINALREPORTOFTHEPOLITICALREFORMCOMMISSION-complete.htm.
23. The St Lucia Constitution Reform Commission Report, 142.
24. Divided government normally refers to a political situation where no single political party controls both the executive and legislative branches of government simultaneously, or where the legislative chambers in a bicameral system are controlled by two different political parties. This is viewed as arithmetic division of power. Under Westminster, divided government in an arithmetic sense can only occur in the context of a minority government or coalition government. In contrast, divided government in a behavioural sense occurs whether or not there is the arithmetic division of power. In this sense it refers to divisiveness.
25. Eight thousand nine hundred and thirty-nine persons supported the establishment of an Independent Elections and Boundaries Commission compared to the 13,207 persons who voted against the bill. In relation to Bill no 4 – A fixed date for elections, 14,508 persons voted against the bill compared to 7,075 persons who supported. Nearly three times as many persons rejected term limits for the prime minister as those who support it. The results of the referendum showed a mere 5,393 yes votes to 15,270 persons who cast a no against the bill. See http://nowgrenada.com/2016/11/results-grenada-constitution-referendum/ for more details.
26. Stuart Weir and David Beetham, *Political Power and Democratic Control in Britain: The Democratic Audit of the United Kingdom* (London: Routledge, 1999), 47.
27. Ryan, *Winner Takes All*, 130.
28. While West Germany was the only country practising the mixed-member electoral system, since the 1990s a number of other countries have followed suit. In 1993, New Zealand opted for the system. Japan, Venezuela, Bolivia, Mexico, and Israel, for example, have mixed member systems. In the 1990s, Russia and a number of other COMECOM countries such as Albania, Armenia, and newer states of Croatia, Georgia, Hungary, and Lithuania

also adopted mixed-member systems. In the UK, Scotland and Wales also adopted mixed-member systems, while in Britain itself, a Royal Commission Report of 1998 recommended the adoption of the system.

29. Matthew Soberg Shugart and Martin P. Wattenberg, 'Mixed Member Electoral Systems: A Definition and Typology', in *Mixed-Member Electoral Systems: The Best of Both Worlds?* eds. Matthew Soberg Shugart and Martin P. Wattenberg, 9–24 (London: Oxford University Press, 2001).

30. Ibid.

31. Soberg Shugart and Wattenberg define linkage as follows: 'Linkage refers to whether votes are transferred from the nominal tier to the list tier, or whether the number of list seats a party receives is based in some way on how many nominal-tier seats it has won.' Ibid., 1.

32. Ibid., 9–24.

33. Soberg Shugart and Wattenberg, eds, *Mixed-Member Electoral Systems*, 1.

34. Among other things the Grenada 2006 Commission called for the establishment of a unicameral Legislature comprised of the 15 established seats, elected on the electoral principle of first-past-the post, and an additional 13 seats, selected on the basis of the percentage of votes each political party has received in the general elections. It further recommended the retention of the system of elections under the 'First-Past-The-Post' system, and that the successful candidates be referred to as 'Constituency Representative Members of Parliament' or simply 'Constituency Representatives'. Additionally, the Commission recommended that a number of seats in the National Assembly be allocated to persons chosen by the leader of each political party that contested the general elections for constituency representative members of Parliament. Those seats shall be allocated on the basis of the percentage of votes received by each party that contested the elections. See Redrafting the Grenada Constitution, 2006. Retrieved from http://www.gov.gd/egov/docs/legislations/constitution/re-drafting_grenada_constitution.pdf.

35. See Paul Sutton, 'Westminster Challenged, Westminster Confirmed: Which Way Caribbean Constitutional Reform?', *Journal of Eastern Caribbean Studies* 38, nos. 1 and 2: 63–79, at 76.

36. See the Report of the Constitutional Reform Commission of Saint Lucia, 27.

37. Ibid., 26.

38. Ibid.

39. Ibid., 27.

40. Noted by Allan R. Brewer-Carías (1999). Venezuela 2009 Referendum on Continuous Reelection: Constitutional Implications. Retrieved, http://www.ascoa.org/files/I,%201,%20984_%20VENEZUELA%202009%20REFERENDUM%20ON%20CONTINUOUS%20REELECTION_%20New%20York%20coa.pdf. July 21, 2015.

41. Brewer-Carias, 1.

42. See Fixed-term Parliaments Bill – Constitution Committee, chapter 2. Retrieved from http://www.publications.parliament.uk/pa/ld201011/ ldselect/ldconst/69/6904.htm, November 21, 2014.

43. Ibid.

44. Ibid.

45. Ibid.

46. Ibid., chapter 4.

47. The St Lucia Constitution Reform Commission Report, 2011, 143–44.

48. Final report Electoral Observation Mission to the Referendum on Constitutional reform in St Vincent and the Grenadines, November 25, 2009. Retrieved from http://www.caribbeanelections.com/eDocs/election_reports/ vc/VC_OAS_2009.pdf.

49. Final Report of the Political Reform Commission, January 2000.

50. Grenada Reform Commission, Recommendations by Grenada Constitution Review Commissions, 2014. Retrieved from http://www.constitutionnet.org/ files/recommendations_by_grenada_constitution_review_commissions.pdf.

51. Ibid.

52. Ibid., 2014, 26.

3 Are Commonwealth Caribbean Parliaments Now the Least Dangerous Branch of Government?

Derek O'Brien

Introduction

Criticisms of the performance of Commonwealth Caribbean parliaments are legion.[1] Most of these criticisms focus on the relationship between the legislature and the executive and the dominance of the former by the latter. This is attributable to a number of factors. Firstly, the first-past-the-post electoral system, which is the electoral system of choice across the region, with the exception of Guyana, has tended to produce disproportionately large majorities for the winning party. The post-independence era has thus witnessed a number of occasions when the opposition parties in general elections have been effectively annihilated in terms of seats in parliament, leaving the winning party to govern virtually unopposed.[2] Secondly, the comparatively small size of the region's parliaments and the absence of a cap on the number of ministers who can be appointed by the prime minister mean that Commonwealth Caribbean parliaments are dominated to an extraordinary degree by members of the government.[3] In turn, these ministers are bound by the doctrine of collective responsibility, which requires them to toe the government line in parliament. This has made it virtually impossible for any government to be dismissed on a vote of no confidence. Thirdly, while the inclusion of a nominated element – either within a single legislature or in the Upper House in those countries with bicameral legislatures – was intended to serve as something of a bulwark against executive dominance, the fact that in a number of countries the majority of senators are appointed and can be removed on the recommendation of the prime minister has more or less completely undermined this objective.[4] Finally, their small size has meant that the region's parliaments have been unable to resource the kind of network of departmentally related committees which, in other countries, play such a crucial role in scrutinizing the executive.[5]

Though it is relevant to the discussion that follows, this chapter does not dwell on executive dominance of Caribbean parliaments, but rather focuses on a different relationship, namely that between Commonwealth Caribbean parliaments and the courts, by critically examining two relatively recent judicial developments. The first concerns two judgments of the Supreme Court of Belize in which the Court overturned laws enacted by the Belizean Parliament to amend the Constitution. These laws had been passed in accordance with the express provisions for constitutional amendment as laid down in the Constitution itself. The second concerns a judgment of the Caribbean Court of Justice (CCJ), *Myrie v Barbados*,[6] in which a decision taken by the Conference of Heads of Government of the Caribbean Community (CARICOM) was held to have superior legal force, at least at the regional level, to laws enacted by the Parliament of Barbados. These developments are analysed through the lens of two competing visions of democracy: *political* constitutionalism, which prioritizes representative parliamentary democracy, and *legal* constitutionalism, which privileges the role of the courts as the ultimate bastion of democratic values.

In conclusion, I argue that even if these developments can be defended by reference to legal constitutionalist principles, the resulting erosion of the authority of Parliament at both the national and regional level may be just as great as the erosion of parliament's authority resulting from the dominance of the executive, and with just as undesirable consequences from both a political and a legal constitutionalist perspective.

Part I: Amendments to the Constitution

Though they may have been modelled on the UK Parliament, Commonwealth Caribbean parliaments do not enjoy the legislative supremacy traditionally associated with the UK Parliament. According to A.V. Dicey:

> [This] means neither more nor less than this, namely that Parliament... has, under the English Constitution the right to make or unmake any law whatsoever; and further, that no person or body is recognised by the laws of England as having the right to override or set aside the legislation of Parliament.[7]

Instead, Commonwealth Caribbean parliaments' law-making powers are 'subject to the Constitution'. Here, I want to examine what this means in relation to laws enacted by Parliament with a view to amending the constitution. Traditionally, it has been assumed that so long as Parliament complies with any procedural requirements laid down by the constitution there are no limits on parliament's power to amend the constitution. For example, in *obiter dicta* in *Hinds v The Queen*,[8] Lord Diplock, delivering judgment for a majority of the Judicial Committee of the Privy Council (JCPC), declared that:

> Where...a constitution on the Westminster model represents the final step in the attainment of full independence by the peoples of a former colony or protectorate, the Constitution provides machinery whereby any of its provisions, whether relating to fundamental rights and freedoms, or to the stratum of government and the allocation to its various organs of legislative, executive or judicial powers, may be altered by those peoples through their elected representatives in the Parliament acting by specific majorities, which is generally all that is required.[9]

This assumption has, however, been challenged in two recent decisions of the Supreme Court of Belize: *Bowen v Attorney General Belize*[10] and *British Caribbean Bank Ltd v Attorney General Belize.*[11]

In the first case, *Bowen*, a group of landowners sought to challenge the constitutionality of the Belize Constitution (Sixth Amendment) Bill 2008 (the Sixth Amendment). The Sixth Amendment was intended to enable the government to exploit the recent discovery of oil in the country. Clause 2 of the Sixth Amendment, accordingly, sought to disapply the protection afforded by section 17(1) of the Constitution to the owners of:

> [P]etroleum minerals and accompanying substances, in whatever physical state located on or under the territory of Belize...the entire property and control over which are exclusively vested, and shall be deemed always to have been so vested, in the Government of Belize.

The purported effect of the legislation was thus to deny to the owners of any such interests in land the right to apply to the courts for compensation in the event of being arbitrarily deprived of their interests in the land by the state.

Lawyers for the attorney general argued that, since the Sixth Amendment had been approved by the special three-quarters majority required by section 69 of the Constitution, this was sufficient to dispose of the claimants' challenge to its constitutionality. Chief Justice Conteh, however, disagreed. In his view, the law-making powers of the Belizean Parliament were not unlimited: the Belizean Parliament cannot legitimately make laws that are contrary to the 'basic structure' of the Constitution itself.[12] In the chief justice's view, this included not only the fundamental rights guaranteed by Chapter II of the Constitution – in particular the right to redress from the courts for the arbitrary deprivation of property by the state – but also the principles, ideas, beliefs, and desires of the people of Belize as enshrined in the Preamble of the Constitution. These include, among other things, respect for the rule of law and the right of the individual to the ownership of private property.

The chief justice also had regard to the principle of the separation of powers, which had previously been recognized by the JCPC in *Hinds v The Queen* to be an implied feature of the Westminster-type constitutions adopted by Commonwealth Caribbean countries upon independence. In that case, the issue confronting the JCPC was the enactment by the Jamaican Parliament of the Gun Court Act, which created a Gun Court with three divisions, one of which was a Full Court to be manned by three resident magistrates with jurisdiction to hear serious non-capital offences. The effect of the Act was thus to permit resident magistrates to try offences previously only triable on indictment before a judge of the Supreme Court. In the JCPC's view, the attempt by the Jamaican Parliament to vest in a court composed of members of the lower judiciary a jurisdiction that formed part of the existing jurisdiction of the higher judiciary violated the principle of the separation of powers implied in the Constitution, because members of the lower judiciary did not enjoy the same security of tenure and protection of their independence from political pressure as those of the higher judiciary. In other words, the separation of powers between the executive and the judiciary, which was guaranteed by the Constitution, had been breached. Accordingly, the Gun Court Act was held to be void. Though the factual matrix may have been different in *Bowen*, Chief Justice Conteh concluded that the denial of access to the courts for compensation for the arbitrary deprivation of their property by the state would equally violate the principle of the separation of powers.

But, was the fact that, unlike the Gun Court Act, the Sixth Amendment had been approved by a special majority of the National Assembly to count for nothing? In the chief justice's view, section 69 was a mere 'manner and form' requirement, no more than a 'procedural handbook',[13] and was certainly not determinative of the constitutionality of legislation enacted by Parliament. In addition to the formal procedures laid down by section 69, any prospective amendment of the Constitution had to conform to the Constitution's *normative* requirements as captured by section 68, which provides that all laws enacted by Parliament must be 'subject to the Constitution'.[14] Any other view would entail subordinating the supremacy of the Constitution in favour of parliamentary supremacy because it would mean that once the required majority for an amendment is obtained, then absolutely no constitutional provision would be beyond alteration or revocation.[15]

Following the judgment, the government amended Clause 2 of the Sixth Amendment to provide that nothing in the amended section 17 would affect the rights of the owner of any private land beneath which any petroleum deposits are located to receive royalties from the government.[16] This was not, however, to be the end of the confrontation between the government and the courts with regard to Parliament's law-making powers. In the second case, *British Caribbean Bank Ltd*, which followed hard on the heels of *Bowen*, the Supreme Court was confronted with the government's attempt to respond to an earlier decision of the Court of Appeal to invalidate the Belize Telecommunications (Amendment) Act 2009 (TCA 2009) and, at the same time, to introduce an amendment to the Constitution to circumvent the ruling in *Bowen*.

The purpose of the TCA 2009 had been to enable the government compulsorily to acquire the properties, rights, and interests held by the applicants in Belize Telemedia Ltd, a major provider of telecommunications services in Belize.[17] The Court of Appeal, however, held that the TCA 2009 contravened the right to property under section 17(1) of the Constitution because it did not prescribe the principles on which reasonable compensation was to be paid for the acquisition of the applicant's property within a reasonable time. The TCA 2009 was, accordingly, declared to be void.

The government's response to this judgment was twofold. Firstly, the government secured the enactment of the Belize Telecommunications (Amendment) Act 2011 (TCA 2011), which sought to address some of the problems with the TCA 2009 that had been identified by the Court of Appeal. Secondly, the government secured the enactment of the Belize Constitution (Eighth) Amendment Act 2011 (the Eighth Amendment). The Eighth Amendment not only sought to disapply the 'supreme law' clause of the Constitution to 'a law to alter any of the provisions of this Constitution which is passed by the National Assembly in conformity with s 69 of the Constitution', but also expressly declared that 'the provisions of [s 69] are all-inclusive and exhaustive and there is no other limitation, whether substantive or procedural, on the power of the National Assembly to alter this Constitution'. As the Prime Minister, Dean Barrow, frankly admitted, this was in direct response to the judgment of the Supreme Court in *Bowen*.[18] Additionally, the Eighth Amendment added a new Part XIII to the

Constitution, the effect of which was, first, to define the meaning of 'public utilities'; second, to vest majority ownership and control of all public utility providers in the government; and, third, by section 145(1) and 145(2), to declare that the government's acquisition of such public utilities was duly carried out for a public purpose.

The government's efforts to circumvent the restrictions imposed on Parliament's law-making powers by the judgment in *Bowen* were, however, ultimately, to prove unsuccessful, as a challenge to the constitutionality of the Eighth Amendment was upheld by the Supreme Court. Concurring with the judgment of Chief Justice Conteh in *Bowen*, the Supreme Court held that the National Assembly is not legally authorized to make any amendment to the Constitution that would remove or destroy any of the basic structures of the Constitution of Belize.[19] Since the cumulative effect of the Eighth Amendment was to prevent the Court from determining whether the deprivation of property by the government was for a public purpose, the Eighth Amendment offended the principle of the separation of powers and the basic structure of the Constitution. To this extent, the amendments to the Constitution were unlawful, null and void.

It is impossible at this point to predict with any certainty whether the invocation of the basic structure doctrine by the Supreme Court in *Bowen* and in *British Caribbean Bank Ltd* will be followed by other courts in the region. It is certainly difficult to reconcile with the dicta of Lord Diplock in *Hinds*, which did not contemplate there being any implied limit on the legislature's power to alter the Constitution. However, the JCPC's jurisprudence is no longer binding on those countries in the region that have ratified the CCJ's appellate jurisdiction – Barbados, Guyana, Belize, and Dominica. Moreover, the invocation of the basic structure doctrine has been endorsed by some of the region's leading jurists, who argue that, 'in fragile Caribbean democracies in which the legislature is often an extension of the executive, there is something to be said for the robust approaches in defence of core constitutional values.'[20] Tracy Robinson also argues that the basic structure doctrine offers 'a way in which the courts can protect democracy when other bodies exceed their authority.'[21] All that can be said with any certainty at this stage is that if other courts in the region do follow the lead of the Supreme Court in Belize, this will represent not only a significant departure from the traditional view of the region's parliaments' law-making powers but also a significant invasion by the courts of parliament's constitutional sphere in relation to constitutional amendment.

Part II: the CCJ's Judgment in *Myrie v Barbados*

In 2006, disappointed with the pace of regional integration first begun in 1973 with the ratification of the Treaty of Chaguarmas (ToC) and the establishment of the Caribbean Community and Common Market, the region's Heads of Government decided to accelerate and deepen efforts at regional integration by providing for the creation of the Caribbean Single Market and Economy (CSME) under the Revised Treaty of Chaguaramas (RTC). At the same time, the regional court, the CCJ, was vested with an original and exclusive jurisdiction to interpret and apply the RTC.

Amongst various other freedoms, such as free movement of services and capital, the RTC provided for the free movement of skilled CARICOM nationals seeking employment in another member state. A year later, in July 2007, the right of free movement for CARICOM nationals was expanded as a result of a decision of the Heads of Government at their annual Conference to permit *all* CARICOM nationals to be granted a right of entry and an automatic six month stay upon arrival in another Member State, subject to the right of Member States to refuse entry to undesirable persons and those who might become a charge on public funds (the 2007 decision). It was this 2007 Decision which was at the crux of the CCJ's judgment in *Myrie v Barbados*,[22] as the CCJ had to determine the nature of the legal relationship between decisions taken by the Conference of the Heads of Government at the regional level ('Community law') and the laws enacted by the national parliaments of member states ('national law').

The claimant in this case, a Jamaican national, had been refused entry by immigration officials upon her arrival in Barbados. In addition, the claimant had been subjected to insults based upon her nationality and to an unlawful body cavity search in demeaning and unsanitary conditions. Though the claimant also alleged that her fundamental rights and freedoms had been violated and that her treatment had been in violation of the right to non-discrimination on the grounds of nationality, which is guaranteed by Article 7 RTC, the central plank of her case rested upon her right to enter Barbados and to be granted an automatic six-month stay pursuant to the 2007 decision. However, before the CCJ could find that her rights under the 2007 decision had been violated, it had first to adjudicate on two matters: firstly, the right of CARICOM nationals to enforce decisions of the Conference of Heads of Government and, secondly, the relationship between community law and national law.

1. The Enforceability of the 2007 Decision?
By Article 240 (1) RTC:

> Decisions of competent organs taken under this treaty shall be subject to the relevant constitutional procedures of the member states before creating legally binding rights and obligations for nationals of such States.

The government of Barbados accordingly sought to argue that a decision of the Conference could not give rise to rights and obligations enforceable against member states by the nationals of member states unless and until the decision had been incorporated by national parliaments into the municipal law of the member state. In the CCJ's view, however, this argument was mistaken because it was based on the orthodox dualist approach to international law, which requires the provisions of an international treaty to be incorporated into the domestic law of a state before the treaty can be enforced under the national law of that state. Here, however, the question was not whether the decision was enforceable at the *domestic* level, but rather whether it was enforceable at the *community* level. In the Court's view, Article 240 RTC was concerned exclusively with the creation of rights and obligations at the *domestic* level and their enforceability in *domestic* law.[23]

To accept the submissions of the government of Barbados on this issue would, in the CCJ's view, have been a retrograde step. It would have meant, effectively, that the states had not progressed beyond the voluntary system that had been in force prior to the CSME. It would also have prejudiced the attainment of the aims and objectives of the CSME if binding regional decisions could be invalidated at the community level by the failure on the part of a particular state to incorporate those decisions locally. If domestic incorporation were a condition precedent to the creation of community rights, an anomalous situation could be created in which some member states had incorporated the decision and others had not. In the CCJ's view:

> This would be untenable as it would destroy the uniformity, certainty and predictability of Community law.[24]

2. The Relationship between Community Law and National Law
As the CCJ readily acknowledged, the grant of a right of entry and an automatic six month stay granted by the 2007 decision was wholly inconsistent with the immigration laws enacted by the Parliament of

Barbados. In the Court's view, however, this inconsistency was of no consequence because:

> The original jurisdiction of the Court has been established to ensure observance by the Member States of obligations voluntarily undertaken by them at the Community level. The Court is therefore entitled, if not required, to adjudicate complaints of alleged breaches of Community law *even where Community law is inconsistent with domestic law* (emphasis added). It is the obligation of each State, having consented to the creation of a Community obligation, to ensure that its domestic law, at least in its application, reflects and supports Community law.[25]

The logic of regional integration between a community of states necessarily entailed, in the Court's view, the creation of '*a new legal order*', which required the member states to accept certain limits, albeit relatively modest, in particular areas of national sovereignty. Henceforth:

> Community law and the limits it imposes on the Member States must take precedence over national legislation, *in any event at Community level* (emphasis added).[26]

While claiming to eschew the supranationalism which is such a distinctive feature of the European Union, and to denounce the applicability of the principles of 'supremacy' and 'direct effect', as developed by the European Court of Justice,[27] to the Caribbean regional integration project, the CCJ's judgment in *Myrie* still manages to make remarkable inroads into the law-making powers of Commonwealth Caribbean parliaments in at least two respects. Firstly, the judgment means that national parliaments are no longer the only bodies capable of granting rights to their citizens which can be enforced against their governments. Henceforth, the Heads of Government of the member states can create rights for CARICOM citizens by reaching unanimous decisions at their biannual conferences. Secondly, the judgment means that decisions taken by consensus by the Heads of Government of the member states can, effectively, trump the laws made by their national parliaments in so far as the latter are inconsistent with the former.

Though it is tempting to say this is no different from the relationship between the UK and the European Union under *European* community law, the comparison is, in fact, quite mistaken. In the UK, community law trumps national law, not as a result of a decision of the European Court of Justice, but as a result of an Act of the UK Parliament: s. 2(1) of the European Communities Act 1972. This has been confirmed by s.18 of the European Union Act 2011, which provides that:

Directly applicable or directly effective EU law (that is, the rights, powers, liabilities, obligations, restrictions, remedies and procedures referred to in section 2(1) of the European Communities Act 1972) falls to be recognised and available in law in the United Kingdom only by virtue of that Act or where it is required to be recognised and available in law by virtue of any other Act.

The same cannot be said for any of the member states of CARICOM. There is, as yet, no Act passed by a Commonwealth Caribbean Parliament which expressly provides that CARICOM law trumps national law. Yet this is, to all intents and purposes, the practical effect of the judgment in *Myrie*.

Part III: Interpreting the Constitutional Impact of the Invocation of the Basic Structure Doctrine and the *Myrie* Judgment

1. *A Political Constitutionalist Analysis*

When using the term political constitutionalism public law scholars are referring to the belief that representative democracy is the paramount principle upon which the Constitution is founded.[28] Advocates of political constitutionalism put their faith in the political process, which includes regular free and fair elections and, in between elections, a Parliament which is capable of rigorously scrutinizing the actions and politics of the government. It will be readily appreciated that in the context of the Commonwealth Caribbean, with the constraints on local parliaments' ability to scrutinize the executive for the reasons listed in the 'Introduction', it is that much harder to make out a case for political constitutionalism. Notwithstanding these manifest inadequacies, political constitutionalists would argue that in a democracy the political process nevertheless remains the most *legitimate* means of guarding against unconstitutional behaviour by those in authority. The role of the courts in scrutinizing the government or the legislature ought to be fairly limited because, being unelected and unaccountable, judges lack democratic legitimacy.

But the arguments advanced by political constitutionalists are not solely normative, they are also instrumental. Political constitutionalists thus assert that the political process can deter governments from doing unconstitutional things. This may be because members of Parliament might think badly of a government that behaved unconstitutionally and might refuse to support that government in a vote of confidence in parliament. This is unlikely, it has to be admitted, in the Commonwealth Caribbean context, for the reasons outlined above. However, political constitutionalists additionally assert that the political process provides a corrective if the government behaves unconstitutionally because the people will vote for a different party at the next general election, believing that the new government will conduct itself in a more constitutionally acceptable manner. While it is true that elections in the Commonwealth Caribbean have not always been adjudged to be free and fair – Antigua and Barbuda and Guyana being two particularly egregious examples of countries in which the outcome of elections has been contaminated by electoral malpractice[29] – elections in the region as a whole have been comparatively free and fair, judged by international standards. This is evidenced by the number of countries in the region that have satisfied Huntington's 'two-turnover test' as a measure of consolidated democracy.[30] That is to say, since independence successive governments across the region have respected the outcomes of elections and have peacefully surrendered power to their successors.

Applying these principles to the developments examined in Parts I and II, political constitutionalists would doubtless conclude that parliament's law-making powers ought not to be limited by reference to a concept as nebulous as the basic structure doctrine invoked by the Belize Supreme Court in the *Bowen* and *British Caribbean Bank Ltd* cases. As J.R. Vile has argued, judicially implied limits on a legislature's right to amend the constitution upsets the delicate balance between the people, Parliament and the courts. Though Vile is referring specifically to the US Constitution, his comments apply with equal force to Commonwealth Caribbean constitutions:

> To empower the courts not simply to review the procedures whereby amendments were adopted but also to void amendments on the basis of their substantive content would surely threaten the notion of a government founded on the consent of the governed.[31]

As Vile observes, the solution to a bad or unworkable constitutional amendment is not invalidation by the courts by reference to implied constitutional limits on the legislature's powers, but rather another constitutional amendment repealing it.[32]

Political constitutionalists would also argue that the CCJ should not in the *Myrie* case have held that the laws made by national parliaments are trumped by decisions taken collectively by the Heads of Government at a regional conference. This is especially so if the substance of such decisions has not been included in the governing party's manifesto, has not been debated before the national Parliament and has not been subject to parliamentary scrutiny. From a political constitutionalist perspective, such decisions lack any democratic mandate.

2. A Legal Constitutionalist Analysis

Legal constitutionalists put their faith in the judicial rather than the political system. Legal constitutionalists rely on both philosophical and practical arguments to advance their case. In philosophical terms, they believe that there are certain 'higher law' principles, which are so fundamental as to be immutable. A law that contradicts such principles cannot be a genuine law at all and should not be enforced by the courts. As we have seen, even in a region such as the Commonwealth Caribbean where all the countries adopted codified constitutions upon independence, the idea that there are certain 'higher law' principles might still be important in supplementing the text of the codified constitution. This is because legal constitutionalists believe that the text of the constitution does not necessarily provide an exhaustive statement of all the principles upon which the governmental system is founded. There may be gaps or interstices within even a codified constitution and these may have to be filled by the judges by reference to the principles of 'higher law'. In practical terms, legal constitutionalists point to the dominance of the executive over the legislature, rendering the latter an imperfect mechanism for holding the government to account. To redress the imbalance between the legislature and the executive, there needs to be an external body which can ensure that the political branch of government acts constitutionally. Because the judges are independent the courts are the body which is best suited to discharging that responsibility.

Legal constitutionalists would thus likely view the invocation of the basic structure doctrine by the Supreme Court of Belize in the *Bowen* and *British Caribbean Bank Ltd* cases as necessary in order to preserve individual rights from the threat of a legislative majority. In the context of the disproportionate effects of the first-past-the-post electoral system in the Commonwealth Caribbean, where winning parties have, on occasion, won all the seats in parliament, such majorities are not so unusual. Moreover, in the case of the Belize Constitution there is no requirement for constitutional amendments to be approved in a referendum. Thus, from a legal constitutionalist perspective, the only body standing between the fundamental rights guaranteed by the Constitution and a malevolent legislative majority was the Supreme Court, which was obliged to invoke the basic structure doctrine in order to preserve forever the rights guaranteed by the Constitution. Legal constitutionalists would also, doubtless, regard the judgment of the CCJ in *Myrie,* as a necessary corrective to the failure of the government of Barbados to amend its immigration laws to ensure that they were compatible with a decision taken at the regional level to which the government of Barbados was a party.

Conclusion

For the present, at least, it looks as though the legal constitutionalists are winning the argument, but this victory may come at a cost in terms of a diminution in the status and prestige of Commonwealth Caribbean parliaments. This could be dangerous because once citizens lose their faith in the authority of Parliament and the ordinary democratic process they may turn to extra-parliamentary means in order to bring about change. An additional danger of upsetting the traditional balance of power as between the courts and Parliament is that, if the courts are perceived as becoming too powerful and straying beyond their proper constitutional sphere, governments may respond, as the government of Belize attempted to do, by introducing legislation to place limits on the courts' powers of constitutional review. If this happens, one of the fundamental tenets of legal constitutionalism – namely, the supremacy of the constitution and the protection afforded by judicial review – will be fatally undermined. The victory of the legal constitutionalists in that case will be very much of the pyrrhic kind.

NOTES

1. See, for example, Cynthia Barrow-Giles, 'Regional Trends in Constitutional Developments in the Commonwealth Caribbean', paper prepared for the Conflict Prevention and Peace Forum, Social Science Research Council, January 2010 Retrieved from http:// www.agora-parl.org; and the report prepared by Trevor Munroe, Transparency International Country Study Report: Caribbean Composite Study 2004. Retrieved from http://www.transparency.org.
2. See P. Emmanuel, *Governance and Democracy in the Commonwealth Caribbean: An Introduction* (Bridgetown, Barbados: Institute of Social and Economic Research, 1993).
3. Trevor Munroe, Transparency International Country Study Report.
4. See D. O'Brien, *The Constitutional Systems of the Commonwealth Caribbean* (Oxford: Hart Publishing, 2014), 149.
5. R.A.W. Rhodes, J. Wanna and P. Weller, eds., *Comparing Westminster* (Oxford: Oxford University Press, 2011).

6. *Myrie v Barbados*, CCJ 3 (OJ) 2013. Retrieved from http://www. caribbeancourtofjustice.org/judgments-proceedings/original-jurisdiction-judgments

7. A.V. Dicey, *Introduction to the Study of the Law of the Constitution*, 8th ed. (London: Macmillan: 1915, reprinted Indianapolis: IN: Liberty Fund, 1982), 3–4.

8. *Hinds v the Queen*, AC, 1977, 195. Retrieved from http:// www.bailii.justice. org.

9. Ibid., 214.

10. *Bowen v Attorney General*, BZ 2009 SC 2. Unreported. Available on file with the author.

11. *British Caribbean Bank Ltd v AG Belize* Claim No 597 of 2011. Unreported. Available at: www.belizelaw.org.

12. Invoking the 'basic structure' doctrine which had originally been expounded by the Supreme Court of India in *Golak Nath v State of Punjab*, AIR 1967 SC 1643, retrieved from https://indiankanoon.org/doc/21266288/ and in *Kesavananda v State of Kerala*, AIR 1973 SC 1461, retrieved from https:// indiankanoon.org/doc/257876/.

13. *Bowen*, paragraph 10.

14. Ibid., paragraphs 105–107.

15. Ibid., paragraph 120.

16. For an account of the *Bowen* litigation, see *Prime Minister Belize v Vellos* [2010] UKPC 7.

17. One of the major shareholders in Belize Telemedia Ltd was B.B. Holdings Ltd., the chairman of which was Michael Ashcroft, a major funder of the official opposition, the People's United Party.

18. See A. Fiadjoe, 'Legal Opinion on the Ninth Amendment Bill of Belize' (2011), 20. Available at: www.thehaywardcharitablebelizetrust.com.

19. *British Caribbean Bank Ltd v AG Belize* [paragraph 45].

20. T. Robinson, A. Bulkan and A. Saunders, *Fundamentals of Caribbean Constitutional Law* (London: Sweet & Maxwell, 2015), 200.

21. T. Robinson, 'Our Inherent Constitution', in *Transitions in Caribbean Law: Law-making, Constitutionalism and the Convergence of National and International Law*, eds. D. Berry and T. Robinson, 248–76 (Kingston: The Caribbean Law Publishing Company, 2013), 248.

22. *Myrie v Barbados*, 2013, CCJ 3 (OJ). Retrieved from http://www. caribbeancourtofjustice.org/judgments-proceedings/original-jurisdiction-judgments

23. Ibid., paragraph 52.

24. Ibid., paragraph 53.

25. Ibid., paragraph 52.

26. Ibid., paragraph 69.

27. See Van Gend en Loos (Case 26/62) [1963] ECR 1. Retrieved from http://www. cvce.eu/en/obj/judgment_of_the_court_van_gend_loos_case_26_62_5_ february_1963-en-4b81dcab-c67e-44fa-b0c9-18c48848faf3.html.

28. M. Elliott and R. Thomas, *Public Law* (Oxford: Oxford University Press: 2014), 35.

29. See D.W. Payne, 'Political Financing: Access of Political Parties to the Media', in *From Grassroots to the Airwaves: Paying for Political Parties and Campaigns in the Caribbean*, ed. S. Griner and D. Zovatto, 39–59 (Washington, DC: Organization American States: 2005), 38. See also report of the International Team of Observers at the Elections of Guyana, *Something to Remember* (London: Latin America Bureau, 1980).

30. S. Huntington, *The Third Wave: Democratization in the Late Twentieth Century* (Norman, OK: University of Oklahoma Press, 1991).

31. John R. Vile, 'The Case against Implicit Limits', in *Responding to Imperfection: The Theory and Practice of Constitutional Amendment*, ed. S. Levinson, 191–214 (Princeton, NJ: Princeton University Press, 1995), 198.

32. Ibid.

4 Beyond Westminster in the Caribbean: *A Perspective on the Regional Project*

Patsy Lewis

Introduction

This chapter addresses the question of Westminster from the perspective of the Caribbean regional project. Most of the writings on the Westminster model in the Caribbean have focused on national politics. Few make mention of the regional, and those that do, treat the region as a solution for the problems of Westminster as they appear at the national level. The question of how Westminster inhibits the regional project is not well explored, although I have raised this as a concern in my work.[1] The further task of what a new regional democratic process should look like and how the national project can be transcended to achieve this remains unexplored. This chapter establishes a relationship between certain features of Westminster as practised in the Caribbean, namely the first-past-the-post basis for choosing the government and the predominant role of the prime minister, and the effects of both on the regional integration project. It also discusses ways in which these may be overcome. It does not assume that there is no role for Westminster constitutions, especially in preserving a national space for decision-making and in safeguarding the democratic will of citizens against an intrusive regional project. Nevertheless, its focus is limited to ways in which Westminster inhibits the regional project.

Paul Sutton, in his discussion of Westminster in the Caribbean and the failed attempts at constitutional reform, predicts that reform is likely to occur in the context of a region-wide crisis which forces the countries to consider a regional project, a federation along the lines of the US model.[2] Tennyson Joseph also suggests that the resolution of deficiencies in national constitutions would occur at the regional level in a federation:

> In prescribing a new politics and a new democracy for our Caribbean therefore, our first and most urgent task is to recognize that the first independence revolution has run its course, and that the post-colonial Caribbean state as we know it, has exhausted all its possibilities.

Once we come to that realisation, we will have no choice but to turn our collective attention to *the pursuit of the federal option* (his emphasis).[3]

This tendency to view federation as the best option for resolving some of the weaknesses inherent in the national sphere is not new. In the wake of the collapse of the West Indian Federation and before the formalization of post-independence constitutions for Barbados and the Windward and Leeward islands, Arthur Lewis argued for a federal structure on the following grounds:

...the maintenance of good government requires a federal structure. In a small island of 50,000 or 100,000 people, dominated by a single political party, it is very difficult to prevent political abuse. Everybody depends on the government for something, however small, so most are reluctant to offend it...The civil servants live in fear; the police avoid unpleasantness; the trade unions are tied to the party; the newspaper depends on government advertisements; and so on...The only safeguard against this is federation. If the government in island C misbehaves, it will be criticized openly by the citizens of island E. The federal government must be responsible for law and order, and for redress of financial and other abuses....[4]

He concluded that:

They (political leaders) make federation a question of customs unions, freedom of movement, exclusive lists, concurrent lists and the like. All this is secondary. The fundamental reason for federating these islands is that it is the only way that good government can be assured to their peoples[5] (capitalization removed).

Placing the burden of the democratic defects of national constitutions on the regional project ignores the dynamic interface between national politics and the regional integration project. I have laid the prime responsibility for the Caribbean Community's (CARICOM's) implementation deficit[6] at the feet of national politics. Specifically, I identify two of the features of the Westminster system that contribute to this: the first-past-the-post (winner takes all) basis for electoral victory, and the excessive authority of the prime minister.[7]

First-Past-the-Post

The negative effects of the first-past-the-post feature of Westminster constitutions, which assigns victory to the party commanding the majority of seats in Parliament, have been well recognized. Specifically, it amplifies the victory of parties which may have small majorities or even minorities, by allowing them a lion's share of parliamentary seats, thus marginalizing opposition parties. This is further exacerbated in instances where the winning party secures a large majority. The overwhelming victory of Keith Mitchell's New National Party (NNP) in the 1999 elections in Grenada, and again in 2013, capturing all of the seats in parliament,[8] is an extreme example. Further, it makes the terrain for third parties extremely difficult. By excluding the opposition from government, it ensures that their primary function when in opposition is to oppose the government. Regaining power remains the main focus, contributing to the undue politicization of issues and encouraging partisan approaches to government. Selwyn Ryan (1999) has explored this relationship extensively but his analysis does not extend to its effect on the regional process.

This feature is carried over at the regional level, where the opposition does not have a formal role and where in its absence, the Heads of Government operate as a club. A feature of the governance model of CARICOM decision-making is that this occurs at the regional rather than national level. Heads of Governments arrive at decisions at their summits, then expect these to be implemented at the national level. Thus, decisions are not driven by debates and consensus at the national level which then inform regional action. The natural outcome of this is the politicization of regional issues, which fall prey to national politics once they enter the domestic sphere.[9] This is particularly crucial in cases where implementation requires the input of opposition parties, although constitutions requiring simple parliamentary majorities are not immune. A case in point is the ruling People's National Party's (PNP) attempt to institute the Caribbean Court of Justice (CCJ) as Jamaica's final court of appeal, by simple majority in both the upper and lower houses, which was declared illegal by the Judicial Committee of the Privy Council (JCPC), Jamaica's final court of appeal.[10] Prime Minister Ralph Gonsalves' attempt to introduce the CCJ as St Vincent's final court of appeal as part of a larger programme of constitutional reform, also failed when a majority of the electorate voted to reject the new constitution.

As I have argued elsewhere:

> Legislative changes that can be enacted through simple parliamentary majorities are far less problematic than changes to entrenched constitutional provisions, such as the CCJ represents. This does not mean, however, that such changes may not be highly controversial and, as such, threaten the political fortunes of the particular government at home. In other words, the ability to effect legislative changes on the basis of simple parliamentary majorities does not in itself insulate regional decision-

making from the imperatives of national politics, especially where deep cleavages exist. Ultimately, legislation would be enacted at the national level only if it is not sufficiently controversial as to be turned to the service of national political ambitions.[11]

One element of the continued marginalization of opposition parties in the regional project is the effect on continuity of decisions over time. Unfortunately for regional decision-making, politics in the region are fluid, with a healthy change of administrations after national elections. Cynthia Barrow-Giles has observed that:

> Between 1992 and 2010, over 65 general elections took place in the Commonwealth Caribbean, with at least 25 changes of government. Approximately 14 of these elections were won by parties that were new, or experiencing their first electoral victories, or had been in opposition for three consecutive elections or more.[12]

The result of this is that today's Head of Government is tomorrow's opposition leader who finds himself or herself with no mechanism for contributing to decision-making at the regional level. This alienation of the opposition from decision-making contributes to their oppositionist stance, as illustrated in the case of the CCJ where both former prime ministers Edward Seaga (in Jamaica) and Basdeo Panday (in Trinidad and Tobago), supported the formation of the CCJ but found themselves in the unenviable position of opposing its implementation when no longer in power. Thus, at the regional level, the opposition finds that it has no option but to adopt an oppositionist stance,[13] for to support the government at the regional level would be to weaken its role as opposition at the national level, where its primary concern is to gain power. In this scenario national politics takes precedence over regional concerns. The absence of the opposition from regional decision-making will be discussed later, but it constitutes one of the key impediments to regional implementation and the slow movement of the integration process.

The Excessive Authority of the Prime Minister

The summary of the Organization of American States (OAS) 2002 conference on 'Westminster in the Caribbean',[14] observes that [the] 'excessive authority and overwhelming power constitutionally granted to the prime minister' and 'the further concentration of power due to the ineffective separation between the executive and the legislature' presents a challenge to democracy.[15] Terri-Ann Gilbert-Roberts locates this feature of

Caribbean politics at the heart of the implementation deficit characterizing CARICOM. She argues that in the Caribbean, sovereignty has become embedded in the person of the leader and not the people and is magnified at the regional level in the absence of a regional identity which she defines as 'ideas supported by measureable collective action'.[16]

While this is an important insight into the role of the prime minister and how this carries over into the regional project, with negative consequences for the latter, the relationship is more complex. Despite the dominance of prime ministers at home and within CARICOM decision-making structures, their role at the regional level is somewhat paradoxical. In the decision-making structure of the CARICOM Conference of Heads of Government, prime ministers oftentimes act as lone agents making decisions on behalf of their countries, sometimes without the support of members of their government and party, far less the opposition. In such a scenario, regional decisions are a hard sell, so implementation suffers.

While governments can rule on the basis of parliamentary majority at the national level, they are moribund at the regional level where changes require national input. To state differently, it is difficult to effect regional change in the absence of a national consensus. If looked at from this perspective, then, it is clear that any progress towards a new form of regional governance, federation or otherwise, is contingent on national constitutional change or a regional structure that is able to overcome the effect of partisan politics.

Constitutional Reform

We now turn our attention to a brief discussion of the focus of constitutional changes in the CARICOM region and the extent to which any account is taken of the challenges Westminster constitutions present to the advance of the regional project. Sutton identifies a wide range of issues that have been raised in discussions in the region on constitutional reform. These include:

> ...the repatriation of the constitution; the role of the head of state, including whether they are to be a ceremonial president or an executive president; a limitation on the powers on (sic) the prime minister, including restrictions on the number of terms served; the method of election for the lower house and of nomination for the upper house; improving the powers of the legislature, including a limitation on the number of parliamentarians that can serve on the executive; improving the executive and public service accountability through the creation of an effective legislative committee

system; designing measures and mechanisms to limit patronage and corruption, including consideration of the financing of political parties at elections; reinvigorating local government; and the replacement of the JCPC with the CCJ. [17]

The most relevant concerns to address at the regional level are the marginalization of the opposition (including third parties) inherent in the 'winner takes all' feature of the constitutions; the removal of the Queen as Head of State and her replacement with a president (as already exists in Dominica, Guyana, and Trinidad and Tobago); the entrenchment of the CCJ as the final court of appeal; and a stronger alignment between national constitutions and regional goals so that regional decisions are given legal effect in national constitutions. The first and last would help to address CARICOM implementation challenges.

The approaches toward constitutional reform so far have been, for the most part, to treat these as a purely internal matter. CARICOM, despite its commitment to harmonizing laws and its role in drafting model laws to facilitate legislative commonality in the region, has had no formal input in these efforts to reform post-independence constitutions. Yet, given the similarity of challenges with Westminster systems of governance, and the culpability of national constitutions in hindering CARICOM implementation, is there a case for a regional approach to address these weaknesses? Might the region become an avenue for breaking down national partisanship? Despite a legitimate case for the engagement of the CARICOM Secretariat in this process of constitutional reform, it would be naive to believe that this would be a smooth process, given the current features of regional governance already raised. It is quite likely that the process could follow past patterns of heads of government (HOGs) agreeing on an approach and in the process alienating the opposition parties with the expected results. Such an outcome, arguably, could be circumvented if this takes place at the bureaucratic level within the CARICOM Secretariat. Given the institution's dominance by ruling politicians, it is most likely that this would soon become politicized. Another approach would be to transform the regional decision-making process to take account of these weaknesses. This would be in the direction of expanding opportunities for shaping regional decision-making.

Although the regional project is not at the centre of these constitutional reviews, there is evidence that some account is taken of its implementation challenges, especially in respect of replacing the Judicial Committee of the Privy Council with the CCJ as the final court of appeal, which is not easily facilitated by national constitutions. Of 15 CARICOM states, 12 have implemented the CCJ in its original jurisdiction. The remaining three, the Bahamas, Haiti and Montserrat, are not signatories to the agreement. The entrenching of the Court as the final court of appeal has met with less success, with only four – Barbados, Belize, Guyana and Dominica – accepting it as their final court of appeal. Various recommendations for constitutional reform in Grenada have included provision for entrenching the CCJ as the final court of appeal which, under the existing constitution requires a referendum. The matter appears to have been put to rest when Grenadians voted in a referendum in 2016 against a new constitution which would have entrenched the CCJ. The St Lucia Constitution Commission[18] considered both the adoption of the CCJ (para 381–87) and freedom of movement of CARICOM nationals (para 146–49). In the first instance, it recommended the adoption of the CCJ, but provided no guidelines for how this should be done (para 387) and, in the second, decided that the issue was outside of its 'jurisdiction' (para 149). The Report of the Trinidad and Tobago Constitution Review Commission gave considerable attention to discussing the pros and cons of replacing the Privy Council with the CCJ, but recommended that it should be put to a referendum (para 277 (b)).[19]

In both St Vincent and Grenada constitution reform proposals sought to introduce provisions to facilitate regional integration, more broadly. In Grenada, this included the recommendation for exempting 'federation measures...from the more rigid entrenchment stipulations'[20] of the constitution. One proposal from the Grenada Constitutional Reform Committee (McIntosh, Revised Draft Constitution 2006) was for the inclusion of Article XII of the CARICOM Charter of Civil Society in the constitution.

In St Vincent, the proposed revised Constitution sought to facilitate the adoption of the CCJ by requiring 'a two-thirds majority of the National Assembly...without the further requirement of another referendum'.[21] The 2009 St. Vincent Constitution Act goes further in explicitly acknowledging regional integration. Paragraph 23 obliges public bodies to take account of the country's obligations under CARICOM and the Organisation of Eastern Caribbean States (OECS) and applicable international law.[22] As with provisions governing the adoption of the CCJ, the Act also allowed for a two-thirds majority of the assembly to give legal effect to 'any treaty, convention or other agreement to which St Vincent and the Grenadines is a party, the purpose or object of which is to deepen, widen or otherwise strengthen regional integration in the OECS or in CARICOM whether among themselves or together with any other country or countries'.[23]

The St Vincent experiment in constitutional change[24] which began in 2002 and ended in 2009 with the rejection of the proposed constitution by 55 per cent of the electorate, illustrates some of the challenges in effecting constitutional change even when these could potentially strengthen opposition parties and reduce the prime minister's pre-eminence. Specific proposals to address the exclusion of opposition parties under the existing constitution included a 'mixed system' of traditional first-past-the-post elections and proportional representation in the National Assembly which replaces Parliament; limits set on the size of Cabinet (12 in this case), which ensures that it no longer constitutes a majority; and the inclusion of civil society at the expressed invitation of the prime minister and minority leader (formerly leader of the opposition) to speak to the National Assembly on specific issues, but without the right to vote.[25] It also sought to introduce a number of initiatives that would have weakened the dominance of the prime minister and strengthened that of the leader of the opposition, including the latter's chairing of the Public Accounts Commission, the composition of which would have a majority of opposition members.[26] It would also have removed the prime minister's power to appoint chairpersons of service commissions, inter alia.

Despite broad agreement on these measures up to 2007, the opposition leader made his continued engagement with the Constitutional Review process contingent on certain demands being met. Prime Minister Gonsalves refused to address these, arguing in his response that they were not 'credibly...linked' to the process of constitutional reform.[27] In his discussion of the process in an address at the University of the West Indies, Mona, Gonsalves noted the irony of an opposition party rejecting proposals that would have strengthened its hand and weakened his authority as sitting prime minister.[28]

Democratizing CARICOM

We now assess the structures that exist at the regional level and their potential to break this deadlock. The main avenues for influencing decision-making within CARICOM outside of the formal government-dominated structures are the Assembly of Caribbean Community Parliamentarians (ACCP) and the Civil Society Forum (CSF), introduced in 1994 and 1999, respectively.

The ACCP was established as a 'deliberative body'.[29] It was to comprise representatives either elected or nominated by national parliaments.[30] Presumably, the intention was for representatives to be drawn from parliament[31] although this is not explicitly stated, leaving the door open for selection of persons from outside of parliament. Its functions were restricted to deliberating and consulting on matters falling within the scope of the treaty (article 5), with specific restrictions placed on its ability to address matters falling within the purview of the state (article 5, paragraph 4). Member states are allowed to withdraw from the arrangement (article 14 (2)). The committee was to have met every year at the expense of their governments but have done so on only three occasions.[32]

The ACCP has not been particularly effective. There are some obvious weaknesses that inhibit its efficacy as a mechanism for breaking the oppositionist features of regional politics. First, it depends on government funding for its survival. This presupposes both an interest on government's part in promoting opposition participation and their ability, where there is an interest, in providing the necessary financial resources. Secondly, while it allows for a broader engagement of government members in the regional process, it also stands to replicate the under-representation of the formal opposition that is a feature of the national process. Furthermore, by limiting membership to sitting members of Parliament it continues the disengagement of third parties whether or not they have some popular support. Finally, this is a 'deliberative' and 'consultative' mechanism, not designed to have any real influence on CARICOM decision-making.

The CSF was a response at the regional level to the commitment made in the Charter of Civil Society[33] adopted by the HOG in 1997 to provide a framework for wider consultations:

> The States undertake to establish within their respective States a framework for genuine consultations among the social partners in order to reach common understandings on and support for the objectives, contents and implementation of national economic and social programmes and their respective roles and responsibilities in good governance (ARTICLE XXII).

The CSF has functioned on an ad hoc basis rather than as a structured avenue of engagement with CARICOM. The first meeting with the HOG was held in 2002, in Liliendaal, Guyana, out of which came the 'Liliendaal Statement of Principles on Forward Together',[34] which called for mechanisms to further 'continuous dialogue' with civil society, inter alia.

In 2010, the CSF benefitted from an EU-funded project, justified under
the terms of the Cotonou Partnership Agreement and the CARIFORUM–
EC Economic Partnership Agreement (EPA) for civil society consultation,
to establish a 'model framework' for national and regional consultation.
Based on a series of meetings with some 400 civil society representatives,
a framework for the more structured engagement of civil society groups
within CARICOM was adopted in 2011.[35] This framework would allow
for 'direct access to policymakers at the national level'; incorporation of a
formal mechanism for engaging civil society within CARICOM governance
structures; and a system for 'reporting the decisions being implemented
as a result of consultations with Civil Society'.[36] Tillman Thomas, former
Prime Minister of Grenada, then Chair of CARICOM, in an address entitled
'Re-energising CARICOM Integration', went further in recommending
the 'establishment of a Permanent Forum of Non-State Actors with formal
membership of all Councils of the Community, according to subjects
under consideration' and that HOG 'Agree on a timetable for the provision
in each member state of a legal basis for the CARICOM Charter of Civil
Society, thereby authorising the composition of the office holders, rules of
procedure and access to public funds'.[37]

This discussion identifies one of the more glaring weaknesses of the
CSF to broaden CARICOM's decision-making process, the absence of
formal structures entrenching it within the regional governance structure.
Thomas's recommendations, if implemented, would entrench the CSF in
CARICOM decision-making structures, providing a more legitimate basis
for its engagement. Another weakness is the absence of clear sources of
funding to underwrite this process. The reliance on European Development
Fund (EDF) financing to engage civil society in a critical discussion of the
problem suggests some of the dangers inherent in the region's failure to
take on this responsibility. The consultation process was located within the
EU's commitment under the African, Caribbean and Pacific States (ACP)
and the CARIFORUM–EC Economic Partnership Agreement to deepen
consultation with civil society and its commitment to advancing the
CARICOM integration process and, in particular, the CSME. This hardly
appears to be an internally driven process. Kristina Hinds-Harrison has
identified the lack of conceptual clarity as one of the challenges in engaging
with civil society.[38] Pointedly, it is not clear from various usages of terms
such as 'stakeholders', 'social partners', civil society' who government
means to engage. Furthermore, the focus on civil society, used to refer to

formally organized sections of society, stands to marginalize sections of the society that are not organized in formal organizations.

The Way Forward

Drawing from the discussion above, it is clear that regional structures as currently exist do not provide an adequate vehicle for popular engagement. The ACCP would have to be entrenched, adequately funded and revised to provide a greater role for opposition parties both within and without parliament. Its duties must also go beyond advising and consulting to directly influencing decision-making. This would allow for reviewing decisions of HOG and placing issues on the regional agenda. This should give them a more vested role in the implementation of CARICOM decisions and go some distance towards the de-politicization of regional issues. These measures could be supplemented with mechanisms at the national level to allow for political consensus on positions to advance at the regional level. It is unlikely that either the revised ACCP or mechanisms for achieving a consensus among local parties on regional issues would be able to maintain a clear distinction between national and regional issues. In most instances, this is an artificial divide given that the regional project is meant to advance national interests. It is difficult to break the tradition of oppositionist politics without some reform at the national level to bring the opposition into political decision-making. Short of constitutional reform, this could occur through a deliberate regional initiative to entrench regional decision-making in popular national structures.

It is not sufficient to rely on the deeper engagement of opposition parties to break the implementation deadlock and democratize the regional project; nor is the CSF, even if it were entrenched and its participation well funded, a sufficient model for engaging the populace. It is important, given the reality that most of our people are not organized into formal structured organizations, that mechanisms are developed to provide for their direct intervention, including voting on crucial decisions. As Gilbert-Roberts puts it, this requires 'the transformation of the meaning and role of sovereignty in Caribbean politics' towards a more popular conceptualization of sovereignty, which invests sovereignty in the region's people, rather than its political leaders.[39] My own view is that small societies provide opportunities for the exercise of direct democracy that have not been explored. Tennyson Joseph points to the potentially positive role that technology can play in the democratic process,[40] although we need to be mindful of the possible ways in which technology can alienate sections of the society – the old and poor.

Conclusion

I end where I began, with suggestions by both Joseph and Sutton (echoing Lewis, in an earlier period), that federation might be the means for addressing change to Westminster constitutions in the Caribbean. Arthur Lewis, writing in the wake of the collapse of the West Indies Federation and attempts to construct a federation with the remaining units, suggested that, '[the] Federal Government had been handicapped by the absence of organized party support, since the so-called West Indian Federal Labour Party was just a collection of diverse local groups'.[41] The formation of a regional party, in and of itself, is not a sufficient condition for addressing partisan politics but may, in all likelihood, lead to a shifting of domestic partisan forms to the regional level. Further, it holds the danger of greater marginalization of citizens from the centres of power when politicians are distanced from popular reach. Joseph, even as he questioned why a Caribbean Integration Party has never been formed, rejected the party as a vehicle for the expression of regional aspirations on the ground that it had been transformed in the post-colonial period 'from an instrument of liberation' to one of 'oppression', arguing that it should be 'smashed' and 'put aside...forever'. In its place, he recommends a shift to grass roots forms of organization with 'a pan-Caribbean agenda and a pan-Caribbean structure.'[42]

The dangers of the pre-eminent role of the prime minister in small countries are well known. Arthur Lewis made a clear case for this. What is less explored are the potentially positive outcomes for democracy of the closeness of the prime minister and other political figures to their nationals. Throughout the Caribbean and, in particular the OECS, prime ministers do not operate as distant figures but are easily accessible. Moreover, they are expected to take a personal interest in people's lives. This goes beyond the 'patronage/clientist' dynamic that Carl Stone identified as typifying the Jamaican political culture,[43] although this must be guarded against in small states. Rather, it is a perspective that views the prime minister as having an intimate role in improving citizens' lives. This is an environment that makes the implementation of structural adjustment policies difficult, which may or may not be a good thing. This aspect of Eastern Caribbean political life requires further exploration by social scientists to identify not only its weaknesses, but also its potential for enhancing democracy. Under what conditions, for instance, could popular expectations of the role of the prime minister act as a check against the prime minister functioning as the leader of party supporters, rather than of the country? Establishing whether this is a desirable feature of national politics in small states is important in shaping our vision of what regional governance should resemble. Whether at the local or regional level, how people conduct politics is important. This observation also holds when considering Westminster constitutions. The inhibitors to regional action may well act as a brake on regional decision-making that may circumvent the national will. The challenge is to find a model that allows for a more democratic engagement of people in regional decision-making.

Unlike Sutton and Joseph's identification of the federal form as the model for addressing the constitutional changes required in the region, I would hesitate to prescribe a particular model. In my study of the OECS Political Union Initiative, I cautioned against prescribing the precise form that political processes should take. Rather, [it] is important that in defining and fashioning such arrangements the attachment to formal sovereignty which remains strong in some CARICOM territories be considered, as well as the cracks which have emerged in federations in Canada, the former Soviet Union and Yugoslavia. These experiences suggest the need for creativity in forging new types of political relationships to balance the strong nationalistic and individualist characters of Caribbean islands with the requirements for common political action. This might require the emergence of a political form, new and uniquely developed to suit the specific requirements of the region, and built to respond to challenges as they emerge.[44]

To conclude, it is difficult to 'fix' national constitutions outside of a regional project of constitutional reform. This approach offers not just the prospect of a less politicized process but also allows for changes that would advance the regional project by making the domestic implementation of regional decisions simpler. Unfortunately, the pre-eminence of Heads of Governments in CARICOM decision-making would suggest that significant reforms to de-politicize regional decision-making would have to be effected in order for CARICOM to play this role. Ultimately, the transformation of national constitutions is not a matter for individual states but a regional concern. The momentum must shift to the regional level with transparent mechanisms to guard against undue politicization put in place.

NOTES

1.   Patsy Lewis, 'The Agony of the Fifteen: The Crisis of Implementation', *Social and Economic Studies* 54, no. 3 (2005): 145–75.

2. Paul Sutton, 'Westminster Challenged, Westminster Confirmed: Which Way Caribbean Constitutional Reform?' *Journal of Eastern Caribbean Studies* 38, nos. 1 and 2 (2013): 63–79, at 77.

3. Tennyson S.D. Joseph, 'Towards a New Democracy and a New Independence: A Program for the Second Independence Revolution', paper presented at a 'Common Sense Convois', Lloyd Best Institute of the West Indies, The Magdalena Resort Hotel, Tobago, March 24, 2012.

4. Arthur Lewis, *The Agony of the Eight* (Pamphlet, c1965), 16–17.

5. Ibid., 20.

6. Lewis, 'The Agony of the Fifteen'.

7. For a summary of the features of Westminster constitutions see Sutton, 'Westminster Challenged, Westminster Confirmed', 63–79.

8. In 2013, this was achieved with 58.8 per cent of votes, with a voter turnout of 87 per cent. In 1999, the voter turnout was much less, 56 per cent, with the NNP winning a majority of 62.22 per cent of the votes to capture all of the 15 seats. See International Foundation for Electoral Systems, February 19, 2013, and January 18, 1999. Election Guide Democracy Assistance and Election News. Grenada: Election for House of Representatives. Retrieved from http://www.electionguide.org/elections/id/537; www.electronicguide.org/elections/id/236 (accessed 17 May 2016).

9. In my study of the failed OECS political union initiative, I lay a significant portion of the blame for its failure at the door of the partisan character of our political system (Patsy Lewis, *Surviving Small Size: Regional Integration in Caribbean Ministates.* [Jamaica, Barbados, Trinidad and Tobago: University of the West Indies Press], 114).

10. The JCPC, which heard the case, accepted the argument that a court with influence over Jamaican courts entrenched in the constitution, should itself be entrenched; this, despite the JCPC not being itself entrenched in the Jamaica constitution. Thus adopting the CCJ as Jamaica's final court of appeal would require a two-thirds majority in favour in both houses.

11. Lewis, 'The Agony of the Fifteen', 156.

12. C. Barrow-Giles, 'Democracy at Work: A Comparative Study of the Caribbean State', *The Round Table* 100, no. 414 (2011): 285–302.

13. Lewis, 'The Agony of the Fifteen', 158–59.

14. Cited in Sutton, 'Westminster Challenged, Westminster Confirmed', 64.

15. This includes the appointment of key positions in the civil service, control over the date of elections and proroguing of Parliament. See Ralph Gonsalves, 'The Quest for Constitutional Reform in St Vincent and the Grenadines'. Address delivered at the 'Beyond Westminster in the Caribbean' Conference, SALISES, UWI, Jamaica, September 11, 2014, 28–29 for a discussion of these and his attempts, through constitutional reform, to curtail these. Two examples of the use of the power to prorogue parliament, were Tillman

Thomas's proroguing of Parliament in September 2012 to stave off a vote of no-confidence from a member of his government, before dissolving it the following January in advance of elections; and in Guyana, where President Donald Ramotar prorogued Parliament in November 2014 to evade a no-confidence vote from the opposition.

16. Terri-Ann Gilbert-Roberts, *The Politics of Integration: Caribbean Sovereignty Revisited* (Kingston: Ian Randle Publishers, 2013), 235.

17. Sutton, 'Westminster Challenged, Westminster Confirmed',73.

18. 'St. Lucia Constitution Commission Draft Report'. Third Draft for Discussion (mimeo).

19. 'Report Trinidad and Tobago Constitution Reform Commission December 27, 2013, 44.' Retrieved from http://www.reformtheconstitution.com/wp-content/uploads/2014/01/TTCRC-Report-Web.pdf (accessed 3 December 2014).

20. CRC 1985, 87, 90, clause 193 (7), 194, cited in 'Grenada Constitutional Reform: Recommendations by Grenada Constitution Review Commission. Collected and Compiled by Francis Alexis for Grenada Constitution Reform Advisory Committee'. 6 February 2014. Signed 5 January 2014. Grenadaconstitutionreform.com/docs/Recommendations_by_Grenada_Constitution_Review_Commissions.pdf. Accessed 16 August 2014.

21. Cited in Ralph Gonsalves, 'The Quest for Constitutional Reform', 25. See St. Vincent Constitution Act 2009, para 74 (5 (a), (b), 77–78.

22. 'St. Vincent and the Grenadines Constitutional Act, 2009', 15. (Passed in the House of Assembly on the 3rd September, 2009). Fourth Session of the Eighth Parliament of Saint Vincent and the Grenadines 58 Elizabeth II Bill for an Act to Provide a New Constitution for Saint Vincent and the Grenadines. http://www.hsph.harvard.edu/population/womenrights/stvincent.constitution.09.pdf.

23. 'St. Vincent and the Grenadines Constitutional Act 2009', para 74(b), 78.

24. For a detailed discussion of this process and its outcomes, see Matthew Louis Bishop, 'Slaying the 'Westmonster' in the Caribbean? Constitutional Reform in St Vincent and the Grenadines', The *British Journal of Politics and International Relations* 13 (2011): 420–37.

25. Gonsalves, 'The Quest for Constitutional Reform.'

26. Ibid., 29.

27. Ibid., 8.

28. The occasion was the conference jointly hosted by the Sir Arthur Lewis Institute for Social and Economic Studies and the Institute of the Americas, University College London, entitled, 'Beyond Westminster in the Caribbean', September 11, 2014.

29. CARICOM Secretariat, *Agreement For The Establishment Of An Assembly Of Caribbean Community Parliamentarians*, 1, http://caricom.org/jsp/community/accp.jsp?menu=community (accessed September 9, 2014).

30. 'The Assembly shall consist of representatives of member states and associate members elected by their Parliaments or appointed in such manner from their membership as the Parliaments shall decide' (Article 3 paragraph 1). It provided for up to four representatives from each member state and two from associate members (paragraph 4).

31. Article 4 (paragraph b) supports this interpretation as it lists among the objectives a commitment to 'provide opportunities for involvement in the issues of the integration process by members of Parliament in each Member State and Associate Member, in addition to those who now participate'.

32. The ACCP's inaugural meeting was held in Barbados, May 1996, followed by meetings in Grenada (October 1999) and Belize (November 2000). For a discussion of these see Gilbert-Roberts, *The Politics of Integration*, 114–16.

33. CARICOM Secretariat, 'Charter of Civil Society for the Caribbean Community', Georgetown: CARICOM Secretariat, 1997.

34. CARICOM Secretariat, The Liliendaal Statement Of Principles On Forward Together, 2002. http://caricom.org/media-center/communications/statements-from-caricom-meetings/the-liliendaal-statement-of-principles-on-forward-together (accessed 25 July 2016).

35. 'Technical Meeting of Civil Society and government Representatives in Paramaribo', Suriname, November 7–8, 2011. CARICOM Secretariat, Press release 417/2011 (November 11, 2011). CARICOM Civil Society-Government Forum Agrees On Structure For Improved Interaction. http://www.caricom.org/jsp/pressreleases/press_releases_2011/pres417_11.jsp (accessed September 8, 2014).

36. Cecelia Babb, 'Draft Report National Consultations Caricom Civil Society Participation and Engagement in Regional Integration Project', January 24, 2011, 3–4. http://www.cpdcngo.org/cpdc/attachments/article/107/CPDC%20Report%20of%20CARICOM%20National%20Consultations.pdf (accessed September 8, 2014).

37. Tillman Thomas, Prime Minister of Grenada, 'Re-Energising CARICOM Integration', 2011, 10. http://www.normangirvan.info/wp-content/uploads/2011/05/pms-caricom-brief-final-3-april-1011-1.pdf (accessed September 9, 2014). Thomas was reporting on the deliberations of an ad hoc group, which he had established, to propose solutions to CARICOM's implementation deficit.

38. Kristina Hinds-Harrison, 'Civil Society Consultation in the Caribbean Community (CARICOM): Why Conceptual Clarity Matters', *Journal of Eastern Caribbean Studies* 38, nos. 1 and 2 (2013): 1–34.

39. Gilbert-Roberts, *The Politics of Integration*, 246.

40. Joseph, 'Towards a New Democracy', 37–38.

41. Lewis, *Agony of the Eight*, 11.

42. Joseph, 'Towards a New Democracy', 33–35.

43. Carl Stone, *Democracy and Clientelism in Jamaica* (New Brunswick, NJ: Transaction Publishers, 1983).
44. Lewis, *Surviving Small Size*, 200.

5 Westminster Politics: *Democratic Practice and Social Constraints – The Jamaican Experience*

Peter Phillips

It is generally recognized that among what used to be known as the 'new states' in the 1950s and '60s, the so-called Commonwealth Caribbean states that achieved independence in the 1960s and '70s have sustained their democratic traditions. Unlike some other states that were formerly part of the British Empire that assumed independent status in the 1950s and '60s, the Commonwealth Caribbean states have, with one exception, sustained constitutional rule, held regular elections and changed administrations by way of the ballot. They have also for the most part maintained independent judiciaries, and an independent civil service, and preserved the basic rights of the individual.

Specifically, in relation to Jamaica, there have been 16 general elections held since the introduction of Universal Adult Suffrage in 1944, resulting in seven changes of government.[1] Universal Adult Suffrage preceded the assumption of independent statehood. Nevertheless, with independence, the basic political and administrative underpinnings of the Westminster–Whitehall model of liberal democracy was maintained. Since the assumption of independent statehood in 1962, the country has maintained a cadre of impartial, politically neutral civil servants, including an independent judiciary and has maintained the essential individual rights of freedom of association, and assembly and free speech, etc., which are at the core of modern liberal democratic political practice.

Compared with other postcolonial Commonwealth jurisdictions the durability of the 'Westminster model' in the Caribbean is notable. This is unlike much of Africa, such as Ghana and Nigeria in West Africa, or Kenya or Tanzania in the East, where the Westminster inheritance quickly yielded to military government or one-party rule. In hindsight, perhaps this should not seem so surprising.

Africa, with its checkerboard of competing ethnic loyalties and surviving 'traditional' political institutions and ideologies provided a vastly different social and institutional backdrop to postcolonial politics than did the Caribbean. Moreover, in the Caribbean, in form, if not in substance, Westminster patterns have long been exemplified in colonial administration. From the seventeenth century onwards, a local assembly comprised of planters and their managers exercised political authority alongside an appointed governor who constituted the apex of executive authority. Disrupted by the Morant Bay Rebellion of 1865 with the claim of 'free-coloureds' and newly emancipated blacks for participation in political decision-making, direct-rule by the colonial office was to be short lived.

After the re-introduction of restricted suffrage in the 1880s, the political forms of 'representative government' were revived. Essentially, unlike Africa or Asia, the transplanted populations that made up the Caribbean had no other 'indigenous' political models to emulate. Indeed, in large measure, the quest for expanded rights of citizenship and social development championed by progressive advocates from Dr Robert Love in the 1880s and including Marcus Garvey, J.A.G. Smith and N.W. Manley, took the form of a demand for inclusion within the ambit of the representative politics of the day. Love, Garvey, and Smith in particular, experienced different degrees of success in contesting seats in the local assembly – in Garvey's case, the Parochial Board – on the restricted franchise of the times. Garvey was the first to enunciate the demand for Universal Adult Suffrage – a demand ultimately realized in the 1944 Constitution.

Without doubt, the impetus for the extension of Adult Suffrage and for more responsible government was the labour riots of 1938 and the emergence of modern party politics which it precipitated; first with the formation of the People's National Party (PNP) in the immediate aftermath of the upheavals and later with the formation of the Jamaica Labour Party (JLP) in 1943. The elections of 1944, which were won by the Jamaica Labour Party, ushered in a new phase of mass political participation in Jamaica. The political topography which was to define Jamaica's constitutional arrangements and political practice in the ensuing years up to independence and beyond, was all pre-figured in that Constitution. There was to be a bi-cameral legislature, comprised of an appointed legislative council and an elected House of Representatives. Executive authority was concentrated in a governor appointed by the British Colonial Office and an executive council and administrative responsibilities exercised by heads of department under the guidance of a colonial secretary.

The Legislature and indeed, the political life of the country were, by virtue of the expanded suffrage, to be dominated by two main political parties – each with its trade union affiliate. The so-called 'responsible government', defined in terms of elected representatives providing direction to the administrators, was not a feature of the 1944 Constitution. This was to emerge through successive constitutional adjustments, culminating in the assumption of 'full internal self-government' in 1957 and independent statehood in 1962. Significantly however, in the context of the considerable popular agitation and nationalist ferment of the time, there was never any popularly supported demand for an alternative to the Westminster-type constitutional order.

Since 1962, there have been spasmodic attempts at constitutional reform. Initiated in earnest in the late 1970s, these efforts reached a high point in the 1990s with the appointment of a Constitutional Commission in 1992, broadly representative of the main political parties and civil society. Subsequent to its report, a Joint Select Committee of Parliament was to consider and make recommendations. To date, however, with the exception of the promulgation of a new Charter of Rights, there has been no substantial movement on the recommendations of the Parliamentary Committee. More pertinent to the issues under consideration here, however, is that despite suggestions being mooted initially by the PNP for an executive presidency and subsequent proposals for complete separation of powers modelled on the US Constitution, the consensus finally settled on by the Joint Select Committee of Parliament was for the retention of the essential features of the existing constitutional order. Moreover, as I have indicated, there has never been any sustained popular demand for substantial changes to the Westminster institutional forms.

One specific set of concerns raised about the nature of the constitutional and wider political arrangements was the extent to which constitutionally guaranteed rights were actually being enjoyed by the populace. In this view, for example, constitutional guarantees of equal treatment before the courts and against arbitrary arrests, or the right to life, etc., have been denied to many by virtue of police excesses.

The remedy for these and other risks of arbitrary and excessive actions by state authorities was deemed, for the most part, to be secured by the promulgation of a new charter of Fundamental Rights and Freedoms guaranteeing all rights, typical of a 'free and democratic society'.[2] Furthermore, in order to support the observance of these fundamental rights an Office of a Public Defender, charged with the general protection and defence of citizens' rights, was established.

Critical though these issues are, perhaps a more fundamental and certainly more persistent critique of the system of government relates to the quality of governance enjoyed by citizens as a whole. If 'good governance' is defined as 'the exercise of power by various levels of government in a manner that is effective, honest, equitable, transparent and accountable',[3] then by this measure, the post-independence experience of Jamaica has been severely deficient.

There is an extensive literature outlining the dimensions of this deficit and the extent to which 'the Jamaican reality falls short of the ideals of Western Liberal Democracy'.[4] There have been two main vectors to this critique. The first points to the disfigurement of politics by excessive partisanship and the consequential political violence, manipulation of the electoral system, and the emergence of 'garrison communities'. A further dimension of this problem relates to supposed or purported efforts to politicize the civil service and security forces in order to secure partisan advantage. The second main vector concerns the issue of lack of accountability, growing corruption in public life, and declining ethical norms.

Repeated studies, both from international bodies such as Transparency International and from local academic institutions[5] have confirmed the widespread public perception that corruption is a significant and worsening problem in the country. This is generally taken to refer to the use of public office for private gain. The term is also used in reference to a wide range of misdeeds – for example, the sale of public goods such as drivers' licences, customs clearances, etc. to the presumably more egregious circumstances involving presumed alliances between criminal organizations and individuals and political parties and/or elected representatives.

Undoubtedly, these several and manifold threats to 'good governance' have been severe, and in some instances as in the case of political violence and electoral malpractice, threatened basic political stability. Yet, from our current vantage point what is most striking is the capacity of the political system to reform. Certainly, some efforts at reform have been more successful and far-reaching than others. Among the more successful measures was the formation of the Electoral Advisory Committee which subsequently evolved into an Electoral Commission. This took electoral administration out of the hands of direct governmental direction and control and placed it with an independent commission with a majority of 'independent' members drawn from civil society. The summary effect of this, and various ancillary reform measures, initiated by the Commission such as the power to void electoral results marred by violence, and the power to demarcate constituency boundaries, etc. has been a steady reduction of incidents of political violence to negligible levels since the low-point of the 1980 elections.

Similarly, the passage of ordinary legislation codifying the autonomy of the Commissioner of Police with respect to operational decisions and the implementation of other reforms such as the establishment of an anti-corruption branch and an informal agreement to secure bi-partisan consensus regarding the appointment of a Police Services Commission have rolled back the perceived spectre of a politicized police force and, along with stepped-up international cooperation, have resulted in greater operational efficiencies. One fundamental consequence of all this has been to reverse the onslaught of organized crime linked to the international trade in illegal narcotics and thereby reduce, if not entirely eliminate, what had been a bourgeoning link between the political parties and organized criminal groups.

Progress in the battle against corruption and its threat to 'good governance' has not been as clear-cut. Corrupt conduct by public officials, including elected representatives and the potential threat implied to public institutions and the integrity of the political process has been long-standing. Certainly, it has been around from the inception of independent statehood and even into the era of internal self-government.

Beginning with the passage of the Parliamentary Integrity Act 1973, there have been numerous and significant legislative initiatives focused on this problem. These include the Contractor General Act of 1986 and the establishment of the Office of the Contractor General to oversee public procurement processes and The Corruption Prevention Act of 2003, which established the Corruption Prevention Commission and required public officials to provide annual reports as to their financial status. Access to Information legislation was also passed, permitting greater transparency for public decisions.

Yet, for all this, the problem persists. It is manifest in the public perception that high-degrees of public corruption exist and it persists – as it can only do – in small society settings where stark and grotesque displays of wealth by public officials and rumours of misbehaviour continue without any prosecutions or convictions of senior public officials. One remedy proposed, and currently being pursued, is for a single anti-corruption agency to be established which would combine investigative functions with some prosecutorial authority.

Viewed from the perspective of long historical time however, the greatest potential threat to the stability of the constitutional and institutional underpinnings of the political system has been its persistent inability to deliver sustained economic growth and employment sufficient to satisfy the aspirations of the population as a whole. The numbers are stark and sobering. For 40 years, the average annual rate of growth of GDP has been less than one per cent. Over the same period, the public debt has risen by more than 600 per cent, amounting in 2013 to close to 150 per cent of GDP making Jamaica one of the most highly indebted countries in the world. In turn, the resultant low growth and stagnating per capita incomes are the root of many of the social ills confronted by Jamaica over the same period. Serious crimes, including murder, have risen sharply, propelled to a significant degree by Jamaica's emergence in the 1980s and '90s as a platform for international narcotics trade flowing between South and North America. In turn, this helped spawn organized criminal networks which sought to embrace marginalized urban youth within their compass. An increasingly overwhelmed courts system and underfunded social services all helped to reinforce a vicious cycle of economic under-performance and social marginalization.

All of this experience of high-debt build-up and economic under-performance, social marginalization, and crime, begs the question as to whether there is any future for the country's constitutional arrangements and the political practices which underlie these phenomena. Similarly, we may ask the same question in relation to the issues of political violence, electoral malpractice, or corruption which emerged at varying times as threats to the political system and constitutional stability and integrity.

What seems clear from the documented historical experience is that excessive partisanship, (termed 'political tribalism' in the popular vernacular) expressed in the quest for power has been a continuing feature of our political practice. Violence perpetrated in the search for electoral advantage for example, or the creation of geographically distinct politically homogenous 'garrison communities' in which uniformity of party allegiance is enforced by the threat of physical violence is all antithetical to the basic assumptions underlying 'Westminster' political practice.

As noted Trinidadian political scientist Selwyn Ryan makes clear, 'a most important assumption' of the Westminster paradigm is that 'society is socially and institutionally homogenous', and that its basic values and behavioural notions are 'widely if not universally shared'.[6] Competitors for power must share a common view as to the 'rules of the game', not only with respect to the requirements of the contest itself – that is to the electoral process – but also with respect to how 'power' is to be exercised subsequently. It is this assumption of common interest that prompted Edmund Burke to observe in eighteenth-century England that:

> Parliament is not a congress of Ambassadors from different hostile interests which interests each must maintain as an agent and advocate against the other agents and advocates; Parliament is a deliberative assembly of one nation, with one interest; that of the whole.[7]

The ideal as described by Burke may never have been attained even in Britain, and will always have, of necessity, an asymptotic quality; pursued but never completely attained. The fact is however, that the prospects for attaining the ideal would be very much affected by the social environment in which the Parliament existed. In the case of Britain, Parliament and its deliberative traditions and the solidarities of nationhood had a long history preceding the formation of strong and institutionalized political party loyalties. In the vastly different socio-historical context of the Caribbean however, defined as it was by strong subcultural divisions, and sharply inscribed race–class hierarchies, the prospects of the emergence of a core of shared national values and interests would have been sharply curtailed. Moreover, as Carl Stone in his pioneering work pointed out, political participation generally in the context of a highly unequal pattern of income distribution took place primarily on the basis of political clientelism and the search for individual benefits through party-structures. 'The very idea of politics is for most members of the Mass Public synonymous with "party politics"'.[8]

In any event, mass participation in the electoral process, in Jamaica took place simultaneously with the formation of political parties, and party loyalties were often stronger than loyalties to the collective which in any case emerged as a functioning sovereign entity more than two decades after the formation of the two main parties that came to dominate modern political life in the country.

Viewed from this vantage point, the viability of Westminster style political institutions, and the 'establishment of successful nationhood' has depended on the society's capacity to curb the excesses of partisanship and sectoral interest in favour of the collective. What is more, and somewhat ironic in the context of a system of party politics that emerged from the demands of civil society groups like the networks of National Reform Associations and welfare groups and trade unions which reached a crescendo of activism in the 1930s, is that the political parties once formed tended to diminish independent civic organizations and activity. Independent organizations of teachers, farmers, trade unions, student organizations, etc., were all subordinated to, or permeated by the competition between the two major political parties to the point where most, if not all, lost the reputation and oftentimes the capacity for independent action.

In recent years, this decline has subsided and has even been reversed. The establishment of the Jamaican Confederation of Trade Unions and the re-invigoration of the human rights and environmental movements have been among the more recent examples of this counter-tendency, which has occurred alongside a long-term trend towards the lessening of hardcore party loyalty on the part of adherents of the two main parties.

Conclusion

What then is the way forward in the face of the country's post-independence experience of our constitutional arrangements? As a prelude to charting a 'plan of action' we should first of all acknowledge that the basic institutional structure of the so-called 'Westminster System' has deep organic roots in Jamaica's history. The population has over hundreds of years fought battles to be included within its ambit; the basic institutional structures and the associated roles and responsibilities are universally understood and it has functioned well as a system in preserving basic democratic rights and freedoms – not perfectly, but well. Moreover, the political system as a whole and critical social sectors have over time, successfully withstood and transcended all fundamental threats to systemic integrity and survival that have presented themselves.

The root of all the major systemic threats that have arisen relate to the extent of partisan loyalties that have exceeded loyalty to the collective. In turn, we have suggested that these 'factional' loyalties have their foundation in historically rooted social inequalities of 'plantation society' and 'cultural pluralism', which together have inhibited the emergence of the critical solidarities essential to nationhood. It would follow from this that in charting a course of advancement, the objective should be to constrain and mute the opportunities for the exercise of partisan advantage by party-political authorities managing the state. Equally, future stability and the effectiveness of the constitutional order would seem to be dependent on the widening of the ambit within which independent 'non-partisan' societal interests can find expression.

In order to achieve these overarching objectives, the following immediate tasks arise: First, we need to complete the Constitutional Reform Agenda agreed to by the Joint Select Committee of Parliament on Constitutional Reform in 1998. A critical feature of those reform proposals imposed a requirement for bi-partisan agreement in the selection and appointment of membership to critical offices of state in the Police Services Commission, Public Service Commission and the like. This would go a far way in eliminating the prospect, and the fear, of partisan manipulation of these institutions and state functions generally. Outstanding issues to be settled, including the mode of appointment of the President and the size and composition of the Senate, could be settled quickly with the appropriate political will and willingness to compromise.

Second, a determined effort must be made to strengthen the deliberative capacities of the Parliament. This includes, but goes beyond the issue of adequate parliamentary facilities. Somewhat paradoxically, Parliament has simultaneously been the scene of partisan excess and superficiality and particularly in its consideration of issues in Committee, the site of the most constructive and deliberative undertakings. In my experience the workings of the increasingly well-elaborated system of committees reveal Parliament at its best. Indeed, in recognition of this, the recently promulgated fiscal responsibility framework and the legislative fiscal rules, place specific responsibility on parliamentary committees to monitor and constrain the build-up of public debt and supervise the Public Sector Investment Programme. In turn, for these deliberations to be meaningful, parliamentarians will need much more support in terms of staffing, research facilities, and advice than is presently available.

Third, we need to ensure the passage of legislation to create a single anti-corruption agency with the requisite powers of investigation and prosecution and with appropriate structures for independent (non-partisan) oversight. The suspicion of public corruption has been long with us and despite the passage of various pieces of legislation and the strengthening of extensive requirements for the reporting of income by public officials, there is still a strong perception that public corruption persists and has, in fact, worsened. This saps the public's trust in their national institutions and weakens the capacity for collective action in pursuit of national objectives. Addressing this problem is an urgent national priority.

Finally, there is the challenge to national leadership. Westminster-style politics implies collaborative politics. It implies a commitment to find common cause in the national interest when fundamental issues arise even as the necessary competition between parties takes place as each competes to form the government. Perhaps the biggest test of this capacity now will be the ability of our national leaders to find common cause in reforming the Westminster System.

NOTES

1. Since this chapter was written, Jamaica held its 17th general elections in 2016 with its eighth change of government, this time from the People's National Party (PNP) to the Jamaica Labour Party (JLP).
2. *Constitution of Jamaica* Chapter III, Charter of Fundamental Rights and Freedoms, Section 2.
3. CIDA, *Redefining the Concept of Good Governance* (Quebec: CIDA, 1997), 1.
4. Gladstone Mills, *Westminster Style Democracy: The Jamaican Experience*, Grace Kennedy Foundation Lecture (Kingston: Grace Kennedy Foundation, 1997), 39.
5. See For instance, Lloyd Waller et al., *A Landscape Assessment of Political Corruption in Jamaica* (Kingston: CAPRI, 2007).
6. Selwyn Ryan, *Winner Takes All: The Westminster Experience in the Anglophone Caribbean*, SALISES, Trinidad, 1999, 3.
7. Ibid.
8. Carl Stone, *Democracy and Clientelism in Jamaica* (New Brunswick and London: Transaction Books, 1983), 81.

6 Challenges for Good Governance within the Westminster Framework

Bruce Golding

Much discussion and scholarly work has taken place about the choice of the Westminster system by Jamaica and other Caribbean countries as we transitioned from colonization to independence. Professor Trevor Munroe, in his book *The Politics of Constitutional Decolonization in Jamaica*[1] documents the scant consideration given in the framing of our constitution to any major deviation from the Westminster prototype into which we had been initiated even before, but especially since the introduction of the first Order in Council in 1944. Some have chided the framers of our constitution for undue orthodoxy and conservatism.

It is arguable whether we really had a choice. Some British colonies in Africa, Asia, and the Pacific had varying elements of indigenous organization and administrations that survived colonization and could influence – even if not define completely – their ultimate form of government. In our case, the Westminster system was the only form we knew. Norman Manley argued in 1962 'Let us not make the mistake of describing as colonial institutions which are part and parcel of the heritage of this country.'[2] In the same vein, Dr Lloyd Barnett, in his book *The Constitutional Law of Jamaica*, asserts that:

> the basic principles of the Jamaican Constitution are not the result of political plagiarism or a slavish adoption of current constitutional fashions but are rather the product of three centuries of historical development and a deliberate decision to continue the pattern of a constitutional system which had gradually evolved and in the operation of which the country had acquired considerable experience.[3]

Let us remember, as well, that such advocacy as there was for radical change in 1961 was driven more by anti-colonial passion and a desire for a demonstrable, even if only symbolic, break with the past than by any coherent articulation of an alternative form. It is a fact of history that the drafting of the constitution was put on fast-rapid and completed in record time of less than three months without any broad public consultation. Even if that were not so, it is doubtful that the outcome would have been much different given the apathy of the general population which Dr Munroe also observed. In the end, in the absence of a clear alternative path and given the anxieties about change and uncertainty, the inclination to 'stick with what we know' and the felt need for as seamless a transition as possible triumphed easily.

The debate continues as to whether the Westminster system has been good for us or has failed us. It is a debate that is unlikely to lead to any conclusion because the term 'Westminster' is often used to mean different although not unconnected things. In one instance, it may be simply a constitutional arrangement in which outcomes are determined by the actions and decisions of the functionaries it creates. In another, it may refer to a far more complex scheme that pre-determines and institutionalizes economic and social relations and outcomes. In the latter case, it is often nailed as the principal cause of our many ills – poverty, crime, corruption, alienation of the people, etc. We need to approach such a conclusion with great caution.

Discussions about the Westminster model face the dilemma that there is no fixed model or template that defines Westminster. Many versions exist within and outside of the Commonwealth where it is most prevalent. There are basic elements that must be present: suffrage, guaranteed periodic elections, a largely non-executive Head of State, a directly elected chamber of representatives with a prime minister and cabinet chosen primarily or entirely from and accountable to those representatives, and a separately constituted judiciary. Beyond those basics, Westminster takes off in all sorts of directions and many variations are to be found among its practitioners from New Zealand to Jamaica, from Singapore to Israel. They may be monarchical or republican, first-past-the-post or proportionally representative, a hybrid of both, unicameral or bicameral, unitary or federal, constitution-sovereign, or parliament-sovereign. The real measure of governance in any Westminster-based country, therefore, is not just the existence of the basic elements but how they relate to each other in both structure and practice. Indeed, the late Professor Ralph Carnegie insisted that the notion that all Commonwealth Caribbean states with the exception of Guyana were Westminster models was a myth.

This lack of rigidity that is a significant feature of the Westminster model can be understood from the fact that, in Britain where it originated and which still serves as its point of reference, the constitution is not even written but, instead, is derived from a body of customs, conventions, statutes, judicial decisions and treaties accumulated over centuries. Such a constitutional arrangement might well have unravelled or be easily manipulated were it not supported by a culture that has withstood the passage of time and is intrinsic to the workings of vintage Westminster. It is this culture that neutralizes to some extent the inherent hazard of the pure Westminster model, which is the intense *de facto* concentration of power in the hands of the prime minister that makes it in practice, if not in appearance, a constitutional dictatorship. Separation of powers between the executive and the legislature is an illusion. The ability of Parliament to hold the executive accountable is more imaginary than real.

Only New Zealand has followed the route of an unwritten constitution. In our case no such reliance on culture was even contemplated. Our arrangements had to be put in black and white and in that 'black and white', some significant deviations from the Westminster prototype were introduced as safeguards against its inherent concentration of power. It has been argued that what emerged reflected, in part, Britain's determination to ensure that we adhere to the principles of Westminster. This does not synch with the report of the late Theodore Sealy who covered the Lancaster House deliberations and who said that the British officials thought that we sought 'to provide for too many eventualities' and that the final draft constitution was 'too static in its reliance on the past and...too timid in its caution for the future'.[4] It has also been argued that these safeguards reflected the mistrust that existed between the key political players (the People's National Party [PNP] and the Jamaica Labour Party [JLP]) and the unwillingness of each to leave too much to chance when the other side holds the reins of power. Mistrust, however, is not an unusual feature but, one could argue, an important component of constitution-making. The observation has also been made that most of these measures were nothing new since they already existed in the pre-independence constitution. However, this does not render them insignificant and, in fact, strengthens the argument put forward by Norman Manley and Lloyd Barnett.

Some 20 years ago after serving in both government and opposition for the previous 20 years, I came to the view that the Westminster system was not appropriate for Jamaica. Its winner-take-all character had cemented a level of political tribalism that was not only destructive in and of itself but made it impossible for us as a people and, especially, politicians on opposing sides, to find common cause in tackling problems that transcended political divisions. The people's representatives elected in good faith either had pawned their mandate to an all-powerful executive in the case of those on the government side or in the case of the opposition side were placed where they belonged outside the arena of authority. I concluded then that effective separation of powers with a directly elected president and a separately elected Parliament, each with clearly defined but intersecting powers, would provide a better framework for governance. I campaigned vigorously for such a change.

I subsequently resiled from that position. Separation of powers can either involve constructive, deliberative engagement between the executive and the legislature or it can lead to a debilitating stand-off. It became increasingly apparent to me that if we lacked the culture to make Westminster work, we were not likely to have the culture to make the presidential system work either. What we are witnessing now in Washington, regarded as a mature democracy, between the Obama administration and the Congress where the Republicans control both chambers, illustrates the hazards with which our not-so-mature democracy would have to contend. The US has multiple layers of institutions that keep it going even where political dysfunctionality exists. A major US investor was once quoted as saying that if the president were to be assassinated he would be deeply disturbed; if the Chairman of the Federal Reserve Board were to be assassinated, he would be frightened. We do not enjoy that level of sophistication.

The change in my position did not remove my discomfort with the Westminster system as we have practised it. It meant finding other ways to fix it and, in seeking to do that, I believe that it is better to insert the critical safeguards against excessive executive power in the constitution rather than hope that those safeguards will flow naturally from the separation of powers. This is especially so if both sets of power come from either Old Hope Road or Belmont Road[5] as it is not just possible but likely given our historical voting patterns. In such a situation, those safeguards and that separation are more imaginary than real.

Efforts were made by the framers of our constitution to mitigate the concentration of power in the executive by inserting provisions that did not exist in the classic Westminster model. Indeed, some can be said to have been innovative since they did not appear in the constitution of any other Commonwealth country. It is useful to identify these:

1. The constitution includes a Bill of Rights.

2. The constitution is given supremacy over Parliament. Thus, certain provisions cannot be altered without a two-thirds majority in

each House of Parliament and, in some instances, also have to be approved by the electorate.

3. The Senate is constituted in a way that deprives the government of a two-thirds majority thereby requiring the support of at least one opposition member to alter entrenched provisions of the constitution even if it has an overwhelming majority in the House of Representatives.

4. All the members of the Senate are to be chosen by the prime minister (13) and the leader of the opposition (8), the intention being to ensure that entrenched provisions can only be altered if there is consensus between the government and opposition. This differs from other constitutions framed in the same period such as in Trinidad and Tobago and Barbados where the Senate is comprised of not just government and opposition members but includes independent members chosen by the president or governor general who outnumber those chosen by the leader of the opposition.

5. Appointments to certain critical positions (chief justice, president of the Court of Appeal, Service Commissions) require the prime minister to consult with the leader of the opposition. In mandating consultations, the framers were evidently striving for government/ opposition consensus while according the government the final say.

6. Members of the judiciary, the auditor-general and director of public prosecutions are guaranteed security of tenure and remuneration as well as non-interference from any source.

7. Special protection is given to public officers from arbitrary dismissal or disciplinary action.[6]

This effort was not without flaws. For example, the Bill of Rights was placed on tenuous footing since any of its provisions could be made redundant by passing a law which the government considered to be necessary 'in the interests of defence, public safety, public order, public morality, public health ....'[7] Yet the inclusion of a Bill of Rights any at all was a major triumph over a strongly argued view that it would 'derogate from the sovereignty of Parliament'. Australia, for example, has resisted all efforts to place a Bill of Rights in its constitution.

Some have argued, especially in the ideologically charged period of the 1960s and '70s, that these 'safeguards' were too restrictive and fettered governments from pursuing bold, progressive, transformative programmes that could have changed the course of our history. Others may say thank God for those fetters, otherwise the course of our history would, indeed, have changed.

Some contend that when the Westminster system was first introduced by the 1943 Order in Council, its intention was to break up the emerging national movement and to divide the Jamaican people into two opposing camps, a fissure from which we have never recovered. It is a view that is offered even today based on Ewart Walters' recent book *We Come From Jamaica – the Nationalist Movement 1937–1962* in which he asserts:

> The Westminster system of government...created an artificial fractiousness that left the losing party to oppose, oppose, oppose, regardless...Jamaica could have been much further ahead now, had William Alexander Bustamante remained as a supporter of the national movement in which Norman Manley's People's National Party played a major role, and not the adversary he became."[8] Competitive democracy and political pluralism are, I submit, too high a price to pay for national unity! A question was asked yesterday about the efficacy of liberal democracy...which begs the question: What is a non-liberal democracy?

There can be no question that the checks and balances against executive power were structured around having a government and an opposition – what Trevor Munroe described as 'institutionalized dissent', a core principle of the Westminster system. We were the first Commonwealth country to recognize in the constitution the position of leader of the opposition and to vest in it specific constitutional functions. It has been argued that this was designed to entrench the two-party system to the exclusion of any other but the PNP and JLP. I believe this interpretation is flawed. The specific provision (section 80) identifies the person to be appointed leader of the opposition as 'the member...best able to command the support of a majority of those members who do not support the Government or, if there is no such person, the member... (who) commands the support of the largest single group of such members who are prepared to support one leader.'[9] The provision clearly foresaw the possibility of more than two parties being represented in the House of Representatives. What it did seek to do is not so much to entrench the two-party system but to institutionalize an essential feature of Westminster parliamentarianism – the rotation of power as against the sharing of power, the coexistence of a government-in-office and a government-in-waiting. All third-party attempts in Jamaica since independence have failed, but the reasons for that must be found elsewhere.

Did we make a mistake when we did not get rid of the Westminster system at the start of independence? Is Westminster to be blamed for our lack of progress, for the persistent crises that engulf us? Empirical evidence does not validate such a correlation. Of the two dozen former British colonies in Africa and the Caribbean that gained independence in the second half of the last century (from Ghana 1957 to St Kitts 1983), a half switched soon afterward from the Westminster to the presidential model. Of the other half that retained the Westminster model, 11 are from the Caribbean and only one from elsewhere. On a range of objective criteria, the conclusion cannot be drawn that the Westminster system has been a hindrance to those countries that have retained it. Indeed, the contrary could and has often been argued. The average annual growth rate in the 'Westminster' countries has been 2.6 per cent compared to less than 0.5 per cent in the others. In the UN Human Development Index, all but one of the 'Westminster' countries outrank those with other forms of government with an average index of .723 compared to .521. On the issues of crime and corruption, the former colonies are scattered across the indices with no discernible correlation with their particular form of government.

This is highlighted not so much to argue the merits of the Westminster system but simply to suggest that the failings associated with it may be founded on shaky ground. The fact is that there is a wide range of factors, some of them peculiar to particular countries, which determine performance outcomes and impact different forms of government in both similar and different ways. We have the benefit of hindsight, which our founding fathers did not have. We have had 52 years of hands-on, real-time experience with this constitution. If it has failed us, the blame must be placed at our feet, not at the feet of those who devised it.

Has it failed? The Westminster system has been credited for providing stability to our democratic process, for facilitating orderly transition of power even when our politics was at its most polarized and the fabric of our democracy most severely tested. But it has failed in some important respects: in securing basic human rights for the ordinary citizen, in making government truly representative, in holding accountable those in whom power is vested, in preventing ruinous executive action that has blighted the hopes and potential of generations of Jamaicans. In contrast to those who would have preferred the 1962 constitution to be less restrictive, to better facilitate strong governments and to enable them to be bold and transformational, I have felt that the strictures imposed were necessary but not sufficient. They were not sufficient to prevent the persecution of Rastafarians, the almost daily detention without charge of ordinary citizens, restricting freedom of expression, the abuse of emergency powers, taxation without the approval of the people's representatives, the accumulation of debt that now leaves us with less than 50 cents in the dollar to address the country's myriad of pressing needs. A constitution is not a firewall; it does not absolutely prevent these things any more than does the constitutional right to life prevent murders from being committed. What it can do is fix boundaries, enable violators to be held accountable and appropriate sanctions to be applied. That is the force of deterrence and redress that it must possess.

Most of the former British colonies in Africa, Asia, and the Pacific have rewritten their constitutions at least once, some two or three times. In the Caribbean, Guyana is the only one to have done so although Trinidad did convert to a republic in 1976. The need for review of our own constitution was long recognized...from the 1970s. The political turbulence of that period did not provide an atmosphere in which it could be pursued, given the collaborative approach that the constitution's 'security system' requires. The review process enjoyed much greater traction in the 1990s with the establishment and work of a Constitutional Reform Commission chaired by the late Justice James Kerr and, after his demise, Dr Lloyd Barnett. Its recommendations submitted in 1994 were considered and, in large measure, adopted by a Joint Select Committee of Parliament in 1995. To the surprise of many, there was substantial consensus between government and opposition, including on issues that required a two-thirds majority in both Houses and approval by the voters. But while they are to be commended for this constructive approach, politicians past and present must take responsibility for the inertia that has caused the process of enactment in large measure to languish for 20 years.

We did manage in 2011 to put into effect one important part of the agreed recommendations – the replacement of the Bill of Rights with a much-strengthened Charter of Fundamental Rights which is now justiciable.

What are these elements of constitutional reform that have been languishing for so long?

- We have agreed that Jamaica should advance from a monarchy where Queen Elizabeth is Queen of Jamaica to a republic with our own president as Head of State. This is more than mere formality and even more than repatriating our sovereignty, for the president is to be more than just a ceremonial figurehead. He or she is to constitute a major restraint on executive power. We came upon this approach in 1979 when we sought to fix the electoral system that had been abused and manipulated by successive governments to the point where it had become a national crisis. The governor-general now selects the largest bloc of members of the Electoral Commission, a format that has led to a restoration of confidence in the conduct of elections. This same approach has subsequently been used in the appointments to other sensitive positions such as the contractor-general, Broadcasting Commission, Public Broadcasting Corporation, public defender, children's advocate, political ombudsman and the Independent Commission for Investigations (INDECOM)[10] commissioner. This is a major deviation from classic Westminster. It is difficult to imagine the Queen exercising such functions in Britain.

- It has been agreed that this power of the president to make appointments would be extended to include the chief justice, president of the Court of Appeal and members of the Judicial, Police and Public Services Commissions.

- Provisions would be made in the constitution for impeachment of a wide range of public officials, elected and non-elected, with a five-member impeachment tribunal that must be established within 35 days after each general election.

- Critical bodies such as the Electoral Commission, the Office of the Contractor-General and the Office of the Public Defender now established merely by ordinary statute would be enshrined in the constitution.

- The Senate would be expanded to 36 members (government 20, opposition 14, other interests 2).

- Provisions would be made to widen the *locus standi* for class actions as well as to enable any citizen, acting in the public interest and without having to obtain the prior consent of the attorney-general, to challenge in the courts any action of government.

- Decisions of the director of public prosecutions (DPP) are to be made subject to judicial review.

What is preventing us from moving forward?

There are technical issues that need to be resolved:

- In this new framework, the president becomes far more functional and pivotal than the governor-general in our present dispensation. It is a feature that is not found in any other Westminster-based constitution where the functions of the governor-general/president are mere formality. But it has worked for us. The way in which the president is chosen, therefore, becomes critical. At present, the governor-general is chosen by the prime minister, and we are fortunate to have had a succession of governors-general who have, by and large, exercised their judgment in a commendable way. That, however, is not sufficient for us to rely on in going forward, especially with the significantly expanded role created for the president. It is no mean achievement for the government and opposition to have agreed that the president would be nominated by the prime minister after consultation with the leader of the opposition and would require approval by a two-thirds majority of both Houses of Parliament. In Trinidad and Tobago, for example, the president is chosen by a simple majority of both Houses sitting jointly. The issue that remains to be resolved in Jamaica is whether that two-thirds vote is to be taken in each House separately or with both Houses sitting jointly.

- While it has been agreed that the sensitive appointments to be made by the President would be subject to a two-thirds majority in each House of Parliament, there is disagreement as to whether it should be by way of affirmative or negative resolution.

- There is disagreement as to whether the two 'other' members of the Senate should be chosen by the president or reserved for other parties contesting the elections that achieve a minimum threshold of votes, failing which they should be reallocated equally to the government and opposition.

The single greatest issue of disagreement, however, has to do with installing the Caribbean Court of Justice (CCJ) as our final appellate court. The government seems unwilling to proceed with any other amendment until this issue is resolved and points to the fact that it can be implemented if the opposition facilitates a two-thirds majority in the Senate. The opposition has maintained its unwillingness to do so, insisting that the matter must be placed before the people in a referendum.

It cannot be beyond the government and opposition to resolve these issues. What is disturbing is that they do not seem to be even making an effort. These issues are nowhere on any agenda. There is no joint select committee at work, no Vale Royal meetings taking place. These are issues that do not stand much chance of being dealt with in the run-up to any elections and that is not far away.

I believe, too, that based on our experiences of the last two decades since those issues were dealt with, we should (a) expand the list of changes already agreed to include other safeguards on which consensus has subsequently emerged; and (b) consider other constitutional changes that can further enhance the quality of governance.

I cite, in particular, the fiscal rules that were recently enacted by Parliament. These establish specific fiscal, wage cost and debt limits, and targets that can be suspended only with the prior approval of Parliament and only in the event of constitutionally declared emergencies or severe economic contraction, the fiscal impact of which must have been certified by the auditor-general. Given our long history of fiscal and monetary indiscretion, I believe these provisions are an important restraint on executive excesses. The problem is that as they now exist by simple statute, these rules could be altered or even repealed sooner or later by a simple resolution of Parliament, notwithstanding the effect it might have on our relations with the multilateral agencies. I believe it is important for good governance for these to be made constitutional requirements.

I believe that the core ministries of government should be specified in the constitution with a limit as to the number of additional ministries that can be created.

I believe that the functions of the Electoral Commission as it is to be enshrined in the constitution should explicitly include the regulation of political financing.

I believe that the procedures for the award of government contracts should be settled conclusively and made into law, criminalizing the more flagrant breaches and rendering null and void contracts obtained by corrupt means.

I support the proposal for the amalgamation of the Office of the Contractor-general, Corruption Prevention Commission and the Parliamentary Integrity Commission into a single anti-corruption agency that would be enshrined in the constitution.

I have long advocated the establishment within the constitution of a special prosecutor with special responsibility for prosecuting cases involving public corruption. I am open as to the question as to whether those functions should be incorporated in the single anti-corruption agency.

Trinidad and Tobago recently made significant amendments to its constitution to establish term limits for the prime minister, provide for the recall of MPs and require a run-off election if a candidate receives less than 50 per cent +1 in a constituency election. Certainly, the first two have long been mooted in Jamaica.

In 2011, the UK established fixed election dates.

I support term limits and, in fact, tabled a bill in Parliament for that purpose in 2010. I support fixed election dates. I have reservations about the power to recall because it is susceptible to manipulation and corruption. I have reservations about run-off election requirements for similar reasons.

The Resident Magistrate's Court constitutes, by far, the largest part of our courts system where the vast majority of cases are tried. Resident Magistrates are technically civil servants and do not enjoy any security of tenure or protection from interference beyond what applies to ordinary civil servants. They are, therefore, exposed to the dangers that the constitutional protection provided to judges of the higher courts is designed to mitigate. Resident Magistrates should be given similar protection.

The need for public sector transformation is an issue the urgency of which is beyond dispute. It is expressed most times in the anguish about excessive bureaucracy, the non-ease of doing business in Jamaica, but it is much more than that. What is required is a strategic realignment within the public sector of responsibility, authority, and accountability. That has constitutional implications as the constitution makes specific provisions for the appointment and management of public officers, some of which are entrenched. Serious transformation cannot avoid a re-examination of those provisions.

Parliament is not just the face but a critical part of the machinery of governance. It currently functions largely as the government's chamber; its preoccupation is with the government's business. Its sittings are viewed by most as boring and uneventful. It can be made to be far more effective as the House of the people's representatives and in holding the government accountable. I had placed before Parliament a set of recommendations to provide for:

a. all oversight committees to be chaired (like the PAC) by a member of the opposition to facilitate more diligent scrutiny of government's activities;

b. each MP to be entitled to make statements to Parliament on matters affecting his/her constituents (duration of no more than five minutes and not more than six such statements at any one sitting);

c. a time limit to be prescribed by which questions tabled in Parliament must be answered and resolutions debated;

d. a requirement that reports from oversight bodies such as the Offices of the Auditor-General, Contractor-General, Public Defender, Political Ombudsman, Children's Advocate, the Integrity Commissions, and the Independent Commission of Investigations must be debated within 30 days of their submission to Parliament;

e. Parliament to have its own legal counsel to avoid the potential conflict of having to seek legal guidance from the chief parliamentary counsel or the attorney-general in considering legislation in the preparation of which they would both have been involved;

f. Access to the Bar of the House while in session by members of the public who may wish to petition the Parliament and can now do so only through an MP who is willing to present the petition on their behalf.

Parliament regulates its own proceeding through its standing orders and that is where these changes would need to be made. But the standing orders can be suspended by simple resolution. I believe section 48 of the constitution that deals with the powers and procedure of Parliament should include specific reference to the standing orders and provide that certain rights of the people's representatives cannot be abrogated by the suspension of the standing orders.

My Final Point

It is said that a country gets the government it deserves. It may also be said that it gets the constitution it deserves – either the one that it demands or the one that it allows its leaders to formulate.

It is arguable whether public interest in matters constitutional is any higher today than it was at the time of independence. Yes, there are more civil society groups and they enjoy exposure through a media that is much larger and penetrative than what existed 52 years ago. But while some of these lobby groups may be reflective of public opinion, they are not representative of the public; some could easily hold their annual general meetings (AGMs) in an ATM kiosk. Politicians tend to view advocacy groups the way Josef Stalin assessed military might when he asked 'How many divisions does the Pope of Rome have?'

The media plays a critical role in shaping public opinion not only in providing an avenue of expression for views that would otherwise be unnoticed but, through that exposure, enabling consensus and momentum to build around broad-based objectives. But that public must be aroused and alert and have views to which the media can provide expression. It must make the governance of the country one of its primary concerns and must educate and inform itself on the issues far beyond those that election campaigns are usually about. Otherwise, the media runs the risk of becoming hostage to those interests that own it or those interests that have access to it, and the rules will continue to be written by the rulers.

Dissatisfaction with the lack of progress, what is seen by so many as the broken promise of independence, has led them to disengage from the political process. I know of persons even among the leaders of civil society activist groups who proclaim with pride that they do not vote – a profound validation of their non-alignment, a demonstration of their 'untaintedness'. Political outcomes are, therefore, determined largely by those who may themselves be dissatisfied but want no fundamental change; they simply want the system to work more in their favour. Bad governance thrives in that environment.

NOTES

1. Trevor Munroe, *The Politics of Constitutional Decolonization: Jamaica, 1944–62* (Kingston: ISER, 1972).
2. Norman Manley, *Jamaica Hansard: Proceedings of the Jamaica House of Representatives 1962* 4:766.
3. Lloyd Barnett, *The Constitutional Law of Jamaica* (Oxford: Oxford University Press, 1977), 24.
4. Theodore Sealy, quoted in L. Barnett, 33.
5. Old Hope Road refers to the home of the People's National Party (PNP) headquarters, while Belmont Road is the headquarters of the Jamaica Labour Party (JLP).
6. See *The Jamaica (Constitution) Order in Council 1962*, United Kingdom Statutory Instruments 1962 No.1550.
7. Barnett, *The Constitutional Law of Jamaica*, 389.
8. Ewart Walters, *We Come from Jamaica: The National Movements 1937–1962* (Ottowa: Boyd McRubie, 2014), 2.
9. *The Jamaica Constitution*, 1962, 108.
10. The Independent Commission for Investigations (INDECOM) was established in 2010 to investigate instances of reported abuse of authority by the police and other arms of the state.

7 The Quest for Constitutional Reform in St Vincent and the Grenadines

Ralph Gonsalves

Introduction

On November 25, 2009, the electorate in St Vincent and the Grenadines rejected a reformed Constitution in a popular referendum by a majority of 55 per cent to 45 per cent of the votes cast. The voter turn-out was moderately high: roughly 65 per cent of the registered voters from a voters' list which contains about 30 per cent more eligible voters than ought to be the case; this voter turn-out reflected a significant popular interest in the constitutional reform exercise. My government spearheaded the campaign in favour of the reformed Constitution; the parliamentary opposition led the 'NO' campaign. Still, one year later, the political party which I have the honour to lead was returned to office in general elections for our third successive five-year term as government, winning eight seats to the opposition's seven.

The journey in this push for constitutional reform in St Vincent and the Grenadines commenced on July 31, 2000, when my political party, the Unity Labour Party (ULP) was in its final few months as the opposition. Of course, the issue of constitutional reform was always on the margins of public discourse since our existing Constitution was proclaimed on Independence Day, October 27, 1979.

So, on July 31, 2000, the ULP, as the then parliamentary opposition, formally launched a publication entitled, *Constitutional Reform: A Discussion*. At that launch, as the ULP's political leader, I pledged that in government, we would pursue vigorously comprehensive, democratic, and effective constitutional reform. In the ULP's Election Manifesto of 2001, this pledge was reaffirmed. Consequent upon our party's overwhelming election to government on March 28, 2001, we acted swiftly to put the appropriate policy framework and relevant programmatic mechanisms in place to give effect to our solemn electoral promise of democratic constitution re-making. I shall highlight some of the signposts along my government's journey on the road of constitutional reform.

First, on October 8, 2002, the House of Assembly approved by unanimous vote, a motion, moved by me as prime minister and seconded in a bipartisan spirit by the Leader of the opposition, Arnhim Eustace, which mandated a review of the Constitution of St Vincent and the Grenadines. Among other things, this motion called for the setting up of a broad-based Constitutional Review Commission (CRC) consisting of 25 persons, and alternates, representing the government, the opposition, civil society, and Vincentians in the diaspora.

The CRC was officially inaugurated on February 10, 2003, in the hallowed Chamber of our House of Assembly. The CRC was amply funded in its work by the government of St Vincent and the Grenadines, and with substantial assistance from the Organization of American States (OAS).

The CRC undertook extensive public consultations with Vincentians at home and abroad, intensively, face-to-face and through the electronic media over a five-year period up to June 2007. Thereafter, a nine-member Constitutional Reform Steering Committee (CRSC) drove public discussion up to Referendum Day in November 2009.

Throughout this entire period, several reports, interim and final, were submitted by the CRC and CRSC to Parliament. Parliamentary debates on the various submitted reports were held. Significantly, on July 17, 2007, all-party unity on constitutional reform was again made manifest in the House of Assembly when a motion moved by the prime minister and seconded by the leader of the opposition, and unanimously passed:

i.   mandated the appointment of the Committee of the Whole House to hold further discussions with the CRSC on the Revised Final Report on Constitutional Reform; and

ii.   authorized the joint body (that is, the Committee of the Whole House and the CRSC) to appoint a Committee of Draftspersons to draft the proposed changes to the Constitution of St Vincent and the Grenadines along the following guidelines:

    a.   A chairperson to be appointed by the Speaker of the House in consultation with the prime minister, leader of the opposition and the CRSC Chairman (Parnel Campbell, QC, former long-serving attorney-general in the NDP government);

    b.   Two members appointed by the Speaker, one on the recommendation of the prime minister, and the other of the leader of the opposition; and

c. The CRSC Chairman as a resource person attached to the drafting panel.

Ten days later, the all-party unity was shattered. Out of the blue, in a letter dated July 27, 2007, from the leader of the opposition to the prime minister proclaimed, for the first time, that the opposition will not participate any further in the constitutional review process unless certain 'things' were 'satisfactorily dealt with'. These 'things' were identified by the leader of the opposition as:

i. We must get the report of the Supervisor of Elections for the 2005 poll;

ii. That the ULP billboards be dismantled;

iii. That Senator Francis publicly explains how he got access to the number of Syrians who voted in 2001 and 2005 elections for the late Michael Hamlett and Senator Francis; and

iv. Mr. Rodney Adams, the Supervisor of Elections resigns his position.[1]

This metaphoric 'bolt from the blue' by the leader of the opposition made absolutely no sense in all reasonable circumstances. So, on August 14, 2007, I replied to him in the following terms:

Dear Arnhim,

I received your letter dated Friday July 27, 2007 on the subject of your party's withdrawal from the formal process of constitutional reform, shortly before my departure for Taiwan and Malaysia recently on July 28, 2007. I have just returned; thus my reply now to you.

It is unfortunate that your party has chosen not to participate any further in the process, especially for the reasons proffered, given all the facts, circumstances, and context. I consider that the issue of constitutional reform is of huge historic significance which ought not to be made a hostage to partisan political fortune.

The government has an unqualified mandate from the people in two successive general elections to proceed with constitutional reform in a most transparent, consultative and democratic way. This we have been doing. Never in the history of the Commonwealth has there been so profoundly a democratic, open, non-partisan, and all-embracing process. This is an assessment which has been made by informed observers, regionally and internationally.

We as a nation owe an enormous debt of gratitude to the members of the Constitutional Review Commission and the thousands of nationals, including those in the diaspora, who have contributed so immensely to the constitutional reform exercise. Thus, neither my government nor I will be party to any action which amounts to a disregard of the commendable, combined efforts of the people as a whole.

Accordingly, the government will continue with all practical dispatch the process of constitutional reform in accordance with the motion passed with the support of the Opposition in the House of Assembly on July 17, 2007, and the supreme law of the land. The door is open, as always, for Her Majesty's Loyal Opposition to participate fully.

I note the four "things" which you specifically raised on page 2 of your said letter. These surely do not, and cannot, credibly be linked to the process of constitutional reform or participation in it. I am prepared, however, to discuss them separately with you at a mutually convenient time at the Prime Minister's Office.

This government has an excellent record of good governance. This is widely acknowledged at home and abroad. Be assured that my government and I are committed as always to a more perfecting of our system and practice of good governance.

All the best to you and your family.

Sincerely yours,

Dr the Hon. Ralph E. Gonsalves

Prime Minister

On May 28, 2009, in the House of Assembly, I made the pitch for the proposed constitutional changes in the following terms:

The changes, for the better, in this proposed Constitution are numerous and wide-ranging. They tackle head-on the weaknesses and limitations of the constitution formulae negotiated with the departing colonial power in 1979. These include: an externally located Head of State of whom the governor-general is the representative; an insufficiently well-formulated bundle of individuals' fundamental rights and freedom and an insufficiently strong enforcement of their protective provisions; a first past-the-post electoral system which, by itself alone, does not provide a sufficiently fair and democratic representation of voters' preferences; the absence of any or any proper mechanisms for the voters to bring their elected representatives to account during their term in office; the highly inadequate and ineffective controls which the legislature exercises over the executive; the excessive powers of the prime minister in the constitutional and political apparatuses; the lack of adequate structures or mechanisms for voters and non-governmental organisations to participate actively on an on-going basis in the governance of the country; the inadequacy of the avenues available to the citizen who suffers from administrative abuses; the limitations on the proper functioning of an effective magistracy; the absence or inadequacy of constitutional provisions governing or regulating the integrity of members of the legislature, senior public servants, and senior public officers; the unnecessary lack of facilitation of regional political integration; and the minimal presence in our Constitution of 1979 of our national spirit and our Caribbeaness.[2]

The Major Constitutional Changes

In my statement to Parliament on May 28, 2009, consequent upon the introduction and first reading of the Constitution Bill, 2009, I sketched the proposed major constitutional changes thus:

1. Guiding Principles and a Young People's Charter

In the existing Constitution, the Preamble admirably lays out certain principles which have guided our nation from time immemorial, namely: the affirmation of our belief in the supremacy of God and the freedom and dignity of man; the recognition that our society ought to be ordered in accordance with a recognition of the principles of democracy, free institutions, social justice and equality before the law; and the realisation that the maintenance of human dignity presupposes safeguarding the rights and privacy of family life, of property and the fostering of the pursuit of just economic rewards for labour.

This preamble has been repeated in full, in the Constitution of 2009. However, the Constitution before us takes the matter much further in articulating a formidable bundle of non-justiciable 'Guiding Principles of State Policy' in 24 clauses of Chapter II of the proposed Constitution. These 'Guiding Principles' include the following: the assertion of the people as sovereign and the true holders of power; the paramountcy of the rule of law; the separation of powers, and good governance; the striving for sustainable economic development and full employment through the workings of a mixed economy; the promotion of justice and legal aid; the right to work; the right to health; the imposition of strictures against the abuse of state power and the building of a more caring and humane society; equality of treatment; the protection and enhancement of the environment; the respecting, protecting, and preserving our historical, cultural, and other heritage; the right to the enjoyment of freedom of culture and to cultural expression; the protection for, and support of, the family; the protection of marriage and the affirmation that marriage shall be a legal union only between a person who is biologically male at birth and a person who is biologically female at birth; the entitlement of special needs and care for the elderly and the disabled; the according of due appreciation to young persons for their contribution to nation-building; the affirmation of equal rights and the same legal status for women and men; the protection of the rights of children; and the equality of children born in and out of wedlock. Together these guiding principles are the essence of our nation's constitutionalism and norms for the conduct of the organs of the state.

Moreover, in Clause 38 of the proposed Constitution, for the first time ever, a deeply-entrenched constitutional protection is provided for a person's 'age of responsibility'. That is to say at the age of 18 years a person may decide for himself his own personal or societal destiny, including, having the right to: marry without requiring the consent of his/her parent or guardian; hold property including land, in his/her own name; dispose of such property without anyone's consent; do, without requiring the consent of any court or other body or person, any of the things which previously could lawfully be done only by a person attaining a higher age. This deeply entrenched constitutional provision amounts to a 'Young People's Charter', in that it has accorded constitutional protection of rights, some of which now exist only under ordinary legislation.

2. Securing Better Fundamental Rights and Freedoms

The Constitution Bill 2009, including its Schedule, better secures our citizens' fundamental rights and freedoms in at least four important respects:

a. By better protecting a citizen's right to life by ensuring that the deterrence of the death penalty for murder will be employed without being subject to judge-made restrictions. Over the recent years, the Privy Council and our Court of Appeal have made it almost impossible to carry out the death penalty for convicted murderers. The Law Courts amidst all their good intentions and impressive judicial learning, have unwittingly devalued the God-given right to the life of innocent persons who are murdered. The people directly in a referendum in November 2009 and through their Representatives in this Parliament have a once-in-a-lifetime chance to assert their support for the death penalty and the right to life. These who murder should forfeit their right to life. So, in Clause 29 (3) of the proposed Constitution it is stated thus:

> 'No objection shall be taken in or by any court to a sentence of capital punishment being carried out within one year after the exhaustion of all proceedings embarked upon and diligently pursued by the person thus sentenced....'

Indeed, we must ensure that the constitutional provision in favour of the death penalty is so tightly-drawn as to make it practically impossible for the Courts to dilute its application. This is a matter to be left to the people and their elected Parliament.

b. By strengthening the provision regarding freedom of expression by explicitly protecting 'freedom of the press' [Clause 34(1)]

c. By extending the constitutional protection of freedom of assembly and association in Clause 35(1) of the 2009 Constitution to include 'the right to participate in collective bargaining activities and agreements, and to form or belong to political parties'. Hitherto, there was an expressed constitutional right to belong to a trade union but a trade union's reason for existence that is to engage in collective bargaining, was not constitutionally protected. Similarly, there was no explicit constitutional right, hitherto, to form or belong to political parties. This and other provisions constitute a veritable 'Workers' Charter'; and

d. By strengthening the constitutional protection from any deprivation of property by specifying that the adequate compensation to be paid for the state's acquisition of a person's property must be paid not only in a reasonable time but in any event in no more than 12 months after the date of the acquisition. This precise time period provides additional comfort to property owners. [Clause 30 (1)]. This provision rightly fortifies our proposed Constitution as a 'Property-Owners' Charter'.

These innovations are in addition to the very strong constitutional protection provided regarding the right to life; the right to personal liberty; protection from slavery and forced labour; protection from inhuman treatment; protection from deprivation of property; protection against arbitrary search or entry; protection to secure protection of the law; protection of freedom of conscience; protection of freedom of expression; protection of freedom of assembly and association; protection of freedom of movement; protection from discrimination on the grounds of sex, race, place or origin, political opinions, colour or creed; and protection of persons detained under emergency.

Further, the proposed establishment, constitutionally, of a Human Rights Commission adds immeasurably to the process and institutional mechanisms of investigating complaints by persons who have suffered wrongs done by public authorities against the basic human rights of complainants whether or not amounting to unconstitutional contraventions of the fundamental rights and freedoms protected by Chapter III of the 2009 Constitution [See Clauses 44 to 48].

Together, the proposed Constitution establishes a "Peoples Charter" in defence and promotion of our fundamental human rights and freedoms.

5. *The Presidency*

Under the proposed Constitution, there shall be an Office of President of St Vincent and the Grenadines. The president shall be the Head of State. His office replaces that of the governor-general. The Queen will no longer be the monarch of St Vincent and the Grenadines though we will remain in the Commonwealth of which she is the titular head. The end of the monarchical system and its replacement by a home-grown, non-executive president is of immense practical and psychological significance. The colonial anachronism of the monarchy for St Vincent and the Grenadines and all which goes with it will be no more. This act of historical reclamation is part of the process of our people coming of age and looking at ourselves through the prism of our own eyes and proclaiming the authenticity and legitimacy of our Caribbean civilisation within our landscape and seascape. Clauses 49 to 65 of the 2009 Constitution detail the provisions regarding the president and the acting president.

6. *Parliament and its Powers*

There is a multiplicity of innovative and beneficial provisions in the 2009 Constitution touching and concerning Parliament and its powers. Among these are the following ten innovations:

a. Parliament (to be called 'the National Assembly') henceforth will be wholly elected on the basis of the traditional first-past-the-post electoral system and a system of proportional representation based on a party list of candidates. Both the government and opposition are agreed on this 'mixed system' although we differ on the actual number of Parliamentarians to be elected. This 'mixed system' provides for a greater representativeness of the people and makes well-nigh impossible a one-party Parliament. There will be no non-elected senator in this new Constitution.

b. A minister of religion under the 2009 Constitution will have the right to stand for election. This was prohibited hitherto.

c. When the Office of Attorney General is a public office, as distinct from an elected one, the holder of that office will have a right of audience, though not a vote, in Parliament. Currently, the 'civil servant' attorney general has no right to be heard in Parliament.

d. The 2009 Constitution strengthens the constitutional authority of the Public Accounts Committee which is expressly chaired by the mnority leader (formerly, the leader of the opposition).

e. In Clause 74(b) of the 2009 Constitution, there is an expressed provision which facilitates the achievement of regional integration.

f. The Clause 78 of the 2009 Constitution permits, as never before, the active participation of civil society invitees in the National Assembly. Clause 78(1) states:

> The Speaker, acting in accordance with the request of the prime minister or the minority leader, may from time to time invite persons from civil society who are not Representatives or other members of the National Assembly to address the Assembly on matters within the special expertise of such invited persons when such matters are being considered by the Assembly.

These civil society invitees shall not enjoy voting rights but shall otherwise enjoy the same privileges and immunities as a member of the Assembly.

g. Clauses 87 and 88 of the 2009 Constitution impose, for the first time, a formal obligation on a constituency representative to report to his constituents at least once every six months on his representational activities. Further, a written report in this regard has to be submitted by the representative to the Speaker. Any default in either respect by the representative may cause the Speaker essentially 'to name and shame' the representative openly in the Assembly.

h. The removal of the disqualification of a person to be elected as a representative if he/she is a citizen of another country by a voluntary act, in addition to being a citizen of St Vincent and the Grenadines (Clause 69(1)]. This provision acknowledges the migrant nature of our citizenry while embracing the fact that they are deeply connected to their homeland St Vincent and the Grenadines.

i. The removal of a referendum requirement for altering several constitutional provisions save and except the most deeply entrenched provisions such as those relating to our fundamental rights and freedoms and their enforcement, the Supreme Court Order, the major governance provisions, the independent Offices such as Director of Audit and Director of Public Prosecutions, the Service Commissions, and the provision regarding the Constitution as the supreme law. Wherever there is no referendum requirement to alter any provision of the Constitution of 2009, a special majority of two-thirds is required in the National Assembly. The majority in any future referendum, however, will be sixty percent instead of two thirds.

j. Clause 84(2) strengthens the role of the minority leader regarding financial matters in a way not available currently. Under the proposed Constitution, the minority leader, by way of a motion (not a bill), can formally propose to the National Assembly any matter regarding taxation, expenditure from the Consolidated Fund, or any such related financial issue of the central government. The opposition had been asking for this every year.

5. *Elections and Elections Machinery*

There is a bundle of innovative provisions, for the better, in the proposed Constitution regarding elections and the machinery for the conduct of general elections. These provisions include:

a. General elections cannot be called before the expiration of four (4) years and nine months after the first sitting of the National Assembly after the previous dissolution of Parliament. Thus, the prime minister cannot call a 'snap' election under the 2009 Constitution. So, for example, if the proposed Constitution is approved by the people in a referendum and by the House of Assembly, the next election has to be called sometime between the end of September and the end of December 2010. Please note that the current Parliament first met for its five-year term after the last dissolution on December 29, 2005.

A special provision exists to address the circumstances under which general elections may be called consequent upon the success of a 'no-confidence' motion.

b. A five-member independent Electoral and Boundaries Commission is to replace the supervisor of elections as the authority charged with directing and supervising the registration of voters and the conduct of general elections. This mechanism will strengthen the pre-existing process of our well-known free and fair system of holding elections. The Commission will also have the responsibility for the determination of constituency boundaries. Clauses 94 to 96 make provisions for this Commission.

c. A 'mixed' electoral system of first-past-the-post constituency elections and a proportional representation system based on simple 'party lists' is being proposed. It is fairer and more representative, but at the same time avoids a situation of a multiplicity of political parties and thus weakened government. There are to be 17 constituency representatives and ten party representatives in the National Assembly, up from the current number of 21 (15 representatives and six senators). This slightly enlarged number will provide for a greater display of parliamentary democracy particularly since the number of Cabinet members will be limited to 12 only!

Under the 'mixed' system the voter will vote once in the usual manner for his Constituency Representative. To determine the number of the ten part representatives to be accorded to each competing political party, all the votes cast in the constituency elections would be tallied up for each competing party by a simple proportional formula set out in the proposed Constitution. Because there are ten party representatives, the quota of votes per seat for party representatives will be ten per cent plus one of the votes cast in the constituency elections.

d.   Clause 98(3) makes the innovative provision that no fewer than six of the combined total number of persons being offered as constituency candidates and on 'the party lists' shall be women; correspondingly no fewer than six shall be men. In this way, we shall ensure a minimum gender representation offered to the electorate. This, and other provisions, elaborate a 'Women's Charter'.

6.   The Judiciary

The provisions for the independence and quality Judiciary remain deeply entrenched and robustly protected. The proposed Constitution makes a stipulation, nevertheless, for a two-thirds majority of the National Assembly to replace the Privy Council by the Caribbean Court of Justice without the further requirement of another referendum.

Moreover, the proposed Constitution contemplates the probability of a regional Magistracy, by whatever name it is designated. This will strengthen the forum before which most civil and criminal disputes are heard. Additionally, the Office of the Magistrate is protected as never before.

7.   The Service Commissions

A Teaching Service Commission is being proposed in the 2009 Constitution in addition to the Public and Police Service Commissions. This amounts to a 'Teachers' Charter' and fulfils a demand of the teachers since 1975. In the appointment of a Chairman of each of these three commissions the president is required to act in his own deliberate judgment, having only consulted the prime minister. Currently, the governor-general makes the appointment of the chairman of the Public and Police Service Commissions on the advice of the prime minister. In short, the prime minister's authority in this regard is markedly reduced. Further, civil society is accorded a representative on the Service Commissions in the new Constitution.

Meanwhile, the public servants, police officers, and teachers are accorded full protection in the terms and conditions of their employment.

8. Local Government

A Constitutional provision is made, for the first time, for the establishment of a system of local government, with special autonomous attention mandated for the Grenadines.

9. Integrity Commission

An independent Integrity Commission is established, for the first time ever, in a Constitution of St Vincent and the Grenadines. This Commission will oversee, monitor, investigate issues relating to 'the integrity' of parliamentarians, and holders of certain prescribed public offices.

10. The Ombudsman

The proposed Constitution establishes the independent Office of the Ombudsman which shall be answerable to the National Assembly. The central function of the ombudsman shall be to investigate complaints by members of the public about maladministration in any public office. This is a vital innovation.

11. The Parliamentary Commission

An innovative, independent ten-member Parliamentary Commission, chaired by the Speaker, is proposed to be established in the 2009 Constitution. Its several functions include exercising the Prerogative of Mercy, proposing nominees for the Office of President to the National Assembly, and deliberating on matters pertaining to good governance.

12. Minority Leader

The proposed Constitution renames the Office of the Leader of the Opposition as the minority leader in an effort to reduce the 'oppositionist' perception of that office. The important functions of the minority leader are spelt out in Clause 126 of the proposed Constitution. The minority leader/leader of the opposition is accorded more power under this proposed Constitution than what exists in any other Constitution in the Commonwealth.

13. The Executive

The effective executive is the cabinet. The proposed Constitution stipulates, for the first time, the appointment of a deputy prime minister and limits the size of the cabinet to 12 members plus the prime minister. That means that the cabinet will no longer constitute a majority of the National Assembly.

14. Reduction Of The Prime Minister's Powers

The proposed Constitution reduces markedly the powers of the prime minister in several ways, including:

a. The constitutional requirement of a more or less fixed date for general elections. There cannot be snap elections anymore outside a very narrow window of opportunity. This is a major limitation on the prime minister's powers.

b. The limitation on the number of cabinet members that a prime minister can cause to be appointed.

c. The removal of the prime minister's power of determining life or death or in reducing any sentence of imprisonment. He would no longer be in charge of the Prerogative Committee of Mercy. That authority would henceforth be in the Parliamentary Commission.

d. The strengthening of the power of the Public Accounts Committee which is chaired by the minority leader and would have a majority of opposition members.

e. The removal of the prime minister's power in effectively appointing the chairpersons of the Service Commissions.

f. The restraints on the prime minister's authority by the sizeable numbers of non-cabinet members in the National Assembly; by the Parliamentary Commission; by the Human Rights Commission; by the ombudsman; by the participatory role of civil society nominees in the Assembly; by effective local government; and by the Electoral and Boundaries Commissions.

g. The removal of the sole effective power of the prime minister in the appointment of the Head of State.

h. The removal of the power of the prime minister to appoint senators.

15. Miscellaneous

There is a range of miscellaneous provisions in the proposed Constitution which improves significantly our Constitutional governance. These include:

a. The provision that the attorney general is prohibited from acting as the director of public prosecutions at one and the same time.

b. A provision relating to the holding of dual or multiple citizenship.

c. A provision against 'marriages of convenience' as the basis for acquiring citizenship of St Vincent and the Grenadines.

d. The availability of a civil society appointee on the Public Service Board of Appeal.

e. The widening of the access to the Constitutional Court (High Court) in relation to the enforcement of the general provisions of the Constitution (except those relating to fundamental rights where there is a specific enforcement provision). Under the current Constitution, the applicant is required to have a 'relevant' interest which has been frequently narrowly interpreted by the Courts. Under the proposed Constitution, the applicant is required only to have an 'arguable' interest. The difference is profound!

Conclusion

Accordingly, on the basis of all that I have said, I urge a 'Yes' vote in the referendum in November.

Meanwhile we have work to do over the next 90 days. I expect to be here, God's willing, on Tuesday September 1, 2009, for the second reading of a more perfect Constitution Bill 2009.[3]

Reasons for Defeat in Referendum

I offer now a summation of the reasons for the rejection of the proposed Constitution in the 2009 referendum. These include:

1. The resistance to political and constitutional change by a population which has had some 250 years of British colonial tutelage. Essentially, they were satisfied with the constitutional arrangements bequeathed to them at the terminal stage of colonialism. They felt broadly comfortable with the existing Constitution, despite an acknowledgement of its several weaknesses and limitations. The seven-year campaign to reform the Constitution did not succeed in undermining the general public's satisfaction with the existing Constitution.

2. The 'No Campaign' for the referendum was better organized and run than the 'Yes Campaign'. The 'No Campaign' had a simple

set of messages and hugely exploited the people's fear of change. Their propaganda was well-financed, and executed through a British public relations firm, Strategic Communications Laboratories (SCL). The 'No Campaign' was conducted from a narrow, partisan political perspective. Because the 'Yes Vote' required a two-thirds majority in the referendum, all the 'No Vote' had to do was to play to the party base of the opposition *plus* those fearful of, or opposed to, constitutional change. The 'Yes Campaign' needed to go beyond the political base of the ruling party; thus, it consciously avoided appeals to the party. In the process, the 'Yes Campaign' ran the campaign with one political hand tied metaphorically behind its back.

3.   A significant slice of the ruling party's supporters were insufficiently motivated to vote in the referendum. After all, a referendum loss still had their party in power.

4.   The army of volunteers and paid canvassers for the 'Yes Campaign' provided much erroneous tracking information about public opinion until quite late in the referendum campaign. This hampered the efficacy of the 'Yes Campaign'.

5.   There were too many issues for the voters to consider in assessing the proposed Constitution. In retrospect, it would have been better to focus on a few reforms, rather than an extensive root-and-branch overhaul. Perhaps, the reforms should have focused on completing the *national* tasks of the social democratic revolution, mainly, the end to the monarchy, the retiring of the Privy Council, and the facilitation of deeper regional integration. Later, the more democratic-centred reforms could have been addressed.

No Retreat on Constitutional Reform

My government has accepted, as it must, the democratic verdict of the people as reflected in the results of the 2009 referendum. More and more, the general public is appreciating the sensible reform proposals which were on offer in the referendum as governance challenges arise on an on-going basis in the functioning of the existing Constitution. Repeatedly, I draw attention to these, so there is no retreat from the agenda for constitutional reform.

At the same time, other national priorities have arisen and the government is focused on them. In time, my party, perhaps with a new generation of leaders, is likely to return practically to constitutional reform. When that occasion arises, the people would be able to build upon the efforts of the 'failed' referendum exercise. After all, a vote of 46 percent for constitutional change, further constitutional decolonization, and enhanced democracy, in a society gripped substantially by the incubus of colonial thought, is still a significant political change.

So, I remain active and hopeful in the vineyard of meaningful constitutional reform. I take solace and guidance from the book Ecclesiastes (chapter 11, verse 4):

> *Whoever watches the wind will not plant;*
> *Whoever looks at the clouds will not reap.*

NOTES
1. Leader of the Opposition Arnhim Eustace to Prime Minister Dr the Hon. Ralph E. Gonsalves, July 27, 2007.
2. Prime Minister Dr the Hon. Ralph E. Gonsalves, Statement to the House of Assembly, May 28, 2009.
3. Ibid.

8 The Westminster Model and the Collapse of the Postcolonial Order

Tennyson S.D. Joseph

Introduction

Paul Sutton, writing on the historical experience of constitutional change in the English-speaking Caribbean, makes two observations that are critical to understanding the essential crux and concern of this chapter. In reference to the 'content' of proposed constitutional reforms, Sutton observes that suggested changes have been rather limited in form and do not overturn the essential basis of the Westminster system. In his view, most of the standard recommendations and related proposals all point to 'modifications' of Westminster rather than its complete elimination. This is seen, for example, in the recommendations pertaining to:

> the role of the head of state, including whether they are to be a ceremonial president or an executive president; a limitation on the powers of the prime minister, including restrictions on the number of terms served; the method of election for the lower house and of nomination for the upper house.[1]

Sutton's second observation is that ongoing efforts at constitutional change have been pursued outside the context of wider and deeper economic and political developments, which would feed organically into a genuine framework for overcoming Westminster. In support of this, he identifies the limited use of the facility of the 'constituent assembly' as the framework for pursuing constitutional change, since the convening of constitutional conventions is normally associated with major crises and the Commonwealth Caribbean has witnessed more stability than crisis.[2] Thus, in the absence of a context of unquestionable and ongoing crisis he concludes that:

> There is no appetite for fundamental constitutional change among the majority in the region and that substantial constitutional change is very much a minority interest; even among the political elites. It also indicates that when constitutional change occurs it is as or more

likely to take the form of amendment to the existing constitution rather than take the form of a commitment to a wholly new one with significant departure from existing norms and practices.[3]

It is Sutton's denial of the immediate presence of crisis, and by extension, his reduced expectation of radical constitutional deviations from Westminster, which provides the substantive point of departure of this chapter. In contrast to Sutton's explanation of conformity to Westminster and mild reform as the consequence of the absence of genuine crisis, this chapter argues instead that much of the region's conformity to Westminster can be explained by the deliberate management of the process of constitutional reform by regional elites who have resisted radical options, despite the compelling nature of crisis conditions which demand such radical transformation. The chapter argues that the post-2008 socio-economic crisis is impacting on the political process in a manner which may overturn Sutton's assumption of commitment to Westminster as the foreseeable constitutional future for the Caribbean. This crisis presents a moment of socio-economic disruption which will have significant implications for the political and governance framework of the Caribbean.

The chapter, therefore, has three main concerns. The first, in keeping with a Marxist analysis of the relationship between economic transformation and political change, is to make a claim that the current moment in Caribbean development presents features consistent with the end of the 'postcolonial' order, and as a consequence, presents a material basis qualitatively different from the one in which Westminster was established as the 'appropriate' model for the Caribbean. While accepting Sutton's claim of the historical reluctance among Caribbean elites to radically overhaul Westminster, the chapter argues that since 2008, a moment of genuine crisis has emerged in the Caribbean, particularly when compounded with the ongoing crises associated with globalization, trade liberalization, the end of the Cold War and all their attendant consequences since the 1980s. The case is thus presented for understanding the present moment as one of collapse of the postcolonial order, and identifies this as the basis upon which a more radical overhaul of the Westminster system is possible.

A second and related concern of the chapter is to demonstrate the ways in which Caribbean ruling elites have used the formal mechanisms of constitutional change to resist the radical overhaul of the Westminster system. A critique of the historical practice of constitutional change in the Caribbean is presented, largely on the grounds that the dominant methods of initiating political reform have tended to be pursued along lines which separate economic considerations from constitutional proposals. Led largely by states, the movements for constitutional change have provided little room for contested economic questions to be reflected in the various proposals. Relatedly, where proposals are forwarded which have direct bearing on socio-economic relations, such as with the inclusion of employment and other economic rights in the preambles, for example, these ring hollow given the absence of any concrete politico-economic framework which can translate intent into reality. The chapter, therefore, examines a number of the constitutional review documents which have arisen from select constitutional review commissions in the Caribbean since the 1990s, highlighting the mechanical separation of constitutional proposals from the socio-economic context in which they are immersed.

The final section examines current debates on the need for constitutional change that have emerged in the context of the global economic crisis. Analysing political discourse in the region since the crisis of 2008, this section suggests how Sutton might have missed the underlying political impulses which have forced issues of radical constitutional change upon the political agenda. To highlight this development, the chapter focuses on Barbados, where debates surrounding the economic un-sustainability of the postcolonial social democratic model have raised questions about the need for deeper constitutional transformation, thus linking the economic with the political in ways that have potentially radical implications for the existing political system. Barbados is chosen because it is arguably the Caribbean society in which the postcolonial social democratic order had been pursued most thoroughly and had been sustained for a much longer period, post-independence. Consequently, Barbados is currently the society in which the discussion on the neoliberal reversal away from social democracy has been impacting most directly on the politics of the country.

It is in the context of an acknowledged crisis of the Barbadian society and economy that discussions on political reform are being linked to specific economic demands, motivated by group and class interests, by sections of the political class who have made public interventions into discussions on the way forward for Barbados. Thus, as will be seen later, the demands for political reform from sections of the business class, for example, have been couched specifically in class terms, and are deliberately geared to ensuring that specific economic concerns are addressed. For example, calls from the private sector for constitutional limits to government spending based on set revenue-expenditure limits, ignore the issue of necessary social protection and social engineering on behalf of weaker groups historically marginalized by centuries of colonial inequalities. Similarly, the voices from the left have vehemently opposed the ongoing attempts to limit the ability of governments to pursue social interventionist stances on behalf of the poor. Whilst still in their early stages of manifestation, these developments suggest the beginning of a process of more radical change, commensurate with a context of 'crisis' highlighted by Sutton. Thus, the more overt class content of the constitutional debate, as well as the unrelenting nature of the economic crisis with its attendant political and social challenges, signal the end of the practice of 'limited' approaches to constitutional change. Indeed, it may also signal the beginning of a process in which the Westminster system is no longer seen as given and natural.

Explaining the Collapse of the Postcolonial Order[4]

The period following the visit of the Moyne Commission in the Caribbean witnessed a series of economic, social, and political developments which in their inter-connectedness constituted the postcolonial order in the Caribbean. In making a case for the collapse of the postcolonial order, it is argued that the framework which had sustained post-Moyne social and economic relations has been destroyed by global and economic developments associated with the rise of global neoliberalism.

There is much evidence to suggest that roughly since the decade of the 1980s, the postcolonial state-society relations established with and since the Moyne Commission have been systematically dismantled. Central to this have been the emergence of neoliberal ideas and practices as the dominant basis of state society-relations in the Caribbean. This has resulted in the reversal of previous strategies of Caribbean postcolonial development and relatedly, it has eroded the socio-economic framework which had sustained Caribbean democracy and has undermined the legitimacy of the political system.

Given the scale and rapidity of the roll back of the interventionist Caribbean state since the mid-1980s, the period between the 1960s and the early 1980s now stands apart as a golden age for postcolonial state construction and economic development. In that period, there was still a large degree of global legitimacy for even the smallest of states to engage in interventionist social and economic re-engineering. After a protracted battle to win the instrumentality of sovereignty, Caribbean societies, with varying degrees of consistency, sought to pursue correctives to the colonial condition. Those correctives required heavy doses of state intervention to widen education levels, to improve health services, housing and other social amenities, and to modernize the civil service, making it more responsive to local as distinct from metropolitan needs.

All of these progressive developments were sustained by a relatively permissive global politico-economic environment, one feature of which was the presence of the Cold War which created space, through non-alignment, for small states to extract maximum advantage. In economic terms, there was both the expectation and realization that the former colonial powers had some responsibility towards their former colonies, as reflected in relatively favourable and preferential global trade arrangements which provided some breathing space for domestic growth and development, particularly around the production of traditional staple commodities. In philosophical terms, the environment was supported by perspectives which were conducive to independence and self-determination and which saw the instrumentality of sovereignty and state intervention as important mechanisms through which national development could be pursued. Implied in the notion of self-determination was the idea of government by the consent of the governed, which in this context implied a close correlation between the social democratic orientation of the state and the legitimating electoral support for political parties. Whilst gaps may exist between philosophy and practice, the sharp differences between what was viewed as ideologically permissible in the early postcolonial period, and the new ideas which now champion the limits to state power associated with neoliberal ideology, must be taken into consideration in understanding the notion of the collapse of the postcolonial order.

In understanding the link between the ongoing discussions on constitutional change and the collapse of the postcolonial order, it is necessary to show how the specific political arrangements of the postcolonial period are being reversed by the economic and ideological shifts associated with neoliberalism. In this regard therefore, it is important to note that some of the principal economic and democratic successes in the Caribbean took place in the 1960 to 1980 period when the postcolonial social contract was given full expression. Whilst several variations among Caribbean countries can be identified in the levels of commitment to the social contract, during this period the state was seen as having a minimal responsibility for social welfare; primary producers of sugar and bananas enjoyed relatively secure incomes through preferential trade arrangements with the former colonial power; and public sector workers were not rendered insecure by anti-statist ideologies that denigrate the public sector while championing the inherent goodness of the private sector. In some countries such as Barbados, the contract extended generously to the provision of free tertiary education, health care, and state-subsidized public transportation for eligible citizens. Underlying these arrangements was a broad agreement to conform to democratic norms, at least in institutional form if not in cultural substance, with a general adherence to social democracy within the political and cultural orbit of the West, while avoiding communism.

These were the broad terms of the postcolonial social contract which sustained Caribbean democracy and development in the first two decades of independence. However, a number of developments in the post-1980 global politico-economic environment destroyed the postcolonial political order and established a framework which sustained the ideology of neoliberalism. For example, the end of the Cold War, ushered in by the collapse of the Soviet bloc, made a mockery of the policy of ideological conformity with the West espoused by the early postcolonial leaders as the basis of their foreign policy development strategy. The expected benefits of 'non-alignment' to which the left-of-centre regimes had adhered simply disappeared. With the end of the Cold War, the Caribbean immediately witnessed reductions in grants and concessionary financing from the dominant capitalist countries as their investment interests shifted to the regions of the former communist world.

Closely coinciding with this development was the emergence of norms of liberalized global trade which eroded the preferential trade arrangements that had previously sustained Caribbean economies. First, with the establishment of the Single European Economy, and later with the formation of the World Trade Organization (WTO) in 1995, the Caribbean experienced sharp declines in income particularly to the rural agricultural sector, and significant economic reversal as a whole, as a result of the loss of preferential arrangements and the move to liberalized trade. Many of the social, political, and economic crises confronting Caribbean society since the early 1990s, such as crime, drug abuse, violence, political apathy, and youth alienation, have been at least partially the result of economic decline in previously protected industries. The uncritical application of neoliberal norms has removed the economic cushions which had previously protected the Caribbean's fragile democracies, with negative implications for the conduct of political life.

Closely aligned to these developments has been the dominance of neoliberal ideas concerning the role of the state, which has reduced the capacity of the state to pursue locally determined priorities. Once globalization had set in, and with the goal of 'attracting external capital' as the dominant concern, Caribbean governments faced increasing difficulty in pursuing policies consistent with privileging the economic and social aspirations of local populations. In this period, the state's size, purpose, and sovereignty have come under attack. The role of the state has been systematically redefined to a set of functions less consistent with resisting externally determined economic objectives. Faced with its own powerlessness, the state has now responded by resisting democracy and by insulating itself from demands for more democratic inclusion. In Barbados, for example, previous lines of communication such as post-cabinet briefings and quarterly press conferences by the Central Bank Governor have been deliberately abandoned, as the state finds itself unable to legitimize and explain its social-democratic reversals.[5] In Trinidad and Tobago and Jamaica, the state has had to resort to more extreme measures such as military 'incursions' and states of emergency in the face of the growing boldness and legitimacy of criminal gangs which in some instances replace the state as the distributor of social and protective services. Whilst Caribbean states from the immediate post-independence period to the 1970s and 1980s had utilized states of emergency in response to political and ideological threats, the experience since the 1980s suggests that gang violence, organized criminal activity, and instances of social banditry have been the basis of such state action, indicating the greater prevalence of social decay, state failure, value-system contestation, and legitimation crisis as dominant new features of the current moment. All of these developments provide the objective socio-economic conditions in which any discussions of 'constitutional reform' must be undertaken.

Finally, though not exhaustively, a central feature of the collapse of the postcolonial order has been the negation of democracy and the return to old colonial notions of power without responsibility.[6] This development is of direct relevance to the specific concern about the relevance of the Westminster system to present-day Caribbean reality. Whilst much focus has been placed on the economic consequences of globalization, it is often forgotten that among its more pernicious consequences have been the erosion of Caribbean democracy. Under classic colonialism, the state enjoyed power without responsibility, under which British colonial officials and their local representatives were able to wield power over Caribbean populations while remaining unelected by and unaccountable to the local population. The colonial state was therefore neither representative of local wishes nor responsible or accountable to any local aspirations.

A major element of the collapse of the postcolonial order has been the reduction in the democratic power of citizens to influence government policy, through the emergence of neoliberal understandings of the state as a facilitator of international capital rather than as a promoter and defender of local aspirations and as bulwark against external encroachment. Whilst both the colonial and postcolonial states have served to facilitate the demands of international capital, what is distinctive about the period of neoliberal hegemony is the extent to which the already limited levels of state intervention have been further curtailed. Whatever the limitations of the postcolonial state, it cannot escape acknowledgement that a critical feature of the independence movement was its democratic possibilities. By the winning of one-person one-vote, citizens could elect governments of their own making and influence decision-making according to majority interests. The Caribbean independence movements therefore moved the centre of decision-making from the Colonial Office in London and placed them in the hands of the local population.

With the heightened impact of neoliberal ideology and its attendant diminution of the state, and the general impact of globalization, all of these earlier conditions and approaches have been undermined and, as argued by Jamie Peck and Adam Tickell, the old colonial problematic of power without responsibility has been re-presented in a new guise.[7] Given the rolling back of the state and the undermining of the nationalist and social interventionist policies which dominated the postcolonial agenda, increasingly more of the critical decisions impacting the lives of Caribbean people are being made in the International Monetary Fund (IMF), World Bank, and the G20, and in the boardrooms of dominant multinational companies, rather than in domestic cabinet rooms. Whilst the power of domestically elected governments to sustain the social-democratic policies of the postcolonial order has decreased, these governments remain no less accountable for actions over which they have little or no control. Whilst under classic colonialism metropolitan rulers enjoyed power without responsibility, today local governments have responsibility without power, and international agencies enjoy power without responsibility.[8] All of this negates the essence of democracy, in which the right to self-determination and government by the consent of the governed are essential features.

It is in such a context that the implications for the inherited constitutional framework can be fully appreciated. The central ideological assumptions of neoliberalism include: the privileging of private capital over the social good; the assumption of the economic sphere as given and natural, whilst the political sphere is artificial and therefore subject to containment; the privileging of the individual over the social; the idea of the state as the facilitator of private capital accumulation at the expense of the protection and enhancement of civil society; the notion that the state should retreat from the economic sphere and should confine itself to security and labour regulation; the claim of the end of ideology and the assumption that all other options are closed; and the notion of the 'death of Politics' which holds that all major political questions have been resolved and the only role left for politics is 'administration', leading to the rise of technocrats and the privileging of 'management' over leadership.[9]

These developments validate the notion of the collapse of the postcolonial order as both a political reality and as a useful analytical tool for understanding the politics of the Caribbean since the turn of the century. Much of the politics of the Caribbean since the early 1990s can be seen as marking a process of adjustment out of the post-Moyne framework. On this basis, efforts at constitutional change and the transformation of the Westminster system will remain ineffective, inadequate and false unless pursued as a deliberate effort at overcoming and responding to the political consequences arising from the collapse of the social, economic, and political arrangements associated with the independence project. In short, efforts at constitutional change will be meaningless unless they are consciously pursued as a response to the collapse of the postcolonial order. An approach that is oblivious to this wider context will result in the exploration of constitutional change as a mere 'technical' exercise, rationalized on the general need to 'modernize' the governance framework since 'the time has come', divorced from the economic environment in which it is immersed.

In contrast, a more appropriate understanding of constitutional change in the Caribbean would necessarily and logically link such change to the ongoing process of ideological contestation and political repositioning which is arising from the fundamental economic and political dislocations occurring in the Caribbean. If the present moment represents the dismantling of the social and economic state-society relations of the postcolonial order then it can be expected that the constitutional and political arrangements of the state will also of necessity be subject to a process of review, overhaul, and change.

However, it is precisely the absence of any organic connection to these objective social and economic under-currents which presents itself as a most problematic feature of the historical and recent examples of the process of constitutional change in the Caribbean. Rather than being the consequence of the need to adjust to social, economic, and political demands from below, the post-1990 experience of constitutional reform has been totally divorced from the wider economic and social relations which those constitutional changes are intended to mediate. This artificial and mechanical separation of constitutional reform from the objective material reality is the deliberate result of the role of formal governments in spearheading movements for constitutional change. Often divorced from civil society and the normal social contestations which would necessarily ensue, constitutional change has been treated as a politically neutral exercise, disconnected from social interests. A major consequence of this has been not only the divorce of the general public from the process, but the political 'barrenness' of many of the proposals, despite the noble intent in many cases, of advancing political development.

The following section analyses the process of constitutional reform in the Caribbean highlighting these weaknesses and pitfalls. The chapter will then examine the politics of Barbados to demonstrate how the collapse of the postcolonial order is impacting the general politics of that country and to show the implications for constitutional reform.

The Pitfalls of State-led Constitutional Change in the Caribbean

Paul Sutton categorizes the experience of constitutional reform in the Caribbean since independence in three phases. The first was the efforts of Trinidad and Tobago and Guyana in the 1970s, which focused largely on the introduction of republican and republican-type constitutions in 1976 and 1980 respectively. The second phase, in the 1990s, was 'associated with rising concerns at deteriorating standards of governance in the region', and resulted in the formation of a number of constitutional commissions in the Caribbean, including 'Jamaica (1995), Barbados (1998), Dominica (1999), Belize (2000), Antigua and Barbuda (2002), St Kitts and Nevis (2002) and St Vincent (2002)'. Finally, Sutton identifies a third phase which he describes as 'ongoing' and 'involves the approval of the draft constitution and its rejection in a referendum in St Vincent in 2009, and continues in the Bahamas, Grenada, Jamaica, St Lucia and Trinidad and Tobago'.[10] To Sutton's list can be added the announced referendum in October 2016 for Grenadians to decide on a new constitution.

All of this heightened activity on constitutional reform suggests a conscious effort to deepen the democratic basis of the inherited independence constitutions. Cynthia Barrow-Giles has provided a useful synopsis of the issues which have dominated the discourse on constitutional change in the Caribbean over the last two to three decades.[11] The main issue has been the need to deepen democracy, strengthen popular participation, and ensure popular confidence in government. This concern has prompted proposals such as the need to curtail the disproportionate power of the prime minister, addressed as 'early as the 1970s Constitution Review Commission of Trinidad and Tobago' (the Wooding Commission Report), as well as to address the possibilities of single party domination. Such concerns were reflected, for example, in the recommendations of the 1990 constitutional reform committee in Jamaica, headed by Carl Stone, which proposed the adoption of a 'presidential model of government that would create the much needed checks and balances on the political executive'.[12]

Other issues identified by Barrow-Giles which have dominated the discourse on constitutional reform in the Caribbean include the 'poor performance of elected leaders' and the need to make parliamentarians accountable.[13] Thus common proposals include the establishment of recall mechanisms; the jettisoning of rubber stamp senates; the implementation of financial and other regulation of political parties; and judicial reform, in particular the distancing of the judiciary from the executive branch.[14] Finally, Barrow-Giles identifies the growing demand for new categories of rights as being central to the more recent thrust for constitutional reform in the Caribbean. She notes that under the issue of rights have arisen 'calls to protect the right to environment and to review the existing grounds of discrimination to include disability, and sexual orientation' as well as gender equality.[15]

There is little doubt that the recent proposals of the various constitutional reform commissions in the Caribbean represent genuine attempts at advancing democracy beyond its inherited Westminster limits and at placing citizens at the centre of government. For example, the St Vincent and the Grenadines Constitutional Bill (2009) included a special chapter that establishes the guiding principles of state policy, privileging the people as the 'true political sovereign of the state'. The section holds that the 'will of the people shall be the basis of the authority of the government' and asserts that in 'formulating and implementing fundamental policy measures… government must constantly act primarily in furtherance of what is in the best interest of the people'.[16] This development stands in stark contrast to the independence constitutions which made no reference to the governmental authority as being vested in the people but essentially reinforced the imperial basis of the new constitutions.

A similar intent at grounding the constitution to reflect postcolonial majoritarian reality is evident in the Report of the Constitution Review Commission of Barbados (or the Forde Commission), which observed that 'the existing pre-amble was…severely criticized by members of the public mainly on the grounds, inter alia, that there is no reference to the historical fact of slavery; it commences with a blatantly anti-historical claim that "the love of free institutions and of independence has always strongly characterized the inhabitants of Barbados"; and that the reference to the "supremacy of God" may plausibly be interpreted as excluding non-Christians from the purview of the Constitution'.[17]

Similarly, in many cases there is evidence of genuine intent to advance Caribbean democracy beyond what has been allowed under the inherited Westminster constitutions. Several Commission reports have been robust in their language, and radical in their objectives. For example, the report of the St Lucian Constitution Review Commission suggests genuinely radical intent and purpose:

> Saint Lucians regarded our Constitution as placing them in the role of window-shoppers, passively standing outside the store-front of Government, looking in, hands pressed against the glass, but unable to influence decision-makers once an election was won…They lamented the fact that they could not hold Government accountable, except through the remote mechanism of an election, by which time the damage resulting from poor decision-making, malfeasance, incompetence or outright contempt for the electorate, might be irreparable or irreversible.[18]

Aware of popular concerns about exclusion, the St Lucian commissioners embarked on widespread consultations throughout and indeed outside St Lucia. Stating that they had a choice of siding either with the people, or with the politicians and political parties, the commissioners' report claimed that they had resolved to side with the people. This process of consultation contrasts sharply with the historical creation of the independence constitutions, which derived from the pens of civil servants in Whitehall.

However, despite the 'progressive' nature of these interventions, the post-1990 efforts at constitutional change have in many instances been too mechanically separated from the material economic sphere to have any direct and meaningful impact on change. This has resulted in depoliticizing both the process of review as well as the recommendations emanating therefrom. In this way, constitutional reform has been sanitized from any contentious political questions.

In the case of Belize, for example, the commissioners admitted to being caught between their obligations to the government on one hand, and the demands for greater thoroughness and radicalism from the population on the other. The Belizean commissioners made it clear that their obligations rested with fulfilling the mandate of the government:

> Early in the year, several Commissioners and some in the general public expressed concern over what they perceived as an extremely short time period to effectively carry out such a major task that has far reaching national implications. The Commission noted that a significant amount of work had already been done by several organizations on the issue of political reform, including nation-wide public consultations and that it was not starting from scratch. Additionally, the Commission felt that a longer process could dampen interest in the issue and perpetuate public cynicism about government's inaction on issues of public concern. Eventually, the Commission agreed to organize itself to complete the mandate in the time requested.[19]

Similarly, the report notes another occasion when the Commission was forced to make:

> A request that, during the life of the Commission, the Government put a moratorium on additional political reform measures outside of the various Bills and initiatives already in the pipeline. In doing so, the Commission sought to avoid any public confusion between the mandated work of the Commission and political reforms that the government may implement outside of this process. The Government did agree to this request. While there were a few instances where Government did find it necessary to advance political reform initiatives, the Commission communicated its concern and proceeded with the completion of its mandate.[20]

These observations suggest, therefore, that the post-1990 constitutional changes have not been a response to crisis, but have been 'optional' developments allowed by more or less progressive governments who have felt it necessary to 'update' and modernize the constitutions. The changes were hardly ever, if at all, prompted by clear evidence of social and economic upheavals from below, or followed uprisings around specific constitutional demands. Whilst the impetus for constitutional reform might have been prompted by pressure from organized sections of civil society over specific issues such as sexual rights and democratic demands, it is generally the case that the processes of constitutional reform in the Caribbean were rationalized on the grounds that sufficient time had elapsed since independence to justify a review of 'how the nation's political system has been serving the people'.[21] Thus, despite the 'progressive' intent of many of the proposals which have emerged from state-led Constitutional Review Commissions, there is a clear sense in which these processes have been too mechanically divorced from underlying socio-economic structural forces to have any direct impact on real change.

This is not to ignore the critical role that civil society organizations have played in forcing Caribbean governments to act on the issue of constitutional reform. As seen in the case of Belize, where the commissioners recognized the tremendous public education and sensitization work done by civil society bodies in placing specific demands for constitutional change on the agenda, there are, indeed, instances in which the people are ahead of the governments in spearheading constitutional reform in the Caribbean. However, what is being argued here is the manner in which state-led processes of reform have succeeded in blunting the impact of civil society in shaping the outcomes of constitutional reform.

Given the fact that 'official' commissions have been established as government-directed mechanisms to guide the process of reform, the impetus for change has been removed from organic civil society bodies. This has contained and limited demands for transformation, and has allowed governments to control the pace of change. The preliminary report of the Bahamas Constitution Review Commission, for example, declared boldly that 'those who were expecting a wholesale rewriting of the constitution or radical departure from some of the fundamental principles and conventions of Westminster government will be disappointed. In developing its provisional recommendations, the commission was guided by its terms of reference, which required it to retain its system of parliamentary democracy'.[22]

This experience of constitutional reform being skilfully controlled by governments has been dramatically illustrated in the case of Jamaica, in a study by Trevor Munroe.[23] Munroe shows how a number of far-reaching proposals submitted in the 1990 report by Carl Stone on 'strengthening the roles and performance of parliamentarians' were consciously and deliberately opposed by both government and opposition elected members, who opted instead for 'moderate reform of the Westminster model'. Thus, despite the noble intentions of Constitution Review Commissions in the Caribbean, they have been hamstrung in their actual capacity to translate intent into action due to the exigencies of their functioning as government-commissioned agencies and bodies.

Perhaps, however, the most important weakness in the constitutional reform processes led by states is the 'class-neutral' assumption of their approaches to reform. In the cases studied, there is little evidence of the deliberate identification of the socio-economic crises facing the region or the collapse of the socio-economic framework of independence as factors necessitating the reformulation of government.

One key exception to this perhaps can be found in the final report of the Belize Constitution Commission which noted the prevalence of the feeling that 'the system does not work for the poor' as a motive for reform.[24] This observation notwithstanding, the proposed constitutional amendments in Belize, as elsewhere in the Commonwealth Caribbean, have been largely impervious to socio-economic questions. Quite expectedly, therefore, the proposals from the Belize commission contained little to reflect the concern that the 'system does not work for the poor', except for the inclusion in the preamble of the protection of 'the right not to be denied health care'. Similarly, despite the considerations given to demands for special protections for access to land by Belizeans, the Commission opted not to include 'constitutional amendments related to the protection of the right to land for persons in Belize' as one of its proposals.[25]

Thus, the absence of a link to the socio-economic implications of the collapse of the postcolonial order, the disconnection from the class and social contestations which necessarily ensue from such a fundamental shift in the political economy, and the separation of political reform from the context of economic transformation from below, have removed the element of 'necessity' from the reform process. This has resulted in limited and timid 'reformist' interventions, rather than in radically transformative options.

Whilst government-led constitutional review commissions can serve as conservative mechanisms to control, direct and frustrate change, the proposals from civil society bodies and the content and outcomes of everyday political issues and conflicts provide a clearer reflection of the consequence of the crisis of the collapse of the postcolonial order on Caribbean political life. In other words, while the proposals from official constitutional reform commissions deny the reality of a moment of collapse, the issues which dominate the contemporary politics of the Caribbean, point towards clear demands for radical overhaul of existing constitutional arrangements in light of the overthrow of the economic and political framework, local and global, which had shaped the political order of the Caribbean. It is in this context that Sutton's conclusions on the experience of constitutional reform in the Caribbean can be questioned. His claim that recent constitutional reforms indicate conformity to, and confirmation of the Westminster model, can only be reached when the recommendations of Constitution Review Commissions are viewed in isolation from the political environment. An examination of the politics of the Caribbean in its actual navigation of policy demands and the struggles of contending sectional interests, provides an entirely different picture. When the sectional political contestations resulting from the unmaking of the postcolonial order are examined, far clearer demands for overcoming Westminster can be discerned. The politics of Barbados since the crisis of the global economy in 2008 provides a clear illustration of these tendencies.

The Current Crisis: The Case of Barbados

Despite the assumptions by many that the Caribbean's constitutional future remains firmly tied to Westminster, there is much evidence to suggest that the social and economic disruptions associated with the 2008 financial crisis, and the broader adjustments arising out of the collapse of the postcolonial order, are forcing deeper considerations of overhauling Westminster into the political discourse in the Caribbean. The case of Barbados is useful for examining the manner in which this process is unfolding in the Caribbean.

The contestations over the future of social democracy and of the continuing utility of Westminster are particularly acute in Barbados, in light of the deep impact of the post-2008 economic and social crisis on the inherited postcolonial political-economy. The acute nature of the political contestation in Barbados is intensified by the country's historical position as one of the most advanced and resilient social democracies in the Commonwealth Caribbean, in which citizens have enjoyed a wide range of benefits in state-supported education, health, public transportation, and a comprehensive social security network. In the midst of a sustained

period of economic decline as a consequence of the impact of the global
economic crisis on the Barbadian economy, the main approach of the ruling
Democratic Labour Party (DLP), elected since 2008 and led since 2010 by
Freundel Stuart, has been to signal that the postcolonial social democratic
framework can no longer be sustained. In a speech to his annual party
convention in August 2014, Stuart declared openly that his party did not
see the social democratic agenda as having the same relevance as it did in
the immediate postcolonial period:

> Does the state...owe the same duty to the graduates of secondary tertiary
> institutions, living in modern housing with water borne facilities, driving
> one of the $113,000 motor cars on our roads, and in generally steady white
> collar or blue collar employment, as it is owed to the man or woman of
> 1938 wending his or her way to the canefields, or to the farm with broad
> brimmed hat, crocus bag tied around the waist, and a hoe or fork across
> the shoulder, having just left a modest chattel house without running
> water and often on rented land?[26]

Further, Stuart indicated that his party had 'never contemplated funding
university education for all students indefinitely'.[27]

Fully cognizant of the political fallout from his abandonment of
social democracy, Stuart held that any political opposition was 'perfectly
understandable' because,

> as a country, we have become accustomed to the state providing a
> constellation of privileges which require no payment at all or no significant
> direct payment from the public at large. Once the comfort resulting from
> enjoyment of these benefits and privileges is disturbed, a sometimes
> angry and hostile response is predicted. The truth is that the time has
> come for us to confront certain not always pleasant realities in Barbados.[28]

Reality or otherwise, Stuart was presenting an ideological statement to
legitimize the dismantling of the postcolonial social democratic order.
Suggestive of the deep ideological divisions which have been awakened by
this development, a heated debate on the political future of Barbados and
its development options has ensued, which has made the issue of political
reform inescapable.

The following statement by Reverend Leslie Lett, a retired minister from
the 1970s tradition of liberation theology, provides a sense of the ideological
debate that has emerged in Barbados in response to Stuart's announced
abandonment of social democracy. In a letter to the editor entitled 'Social
Democracy No More', Lett argued that:

The Democratic Labour Party's (DLP) electoral victory in 2008, repeated in 2013, was a mandate to improve social democracy, to have the economy embedded in social relations and not the other way around. This was the promise, hence the 'Barbados is more than an economy...' mantra.[29] And it was believable because the DLP from its birth in 1955 fought for the transformation of Barbados into a social democracy and a just society. We have now been informed that the fight is over; the promise cannot be kept. In a strange bit of logic, the Prime Minister sought...to rationalize his abandonment of social democracy by stating the obvious – that we can't pursue social democracy in 2014 'in the same way in which we pursued in in the 1960s, 70s'. Then find another way to pursue it. But surely, he was not given a mandate to either destroy or abandon it if he was incapable of finding another way.[30]

In the intense ideological debates that have been fomented in Barbados since the 2008 crisis, a number of public interventions have arisen over the need to transform the political system. Significantly, and in confirmation of the disconnection between organic politics and the mechanistically created state-led constitutional review commissions, few of these interventions make reference to the recommendations of the official report of the Constitution Review Commission led by Henry Forde. Instead, they start from the realization that the economic crisis is epoch-shifting and that the political system must be transformed as part of the economic and social reconfigurations which must occur as a result of the collapse of the existing order.

Among the groups and individuals intervening in the discussions on the crisis are the leaders of the trade union movement, representatives of private sector bodies, members of the socialist and pan-African Left such as attorney-at-law David Comissiong, and economists and technocrats who have been insisting on constitutionally determined limits and controls on government spending, with deep implications for democratic practice and policymaking. Not surprisingly, these interventions are motivated by class repositioning for greater influence over decision-making in a context in which the tightened economic circumstances have increased social actors' awareness of the link between political arrangements and their class positional power. In short, classes in themselves are now being transformed into classes for themselves.

Interestingly, the demands for political change are being voiced not only by the representatives of grassroots and workers' organizations but also by elements of the monied sector, frustrated by economic failure and the inability of the political system to respond to their class demands. An intervention by a Barbadian entrepreneur Peter Boos, Chairman of the Barbados Entrepreneurship Foundation, and a particularly vocal critic of the Barbadian government's economic failures, illustrates these tendencies. The following, from a newspaper report, captures the essence of Boos's intervention:

> Businessman Peter Boos is unhappy with the Westminster system of government and is calling on civil society in Barbados to take charge. Additionally, he has suggested that a collective non-governmental body work along with the International Monetary Fund to turn around Barbados' economic fortunes... Boos blames the Westminster model for "facilitating" the current state of affairs in the island and charged there was a "deep and urgent crisis" that must be immediately addressed by the entire nation... "Under our current governance model our elected leaders essentially proceed as they please with often little reference to manifesto promises and virtually zero performance measurements or accountability".[31]

The newspaper article further quotes Boos as charging 'that there was an over-abundance of arrogant ignorance...Pretence and hubris are the order of the day', and that 'there was an absence of real leadership in all sectors' with people in leadership roles often 'compromised or conflicted or fearful while others were corrupt and not fit'. The article concludes with Boos's assertion that 'national governance reform will only occur if all of us get engaged in making change happen and agree to share the burdens of adjustment'.[32]

Clearly evident in this intervention was the nakedly class-driven perspectives which shaped Boos's rejection of the Westminster system. This is seen in his overt call for an acceptance of IMF-driven policies in Barbados and the blame which he places on the political system as standing in the way of civil society's dialogue with the IMF. His perspective can be clearly located in the historical monied class's opposition to the rule of the elected majority.

Given Boos's hint at circumventing the elected element, his comments were seen as offensive by the political directorate, elements of which were quick to expose the class basis of his intervention. Whilst making no direct reference to the speech, the prime minister of Barbados used the opportunity of a tribute to a departed former member on the parliamentary floor, to launch into a defence of the 'political class' and by extension, a criticism of those whom he accused of wishing to wield political power without seeking a mandate from the people. The *Barbados Today* newspaper reported Prime Minister Freundel Stuart as rejecting 'the idea of changing the system of governance in Barbados', and insisting that 'he will not allow the democratic rights secured for Barbadians to be rolled back by "elitists and snobs"'. The paper quoted Stuart as saying that he was happy to defend the political class despite the bitterness that is sometimes evident in parliamentary debates:

> They don't want to dirty their hands by even having to shake the hands of ordinary people. They want to sit in ivory towers, use their wealth or their station in life to qualify them to preside over the destiny of people. I am proud to be a politician. If politics is messy, I enjoy the mess. If politics is dirty business, I am prepared to be dirty in order to uplift the interest of the people of this crown.[33]

The newspaper further quoted Stuart as saying that he frowns 'on all those people who believe that we have now gotten to the stage where you can now push politicians out of the way, undo what was done in the early 1950s, set aside and let privilege and status take over from the democratic procedures to which we have all subscribed and for which we have all fought'.[34] Stuart has also declared: 'We are the political class...I believe in the political class...And wherever therefore we have a chance to support one another, whenever we have a chance to validate the claims of the political class, we have to do so.'[35]

What is revealed here is not simply the accustomed resistance by members of the Caribbean political directorate to proposals for constitutional change. Rather, Stuart's comments indicate the ways in which debates about Barbados's constitutional future have been a central feature of day-to-day political debates, but are not captured in the formal constitutional review exercises established by government. What is significant, however, is not only that class antagonisms had been brought to the surface as a consequence of the failing Barbadian economy but that demands for political reform were now being framed as a necessary step in resolving the economic challenges of Barbados. In a particularly biting commentary, David Comissiong, a leader of the left-of-centre Peoples' Empowerment Party, insisted on the need for political reform, given the current betrayal of the electorate by Stuart's highly favoured political class. Comissiong's intervention provides a clear indication of the manner in which the debate on political reform was being presented in class terms, and his published response to Stuart's 'political class' comment is worth quoting at length:

I, for one, do not consider that politicians constitute a separate social class, but the fact that the Prime Minister of our country perceives himself and his fellow politicians as being members of a special category of persons that is separate and apart from the mass of the Barbadian population, in my view, goes to the very heart of much of what is fundamentally wrong with our Barbadian society today...Now, if we pay close attention to Prime Minister Stuart's words, we see that he is...suggesting that his self-defined 'political class' is one that should 'support one another' and 'validate the claims' of the class whenever possible. It is truly tragic that the Barbadian politicians of this era should perceive themselves (and their fellow Barbadians) in this manner! I would, however, like to correct Mr. Stuart, and inform him that he and his fellow politicians do not really constitute a class, but rather – judging from their behaviour and actions over the past seven years – they seem to constitute what Max Weber, the German sociologist, defined as a 'status group'. And they appear to be an elite 'status group' that is, simultaneously, consumed with its own self-interest, and owned or controlled by Barbados' upper or bourgeois class of big business owners and managers: the same 'snobs' and 'elitists' that Mr. Stuart pretends to disavow.[36]

Of specific concern to Comissiong was the need to reform the system, since Stuart's political class, by spearheading the dismantling of the postcolonial social democratic framework, had removed the element of legitimacy which bound the majority to the system. In Comissiong's view, the system had to be reformed to bring the people's needs into the centre:

If you doubt me, just look at the record of Mr. Stuart's Democratic Labour Party (DLP) administration. His predecessor, the late David Thompson, set the tone when, immediately upon being appointed Prime Minster in January 2008, he attended a luncheon of the Barbados Chamber of Commerce, prostrated himself, and pleaded with the leaders of big business to keep him 'on the right track' with their advice and counsel. He then moved smartly onwards to write off a debt of $20 million that the Barbados Turf Club owed the Government! Since then, Stuart's DLP administration has gone on to funnel almost all of Government's major construction and supply contracts to a handful of elite companies and individuals, and to decimate the hard won social rights and programmes of the broad Barbadian working and middle classes.[37]

Instead of defending the political class, therefore, Comissiong proposed instead to 'downgrade it, and create a new political governance system in which much more power, participation and control is vested in the mass of ordinary citizens'.[38]

Conclusion

Whilst none of this suggests that the implementation of the proposals outlined either by Boos or Comissiong is likely or imminent due either to sustained demand, collective will, or commonality of purpose, their significance lie in the manner in which the current debate has been throwing up direct concerns with the utility and relevance of the Westminster system. What can be seen from the more critical and conflictual tone in the Barbados political discourse, is that the assumed legitimacy and taken-for-granted smugness of the relevance of the Westminster system is coming to an end. What is missed by many is that the collapse of the social and economic arrangements of the post-Moyne era necessarily has implications for the legitimacy of the political system. If the social and economic benefits that cushioned the population are removed, the legitimacy of the political system will come into question, and the perceived failures of the Westminster order will be enlarged. Similarly, with a deterioration of the business environment, the monied classes will resume their historical suspicion and class opposition to the 'black governing class', and demand greater levels of direct participation to give full flowering to their class power, or conversely, insist upon greater constitutional controls upon government economic policy-making power to limit the possibility of damage to their interests.

As the post-2008 politics of Barbados shows, therefore, the condition of crisis which Sutton has identified as a necessary condition for the radical overhaul of Westminster may be emerging in the Caribbean, and the moment may soon arrive when national constituent assemblies to examine new constitutional futures will be organized. Perhaps too, such assemblies may only come after open upheavals, deep crises and irreversible revolutionary conditions. Currently, some Caribbean governments have seen the need for referenda on their country's constitutional futures, and these early democratic steps may soon be followed by deliberately organized constitutional constituent assemblies.

What is clear, however, is that, as the case of Barbados shows, there is much evidence to suggest that the global economic crisis is now placing demands for political transformation more organically into the centre of Caribbean political discourse. This is far more potentially revolutionary than the mechanical treatment of constitutional change, as a state-led exercise guided and controlled by government-appointed Constitution Review Commissions. It is now left to the theatre of actual socio-economic struggle to determine the eventual fate of the Westminster system in the Caribbean.

NOTES

1. P. Sutton, 'Westminster Challenged. Westminster Confirmed: Which way Caribbean Constitutional reform?' *Journal of Eastern Caribbean Studies*, nos. 1 and 2 (2013): 63–79, at 73.
2. Ibid., 77.
3. Ibid., 73–74.
4. Much of the content of this section was delivered as an unpublished public lecture. See Tennyson Joseph, 'Towards a New Politics and a New Representation – A Program for the Second Independence Revolution' (Public Lecture, Lloyd Best Foundation, Caribbean Convois, Tobago, Trinidad and Tobago, March 25, 2012).
5. In May 2011, the Governor of the Central Bank issued a letter to its staff indicating that 'Nation/Sun staff will not be invited to any future press conference or media event hosted by myself as governor of the central bank.' See *Stabroek News Online*, 'Barbados Central Bank Governor Bans Nation Newspaper', May 11, 2011. http://www.stabroeknews.com/2014/news/regional/05/11/barbados-central-bank-governor-bans-nation-newspaper/ (accessed August 13, 2016).
6. Jaime Peck and Adam Tickell. 'Jungle Law Breaks Out: Neo-liberalism and Global-local Disorder', *Area*, no. 4 (1994): 317–26, at 324–25.
7. Ibid.
8. Ibid.
9. Rex Nettleford. *Inward Stretch, Outward Reach: A Voice from the Caribbean* (Basingstoke: MacMillan Caribbean, 1993), 21.
10. Sutton, 'Westminster Challenged', 64.
11. Cynthia Barrow-Giles, 'Regional Trends in Constitutional Developments in the Commonwealth Caribbean', paper presented for the Conflict Prevention and Peace Forum, Social Science Research Council, USA, 2010.
12. Ibid., 11–13.
13. Ibid., 13.
14. Ibid., 13–16.
15. Ibid., 19–20.
16. Government of St Vincent and the Grenadines. *Constitutional Bill* (2009), 10.
17. Government of Barbados, 'Report of the Constitution Review Commission' (1998), 17.
18. Government of St Lucia, 'Report of the Constitution Reform Commission' (2011), 33.
19. Government of Belize, 'Final Report of the Constitution Review Commission' (2000), para. 1.19.

20. Ibid., para. 1.20.
21. Ibid., para. 1.4.
22. The Bahamas Constitutional Review Commission. Preliminary Report and Provisional Recommendations (2006), Foreword . http://islandwoo-ivltripod. com/whatsupbahamas/id13.html.
23. Trevor Munroe, *Renewing Democracy into the Millennium: The Jamaican Experience in Perspective* (Kingston: The Press University of the West Indies, 1999), 42–48.
24. Belize 'Final Report', para. 2.1. One possible explanation for the more radical expressions of intent in the Belize Commission's report is the more active role played by civil society groups in shaping the discussion on reform. Particularly critical in this regard was the role of the Society for the Promotion of Education and Research (SPEAR) in spearheading (no pun intended) a public education campaign since the mid-1990s and in creating a more active mass movement behind reform than is evident elsewhere in the Caribbean region (See para 1.4 of the final report of the Belize Constitution report for a background on the role of radical civil society movements in shaping the reform process in Belize).
25. Belize 'Final Report', para. 2.14.
26. *Barbados Today*, 'Those Who Have Ears, Let Them Hear', August 18, 2014, 2.
27. Ibid., 2.
28. Ibid.
29. One of the slogans of the DLP before and after the 2008 General election was 'Barbados is more than an economy, it is a society'. This was meant as a denunciation of the BLP's focus on economic development. By resorting to a more far-reaching dismantling of the social democratic agenda once it had assumed office, the DLP was reinforcing the powerlessness of the independent state. Leslie Lett's reference to the slogan was meant to remind the DLP of its abandonment of its promised commitment to social democracy.
30. Leslie Lett, 'Social Democracy No More', *Daily Nation*, September 2, 2014, 100.
31. *Daily Nation*, 'Boos: Turn to IMF', May 30, 2014, 7.
32. Ibid., 7.
33. *Barbados Today*, 'PM Defends Political Class', June 3, 2014, 4.
34. Ibid., 4.
35. David Comissiong, 'Stuart's Political Class', *Barbados Today*, June 10, 2014, 18.
36. Ibid.
37. Ibid.
38. Ibid.

9 Westminster Shackled: *State Building, State Weakness, and the Democracy Deficit in the Anglophone Caribbean*

Clifford E. Griffin

Introduction: The Democracy Paradox in the Anglophone Caribbean

Anglophone Caribbean states, which began to develop amid a flurry of post-the Second World War state building, constitute a subset of the 'third wave' of countries that underwent transitions to democracy.[1] Beginning in 1944, Britain began to provide these countries with new government institutions and/or assistance in strengthening existing ones in an effort to create the institutional foundations for democratic political development. Such provisions were deemed crucial because states with weak or non-functioning institutions have become the source of many of the contemporary world's most worrisome problems.[2] By the 1980s, their democratic credentials were celebrated amid the euphoria of the two global reform movements then underway. Popularly known as neoliberalism, and considered as '…probably the most important political trend in the late twentieth century',[3] these movements heralded the global trend toward a more uniformly democratic system of governance and a more uniformly market-based, financial, and economic system. Almost a generation later, and with the euphoria having subsided, the apparent failure of these countries to provide effective public safety programmes and policies within the ambit of broader democratic norms[4] continues to raise persistent questions regarding citizen security, the strength of these states, and especially the quality of their Westminster-derived systems of governance.

These concerns are, indeed, justifiable. Table 9.1, which numerically summarizes five governance indicators – government effectiveness: 66.05; control of corruption: 68.44; rule of law: 64.05; and political stability and the absence of violence: 66.01 – indicate that on a scale of 1 to 100, with 100 representing high levels of governance, these countries are running a democracy deficit. While there are variations from country to country, two things stand out: 1) citizen perceptions suggest a strong tendency toward exercising public power for private gain, including both petty and grand forms of corruption, as well as 'capture' of the state by elites and private interests; and 2) much needs to be done to reduce the level of corruption, enhance political stability, minimize political violence, and to reduce perceptions of the likelihood that these governments will be destabilized or overthrown by unconstitutional or violent means, including politically motivated violence and terrorism.

These perceptions exist despite the fact that since the 1970s, Anglophone countries have persisted with open contestation for political office, which, almost without exception, have resulted in peaceful transfers of power. At the same time, however, a pattern has emerged in which electoral outcomes have resulted in a tendency towards one-party dynasties that control Parliament; entrenched, powerful political executives that perennially dominate political decision-making; and creeping authoritarianism in the exercise of political power.[5]

Table 9.1: Average Annual Governance Indicators 1996–2013

	Government Effectiveness	Control of Corruption	Rule of Law	Political Stability Absence of Violence	Voice and Accountability
Antigua and Barbuda	69.94	84.62	80.42	75.35	63.20
Bahamas	82.55	89.59	81.64	80.73	80.25
Barbados	86.23	89.28	83.56	86.14	89.81
Belize	47.7	52.14	47.42	53.75	69.82
Dominica	68.62	73.18	70.44	74.97	80.21
Grenada	63.71	72.92	59.82	66.57	70.35
Guyana	48.71	36.23	35.31	29.82	54.41
Jamaica	60.22	43.45	38.92	40.05	64.05
St Kitts and Nevis	65.33	74.08	71.94	86.97	82.20
St Lucia	67.94	76.67	72.44	75.25	84.55
St Vincent and Grenadines	67.98	74.22	74.06	77.65	81.33
Trinidad and Tobago	63.62	54.85	52.64	44.92	64.47
Average	66.05	68.44	64.05	66.01	73.72

Source: http://info.worldbank.org/governance/wgi/index.aspx#home

These outcomes, therefore, warrant citizen concern given that democratic institutions and processes should minimize the potential for the domination of, or by, an individual, a group, or a particular interest regardless of whether the nature of the domination is political, economic, or social.[6]

Further, and almost paralleling the neoliberal transformation, the 1980s witnessed the emergence of citizen security as a major issue of concern in light of the rising levels of crime and violence, especially homicides, most of which are attributable to the emergence of the region as a major transshipment point for illegal narcotics originating in South America and destined to the streets of North American and European cities. Additionally, issues of high unemployment, poverty, and income inequality have persisted and have become even more pressing. These developments, therefore, have raised the following probing, yet interrelated, questions: 1) What role, if any, does the inherited governance model play in the apparent failure of Anglophone Caribbean countries to strengthen and protect democratic civic order and enhance citizen security by minimizing or eliminating threats of crime and violence; and to reduce unemployment, poverty and inequality? 2) Are these paradoxical outcomes of their democratic experiment due necessarily to the inherited constitutional order and, if so, will the various constitutional reform agendas being contemplated from Barbados to Guyana to St Vincent and the Grenadines, and to Trinidad and Tobago offer meaningful options for improving the quality of democracy in these countries?

In attempting to answer these questions, the following contentions are made. Contention number one posits that while the reforming of constitutions may be necessary to improve the quality of governance, such interventions will not be sufficient because of the nature of, and the relations that govern the political economy of these countries, particularly the global environment in which they must necessarily function. That is, changing the procedures by which democratic politics operates may be necessary but not sufficient to address, meaningfully, citizen security concerns, poverty, and socioeconomic inequality. Beyond the internal institutional forms, it becomes necessary to examine the substantive dimensions of democracy by focusing on the structural relations – domestic and international – that influence the process and outcome of politics. When viewed from this perspective, what might at first appear to be a paradox of democracy may be, instead, a paradox of globalization (internationalization), which, as Dani Rodrik argues, has produced a 'trilemma' in which these countries are attempting to achieve the impossible: the simultaneous pursuit of economic globalization, national development imperatives, and democracy.[7]

Contention number two holds that Anglophone Caribbean countries, as democracies and as sovereign states, have the right to create and protect their social arrangements. However, because they are weak by design, the reform movements of the 1980s have exposed and exacerbated those weaknesses, limiting their transformative capacity to adapt to the changed international environment. Their weakness has also hampered their ability to defend themselves against internal and external challenges. As a result, not only have they been ineffective in defining the conditions under which they would participate in economic and financial globalization but they also have been 'captured' by internal and external forces, including Transnational Criminal Networks (TCNs) and their local partners. By capitalizing on the weak institutional structures and processes, these forces have suborned state authority such that the last three decades have witnessed the emergence of an environment that has favoured the TCNs and, in turn, put the poor in a position where many consider crime as an option for survival.

To be clear, the quality of democracy in the region is such that there is need for reform of the institutional structures and processes. However, the Westminster-derived model of governance is not the entirety of the problem because the internationalizing agenda has so complicated relations within and between states that the traditional view of democracy as a majoritarian system that provides benefits for all citizens seems overly simplistic. Internationalization and interdependence suggest that concerns over the quality of democracy and efficacy of the Westminster-derived model of governance are rooted partly in their history as colonies and dependent, agriculturally based economies, as well as in large measure in the present realities of economic and financial globalization that began in the 1980s. This means that analyses that focus mainly on the institutional structures to the exclusion of the substantive dimensions of democracy may not yield the rich insights necessary to divine the complexity of factors that would inform the appropriate structural and policy changes for enhancing the quality of democracy and improving citizen security. This chapter, therefore, speaks to the interrelated issues of state weakness, state 'capture', and the adaptive or transformative capacity of these states as they have attempted to address the challenges posed by the forces of internationalization. In so doing, it sheds important light on the democracy deficit in the Anglophone Caribbean.

The Challenge of Internationalization

Democratic state-building in the Anglophone Caribbean began under the 'Bretton Woods compromise', which functioned as a 'shallow multilateralism' that allowed policymakers the latitude to focus on domestic, social, and employment needs while allowing international trade, which had suffered as a result of the Second World War, to recover and flourish.[8] Additionally, it allowed for the removal some of the most highly restrictive provisions to international trade while permitting governments the latitude to implement their own independent economic policies, and to construct their preferred versions of the welfare state. Developing countries, in particular, were allowed to pursue their own strategies for growth with limited interference from external actors.[9] Initially successful, the Bretton Woods monetary region proved unsustainable as capital became internationally more mobile and as the oil shocks of the 1970s reverberated throughout the world. While they were newcomers to democratic development, Anglophone Caribbean countries were simultaneously 'latecomers' to economic development and industrialization. Saddled with economic and technological deficiencies – low level of development, including communication, information, transportation, and technological infrastructure; small and limited private sector; and a narrow economic base – that put them at a competitive disadvantage to their former colonizers and others in the global marketplace, leaders chose the state, rather than the market, as the institution that would guide economic and technological development.

However, the received wisdom governing this new liberalizing agenda held that free-market economic systems and liberal-democratic political systems can and must flourish simultaneously. Workers were transformed into consumers, who became the foundation for middle-class societies, and the principle of consumer sovereignty became the basis of democratic choices of the mix and quantity of goods that are made available in the marketplace. Correspondingly, as political actors, these same consumers constitute the centerpiece of democracy by casting votes to ensure their political sovereignty.[10] International Financial Institutions (IFI) instituted the attendant policies that included a generalized reduction, if not an end, to statist development policies that emphasize central government run industries, central government commitment to social welfare, and central government protection of local industries. A reduced role for government and an enhanced role for the private sector were central to this policy change, which viewed the free marketplace and the private entrepreneur as representing a superior and far more efficient, rational, and dynamic combination of forces for achieving growth and development than the state and its intrusive, protectionist role in economic decision-making. Highlighting this policy change in the Caribbean was the 1984 Caribbean Basin Initiative (CBI), which signalled a shift from aid as government-to-government transfers to aid as trade, as well as changes to the Lomé Agreements on which Anglophone Caribbean states were long dependent.

Anchored in neoclassical economic theory, proponents deduce from its postulates the false notion that liberal democracy equals free market capitalism and that free market capitalism equals liberal democracy. These two conceptual dichotomies underscore at least two problems that confront Anglophone Caribbean states. Problem number one is that although free elections determine which civilian authorities will govern, political stability and electoral democracy are not necessarily assured because, while necessary, multi-partyism and freely and fairly elected governments are insufficient for democratic governance and endurance. Meaningful access to economic and social goods, and reductions in economic and social disparity also matter. A second problem is that these countries continue to experience great difficulty in complying with neoliberalism's economic agenda, which demands the unburdening of the economy from governmental intrusion and, under International Monetary Fund (IMF) guidance, states must allow the free market to determine currency values, curtail many government sponsored programmes, and enforce the payment of low wages.[11] The reality is that the neoliberal agenda has brought together a highly combustible mixture of two reform movements – political decentralization and economic deregulation and privatization. Evidence across the developing world indicates that economic deregulation has tended to bring about economic impoverishment and, with time, increased poverty and inequality, because it drastically reduces the redistributive as well as entrepreneurial role of the state.[12] Given differential access to economic power, the resultant hardships inflicted by neoliberal reforms have weakened the state and limited its ability to pursue national development alongside democracy.

Historically, there has been no economic dimension to the role of liberalism. Creating a necessary role for economics in the liberal democratic process, therefore, presents Anglophone Caribbean countries with daunting challenges. This is because building a modern, market-oriented economy, capable of sustaining relatively high levels of growth is, at best, a slow and difficult process; and attempting to do so simultaneously while creating democratic institutions is fraught with problems. Democracy and the public institutions that support it, such as parliaments, legislatures, judiciaries and political parties, lose prestige and legitimacy when they are unable to provide answers to a country's growing problems of crime, poverty, inequality, unemployment, and violence.

Therefore, to ask about the quality of democracy and efficacy of governance in the Anglophone Caribbean is to ask about the transformative capacity of these states. More than their capacity – the ability to pursue their goals – transformative capacity speaks to the ability, agility, and effectiveness of the state in adapting to external shocks and pressures occasioned by internationalization. To be sure, internationalization has so profoundly impacted these states that it has limited or undermined their ability to pursue their own goals as they see fit. Contributing to the democratic deficit, therefore, has been the relative inability of these countries to reorient their resources internally by building the right coalitions with business and civil society to change the process by which national objectives can best be pursued.[13] It is quite likely that the external environment has been so daunting that it has exposed and exacerbated state weakness and, thereby, the difficulty of deepening democracy as internationalization is intensified.

State Weakness, State Capacity, and State Capture

The emerging consensus holds that countries lacking in capacity and/or will to perform core functions of statehood, including fostering equitable and sustainable economic growth, governing legitimately, ensuring physical security, and delivering basic services are, effectively, weak. This analysis, absent and agreed upon definition, characterizes as weak countries that lack the essential capacity and/or will to fulfil four sets of critical government responsibilities: 1) fostering an environment conducive to sustainable and equitable economic growth; 2) establishing and maintaining legitimate, transparent, and accountable political institutions; 3) securing their populations from violent conflict and controlling their territory; and 4) meeting the basic human needs of their population.[14] This does not mean that these functions are not performed; rather, it means that they are not performed as well as they might. That is, a state's strength or weakness is a function of its effectiveness, responsiveness, and legitimacy across a range of government activities. That said, states exercise many forms of weakness that fall short of outright failure; consequently, designating Anglophone Caribbean countries as weak states does not mean that they are failed or collapsed states.

The weakness of Anglophone Caribbean countries is related, in part, to their history, which has led to their economic, political, cultural, institutional, intellectual and psychological dependence on the outside world.[15] Economically, these countries inherited agriculturally based economies, mainly, and their traditional exports – sugar, bananas, and citrus – have long depended on tariff preferences and special market access. The political links, in turn, determined the pattern of trade and economic alignments, such that a vertical linkage existed between the individual territory and the UK. Endowed similarly with limited natural resources, their political and economic history also limited the development of internal institutional partners, which, in turn, restricted their ability to develop a high level of transformational capacity. This weakness, then, forced them to compete against one another to grant outrageously disadvantageous (to themselves) long tax holidays for metropolitan firms to establish industries, branches and subsidiaries in their territory.[16] In turn, this has led to an historical dependence on the outside world such that many of the strategic decisions that impact their economies are made by foreign governmental and nongovernmental entities. As Eric E. Williams put it:

> The strategic decisions affecting the economies are made outside the [Anglophone Caribbean] national boundaries – by foreign companies and by large international firms. The original mercantilism of the seventeenth and eighteenth centuries has been replaced by the neo-mercantilism of the second half of the twentieth century. Instead of the British or European merchant firm and the absentee sugar plantation owner, the allocation of resources in the Caribbean is now controlled by the large international corporations. This is the case whether one looks at sugar production and refining; the international marketing of other primary products such as bananas; shipping; banking; insurance; manufacturing industries; hotels; minerals such as oil and bauxite; and even many of the newspapers and mass media. The locus of economic decision-making and the dynamics of economic growth continue to rest well outside the territorial boundaries of the Caribbean territories.[17]

Franklin Knight notes that while industrial production has contributed to the GDP of many states since the 1950s, its contribution has not exceeded 20 per cent of GDP, and 'has provided neither sufficient jobs nor sufficient wealth to offset declines in agricultural production and labor absorption'.[18]

As another manifestation of their weakness, external dependence forced them to switch from state capitalism to neoliberal globalization, and this meant trading off important social spending for specified market reforms in order to access credit and markets. The weakness of these countries, therefore, meant that unlike countries like Brazil, China, and India, for example, which have had the transformative capacity that enabled them to continue to pursue economic and financial globalization on their own terms, including state-capitalist development strategies, Anglophone Caribbean countries have not had the capacity to defy IFIs by mobilizing domestic institutions, actors, and resources in support of national development. Weakness and lack of transformative capacity have led to state 'capture', which has strongly affected the ability of these countries to embrace internationalization while simultaneously deepening democracy.

In order to have capacity, a democratic state must have strong and effective institutions over and through which it can fulfil its proper functions. That is, state legitimacy is strengthened by state capacity and autonomy. However, state capacity depends on resources. Because the competence of the state's bureaucracy, the efficiency of its management of public policy, the proper regulation of the economy, and the effectiveness and efficiency in collecting taxes and democratic governance cannot be accomplished by a weak and underfinanced state, then the greater its capacity to utilize force to suppress disruptions and protests, reform the state or social institutions, or pass unpopular legislation, the greater is its legitimacy enhanced.[19] Anglophone Caribbean countries have low capacity, reflecting high levels of public debt, high levels of poverty, and high levels of income inequality, which combine to affect their ability to strengthen democracy and also effectively perform the roles that citizens expect. Table 9.2 indicates that the average gross public debt as a percentage of GDP in 2012 was 84.3 per cent (ranging from a high of 144.9 per cent in St Kitts and Nevis and 143.3 per cent in Jamaica to 35.7 per cent in Trinidad and Tobago); the average per cent of the population below the poverty line is 25.9 (ranging from 37.7 per cent in Grenada and 37.5 per cent and 37.5 per cent in St Vincent and the Grenadines to 9.6 per cent in the Bahamas); and that the average Gini Coefficient score is 0.41 (ranging from 0.35 in Antigua and Barbuda to 0.56 in St Vincent and the Grenadines). These data help to underscore the reality weakness and low capacity of these states and, in turn, their susceptibility to 'capture'.

Table 9.2: Poverty Indicators For Selected Countries

Country	Survey Year	% Below Poverty Line	Survey Year	GINI Coefficient	Gross Public Debt (% of GDP 2012)
Antigua and Barbuda	2006	28.5	2006	0.31	97.8
Bahamas	2001	9.6	2006	0.48	52.6
Barbados	2003	13.9	1997	0.39	70.4
Belize	2003	33.0	2002	0.40	81.0
Dominica	2003	40.0	2002	0.35	72.3
Grenada	2008	37.7	1999	0.45	105.4
Guyana	2003	35.0	1999	n.a	60.4
Jamaica	2003	16.8	2002	0.40	143.3
Nevis*	2007	15.9	2000	0.37	144.9*
St Kitts*	2003	23.7	2000	0.39	
St Lucia	2003	28.8	1996	0.50	78.7
St Vincent and the Grenadines	2003	37.5	1996	0.56	68.3
Trinidad and Tobago	2005	16.7	1997	0.37	35.7
Average		25.9		0.41	84.3

Source: Thomas McDonald and Eleanor Wint, 'Inequality and Poverty in the Eastern Caribbean 2002', Caribbean Development Report. 2, CEPAL, 2009; Andrew S. Downes, 'Poverty and Its Reduction in the Small Developing Countries of the Caribbean', IMF, 2010.

State 'capture' is one of the most pervasive forms of corruption, where companies, institutions or powerful individuals use corruption such as the buying of laws, amendments, decrees or sentences, as well as illegal contributions to political parties and candidates, to influence and shape a country's policy, legal environment, and economy to their own interests. This phenomenon results from efforts by powerful actors – domestic and transnational – who secretly and subtly, seek to weaken, co-opt, disable, or privatize governmental agencies, territory, and the state. These clandestine efforts to systematically distort or displace the state are viewed as the most pernicious manifestation of political corruption. Some commentators maintain that it is in the interest of clandestine groups and transnational criminal networks (TCN) for the state to be functional, if only for the sake of greater profit. While this type of relationship may be viewed as parasitical in more developed economies, it becomes a malignant cancer in less developed countries with weaker, vulnerable governments.

State 'capture', therefore, is to be distinguished from petty corruption; it is manifested as meta-corruption, or grand corruption, in which illicit political finance is used to systematically control public institutions.[20]

A 'captured' state is a weakened state, in which democratic institutions and processes are unlikely to function effectively. While weakened states may still engage in legislative debates, pass, and enact legislation, as occurs in the Anglophone Caribbean, such legislation may not always be in the best interest of society. In other words, a weakened state will necessarily experience great difficulty in enforcing its rightful monopoly on violence; coordinating the activities of the governing institutions; extracting resources to fund itself; promoting citizen participation such that the right sets of societal values are promulgated; and acting as the dominant or central power in society. As 'captured' states, therefore, Anglophone Caribbean countries do not perform as well-functioning democracies because they are not dominant and autonomous, as they should be, nor do they have the capacity to act against internal and external challenges. For example, prior to the 1970s and early 1980s, developing countries, like those of the Anglophone Caribbean, were able to pursue their own independent economic policies, including, where practicable, erecting trade barriers and participating in preferred trading schemes. In this regard, they were able to pursue their preferred version of the welfare state – their own internal social and employment goals – with little to no interference from IFIs. Following the oil price shocks of the 1970s, the IFIs presided over the dismantling of the welfare state, and Anglophone Caribbean country leaders were pressured to open their markets to foreign trade and investment, which resulted in greater inequality and insecurity.

As weak states, therefore, these countries lack the power to resist this pressure to open up their economies unconditionally to international trade and finance. While leaders understood and argued that economic prosperity and political stability are achievable under different combinations of institutional arrangements in labour markets, finance, corporate governance, and social welfare and that countries are entitled to make decisions regarding economic and social policy, IFSs remained steadfast in their programme to replace the welfare state. This steadfastness produced policies that exacerbated the weakness of these countries, and made them increasingly susceptible to state 'capture'.

State 'capture' reflects a systemic failure, which can occur in a country where the systems of checks and balances do not function at all or, at the very least, do not function well. Such a circumstance creates numerous opportunities for law enforcement and government officials, as well as non-government organizations, including 'un-civil' society groups, to maximize wealth and power with such impunity as to benefit particular individuals, groups, and networks. Situations include collusion between businesses and political institutions and leaders that allow them almost unfettered access to the centres of political power. Captured states, therefore, are likely to experience corruption in the political, administrative, and judicial branches of government, and are likely to have areas – especially low-income areas – that are dominated by 'un-civil' society groups connected to the political structure and to TCNs. Evidence of 'capture' can be found throughout many Anglophone Caribbean communities, and is also reflected in the apparent correlation between the rising levels of crime and violence and gang activity that became politically significant in the 1980s, and which has undermined, if not, eroded citizen security and effective governance.

State Capture and Government Effectiveness

One of the primary roles of government is to provide a consistent set of public goods to citizens. To a great extent, this role cannot be effectively fulfilled unless there is a corresponding role for government in economic decision-making because government must be able to determine which business activities will be actively encouraged, which will not, and which will be considered criminal. How the state performs in this capacity – its effectiveness – therefore, affects not only the development of legitimate organizations but illicit ones as well, and where it fails to get the institutions 'right', it invites non-state groups to fill the gaps.[21] Despite having many of the right institutions, the global, political, and economic changes have contributed to erosion in the efficacy of these institutions in the Anglophone Caribbean, and have reduced the ability of governments to deliver on these responsibilities, especially in the historically underserved communities.

As noted above, these countries have become victims of state 'capture' and have experienced severe economic, social, and political dislocations as a result of economic and financial globalization. These dislocations have manifested themselves in the fragmentation of social groups that long relied on the public sector for employment, income, and goods and services, and resultant increases in crime, violence, riots, demonstrations, strikes, human rights violations, and various manifestations of political instability.[22] Entering this space and suborning legitimate political authority, especially in underserved communities, are a number of 'dark (covert) networks' or 'un-civil' society groups associated with TCNs, and reflecting organized gang activity that is loosely, in some cases, and less so in others, affiliated with the dominant political parties. The two most prominent examples are Jamaica and Trinidad and Tobago.

State Capture and Governance in Jamaica

Jamaica has had a fairly lengthy exposure to state 'capture' given that two of the main 'un-civil' society groups, the 'Clansman Gang' and the 'One Order Gang', respectively, have long been associated with the country's two main political parties, the People's National Party (PNP) and the Jamaica Labour Party (JLP), respectively. These two parties and their relationship with these 'un-civil' society groups owe their emergence to the strategies of power formation pursued by Norman Manley and Alexander Bustamante in the wake of the Caribbean-wide labour riots of the 1930s. Paradoxically, while both leaders were allied in the pursuit of a common, nationalist agenda, each had developed an independent power base as the head of different umbrella labour unions. However, perhaps it was political ambition and/or distrust that resulted in a rupture of this alliance in 1942, and the formation of the JLP in 1943 by Bustamante.[23] The resulting two-party system with a strong man at the head, who was simultaneously union leader and party chief, reflected the consequential tight alliance between political party and labor union, an arrangement that became increasingly institutionalized into the emerging political culture. Thus, by the time of the country's formal independence in 1962, both the PNP and JLP had long become aligned with their respective industrial trade unions. An important aspect of this political culture was the tendency towards and the subsequent expectation that the winning party would give preference in employment and contracts to its unionized supporters. This tendency, therefore, motivated supporters of one or other of these candidates/parties to vigorously and violently engage in getting-out-the-vote activities in support of their respective patron.[24] With time, political tribalism between these two parties led to the creation of 'garrison communities' in the inner city, which are strongholds of one or the other party. Among them are Tivoli Gardens (which was built on the bulldozed community of 'Back O' Wall' from which all the residents were displaced and denied occupancy in the new community, and which became a JLP stronghold); August Town; Arnett Gardens (Concrete Jungle created on the same political/strategic model as Tivoli Gardens, and which became a PNP stronghold); Olympic Gardens; Wareika Hills; and Rema.[25] These neighbourhoods, political party enclaves, function like miniature states under the leadership of so-called 'dons', who appropriate and allocate benefits, defend borders, and extract taxes. According to Carl Stone:

> These benefits include employment on government projects, contracts to carry out government projects in the building of economic infrastructure such as roads, bridges, markets and water supplies, and access to facilities such as housing in housing schemes, and highly sought after opportunities for overseas employment in contract labor schemes in the United States.[26]

Mark Figueroa and Amanda Sives describe a garrison community as:

> ...A political stronghold, a veritable fortress completely controlled by a party. At one level a garrison community can be described as one in which anyone who seeks to oppose, raise opposition to or organize against the dominant party would definitely be in danger of suffering serious damage to their possessions or person thus making continued residence in the area extremely difficult if not impossible. Any significant social, political, economic or cultural development within the garrison can only take place with the tacit approval of the leadership (whether local or national) of the dominant party.[27]

In other words, the garrison phenomenon fostered a politics of tribalism that became central to the practice of electoral manipulation in Jamaica, and its political significance extended beyond the borders of these communities to the wider political system.

State 'capture', reflecting a perceptible erosion of state control gathered momentum during the 1970s when the fight for power based on political tribalism began to intensify due in part to rising unemployment and increases in the cost of living. It was during this period that the phenomenon of the 'dons' or 'donmanship (gang leaders) emerged, and stiff competition for leadership became the primary contributing factor to the nature and level of violence and political killings. Some of these 'dons', who were aided and abetted by friends in the Jamaican constabulary, or by police on their payroll, became wealthy, influential and brazenly murderous while raking in millions of dollars.[28] Among the PNP-linked dons were George 'Feathermop' Spence, who, during the 1970s, accompanied then Prime Minister Michael Manley on a trip to Cuba. Others included Anthony 'General Starkie' Tingle and Aston 'Buckie Marshall' Thompson.

Immediate past Prime Minister P.J. Patterson shook the hand of Donald 'Zeeks' Phipps, the Matthews Lane 'don', thanking him for keeping the roads in his area clear during a demonstration against the government. Zeeks, incidentally, paid for the construction of a school in his community, which is named after him. The JLP-linked 'dons' included Claudius 'Jack Parlance' Massop, Lester Lloyd 'Jim Brown' Coke (and his son, 'Dudus' Coke) and Carl 'Biah' Mitchell.[29] During this period, general elections resulted in large numbers of deaths, and the political tribal wars between the two political parties raged. As a University of the West Indies Sociologist put it:

> Just as the political tribe of ancient Greece and Rome was under the leadership of a demagogue so in Jamaica the garrison towns were controlled by the Dons. Entry and exit to and from these communities are controlled by the so-called "top ranking" and gang leaders who have close relationships with the constituency Member of Parliament, get preferential access to contracts and jobs and function as key elements of the local level community political leadership in both parties in these inner city poor areas. These constituencies are made up preponderantly of these "garrison communities" where organised political gangs with high powered M-16 and A.K.47 assault rifles and sub-machine guns control clearly defined political boundaries and territories where political protection insulates them from the reach of the security forces.[30]

This analysis was interpreted to mean that from time to time political influence has impeded the security forces in the performance of their duties. Barry Chevannes noted that the link between the garrison forces and the political leadership of the respective political parties performs two functions: 1) it provides the main conduit for accessing and distributing scarce benefits. The 'top rankings' (gang leaders) thus become the main brokers between the members of Parliament and the local communities; 2) in a transactional sense, the member of Parliament is sure of retaining his territorial support, while the rankings are able to acquire wealth and local power as well as protection from the forces of law and order.[31]

This issue is captured in the opinion pages of the local Jamaican newspapers. The *Jamaica Gleaner* (May 23, 2010) opined on this phenomenon, noting that the notorious Jamaican underworld figure, Christopher 'Dudus' Coke, acted as the 'supreme leader' of the Tivoli Gardens garrison community, and had been instrumental in selecting and electing the parliamentary representative for the community of Western Kingston. With regard to the reach and impact of these garrison communities and, Tivoli Gardens, in

particular, the *Jamaica Observer* (September 1, 2011) opined as follows: '...
In a small society such as ours, it is not possible for Mr Coke to have been
able to run such a "successful" business without the involvement of well-
placed individuals in both the public and private sectors...' And the *Jamaica
Observer* (April 16, 2015) further opined:

> We shudder to think what would have happened to Jamaica had the
> security forces failed to dismantle what was clearly an empire being run
> by Coke, that for decades, operated outside of the laws governing this
> country, and which benefited from political protection.

Thus, by 1980, when crack cocaine entered Jamaica, the link between
TCNs and the corrupting aspects of state 'capture' became more striking,
and the general election became the most violent with 889 homicides – 339
more than during the 1976 election – including 28 police officers. Politically
motivated murders declined while income-generating ones increased as
the transnational nature of state 'capture' became clear during this period
of economic and financial deregulation. Gang members were receiving
financial support from their associate members in the US and Britain,
and were now becoming fully independent of the political parties. Reports
indicate that by the end of the 1980s, the following gangs – Shower Posse,
Spangler Posse, Dog Posse, Tel Aviv Posse, Waterhouse Posse, Banton
Posse, and Dunkirk Posse – had over 5,000 members. With the advent of
the 1990s, a wider array of guns to complement the well-entrenched M16s
and other high-powered rifles of the late 1970s were now falling into the
hands of these 'un-civil' society groups. Since this military-style weapon
is sold only to governments allied to the US and not to the public, the
conclusion drawn was that individuals in the government provided these
weapons to these groups. However, the conventional wisdom reflected a
much more nuanced interpretation of the reality of the pre-1980 violence.
Given that these events were unfolding during the Cold War, and that while
the PNP and its leadership were more ideologically aligned with Cuba
(and the Soviets) while the JLP and its leadership were more ideologically
aligned with the US, the JLP was supplied with weapons by the US and the
PNP was supplied by the Cubans. Whether the conventional wisdom holds
true or not, the reality of political violence in Jamaica during the 1970s
was that M16s and AK47s were in the hands of the respective paramilitary
forces of both political parties. As Kevin Edmonds (2016) argues, Jamaica's
crime epidemic is not fully explainable through the lens of drugs, gangs,
and guns; instead, the roots of this epidemic reflect [in part] connections

with the US Central Intelligence Agency (CIA) and the Cold War. This conclusion demonstrates another aspect of state 'capture', and how it corrupts and undermines the democratic process.[32]

It was the political patronage system that created the foundation upon which 'un-civil' society would eventually emerge in Jamaica. To underscore this point, the *Jamaica Observer* published a story on Prime Minister Edward Seaga, who, on September 27, 1994, issued a news release regarding the previous weekend's shootings in Tivoli Gardens that left five people dead and 12 wounded. The statement read in part:

> I have given to the Commissioner of Police, a list of thirteen men in Tivoli Gardens and Denham Town who are the source of the violence in West Kingston. I have advised the commissioner where they can be found. So far, six of these thirteen men have been taken into custody by the police where (sic) they are being held pending charges. I will continue to advise the police where to find the rest.[33]

However, the ringleader, identified as Christopher 'Dudus' Coke, managed to remain at large. At the time of that statement, Seaga had been that community's parliamentary representative for 32 years, and remained in that role until April 14, 2005, when Bruce Golding, succeeded him as the new JLP leader and the parliamentary representative for that constituency. Ironically, it was 'Dudus' Coke who was partly instrumental in bringing down the government of Prime Minister Golding in 2011. Initially resisting the US request to extradite 'Dudus', Golding eventually relented and issued a warrant for his arrest. This decision prompted a bloody battle between Coke's supporters and the police and army in which more than 70 people were killed. Coke's close relationship with Golding, who was also the representative for Tivoli Gardens, led to suspicions that the government had intervened on Coke's behalf to prevent his extradition to the US, where he was charged as leader of the Shower Posse, a drug gang allegedly responsible for some 1,400 murders.[34] While Golding denied any claims of government interference, it turned out that his party had hired a Washington law firm to lobby on Coke's behalf.

Other striking examples of this type of relationship include Donovan 'Bulbie' Bennett, one of Jamaica's most wanted men for over a decade, who was head of the Clansman gang. It is alleged that because he was a supporter of the ruling PNP, he was able to elude capture until death in a firefight with the police on October 30, 2005. Joel Andem, leader of the Gideon Warriors Gang (and 'don' of August Town community) was the alleged right-hand man of one of the leaders of the PNP. To his many critics, Seaga's claim of personal knowledge of these individuals, as well as Golding's refusal to arrest 'Dudus' speak not only to the nature of the relationship between politics, patronage, and gang-activity but, more specifically, to the nature of state 'capture' and its impact on governance in Jamaica.

State Capture and Governance in Trinidad and Tobago

Despite its enormous wealth derived largely from the oil and gas sector, TCNs have also penetrated Trinidad and Tobago's political and economic system, thereby making the country a victim of state 'capture', and this phenomenon has had a profound effect on the quality of its democracy. Located approximately seven miles away from neighbouring Venezuela, a major source of illegal narcotics and guns entering and transshipping the country, Trinidad and Tobago has long been a central actor in the international illicit drugs trade. Therefore, the role of TCNs and their connections with 'un-civil' society groups as well as other non-state actors in the country cannot be understated.

In 1995, for example, US Drug Enforcement Agency (DEA) officers identified a massive operation in the country when cocaine was discovered in fish that had been packaged for export. Two Trinidadian nationals were extradited to the US, where they were convicted for cocaine trafficking. In December 2000, the DEA once again informed the country's police that six of its nationals had been assigned by a Colombian drug cartel the responsibility of ensuring that the 2.5 tonnes of cocaine aboard the Colombian cargo vessel, *Ricky II*, got a smooth passage while it docked in Trinidad.[35] In August 2011, police seized about £13.5 million worth of cocaine that set off a spate of violence as gangs sought retribution for the losses. The government imposed a curfew and mobilized the military to join police patrols to cope with the violence. And as recently as November 2014, police in Trinidad and Tobago netted a haul of some 102 kilograms of marijuana with a street value of over $1.2 million. The drug, which police said was a special derivative of the marijuana plant, known as 'creepy', is believed to have originated in Colombia.[36]

In December 2013, the DEA was reputedly informed by a local whistle-blower about a shipment of some $644 million worth of prime grade cocaine concealed in more than 700 cans of Trinidad Orange Juice. According to the report, a group of transnational drug dealers shipped the drugs from Port of Spain on November 17 to the Port of Norfolk, Virginia. At least three local business people affiliated with Caribbean Sea Works Ltd and Basics Transport Ltd were identified as prime suspects.[37] Over the previous 18 months, four other consignments departed Trinidad variously on May 26, 2012; October 25, 2012; March 23, 2013; and July 26, 2013. Each consignment was shipped in 20-foot containers with canned juice; each was destined for Norfolk, Virginia; and each was shipped by Caribbean Sea Works Ltd. According to DEA officials, this arrangement began when a South American drug lord believed to be Colombian but posing as Venezuelan, met with a local businessman, who assured the former that millions of dollars worth of cocaine could be trafficked to the US via Trinidad. That initial meeting soon turned into a lucrative trade, with the businessman promising to ensure the cocaine transited Trinidad undetected.[38]

The preceding speaks to two interrelated issues regarding state 'capture'. Issue number one holds that it is less the quantity seized and more the quantity that enters and is transshipped through the country that is relevant to the connection between TCNs and state 'capture'. Issue number two is the fact that this volume of drugs trafficked can take place only with the complicity of powerful and well-connected individuals at various levels of society, including business elite, customs and law enforcement, and members of the political class. What is noteworthy is that except for Dole Chadee in 1994, no major drug kingpin has been arrested in the country to date; instead, only local street hustlers.[39] Moreover, police efficacy is assessed largely on the number of crimes that have been cleared up and neither on the number of homicides solved nor the frequency with which drugs are interdicted. To underscore this point, one senior security services official commented: 'for all the mayhem street gangs in Port of Spain create, far more drugs pass through Trinidad on their way to Europe and America'.[40]

And the corruption that has been spawned by this illicit activity carries over into other aspects of society as well, and involves various 'un-civil' society groups, especially those in many of the depressed communities throughout the country. Run by so-called 'community leaders' (gang leaders), not only are these 'un-civil' society groups involved in drug-related activities but also are responsible for delivering blocks of votes in return for the control of public works projects and other government funding. The country's East–West corridor contains a number of depressed communities that are afflicted with high levels of unemployment, subpar infrastructure, and limited access to basic public services and, like Jamaica, it is in these areas that issues of government efficacy and citizen security are most concerning and compelling because they account for the vast majority of crimes, especially homicides, in the country.

In order to offer temporary economic relief while providing life skills, the government has, over the years, introduced a variety of programmes, including: the Unemployment Relief Programme (URP) introduced in 1992, which provides three consecutive two-week jobs and allows re-registration after a three-month break; the one-three-year long, Community Environment Protection and Enhancement Programme (CEPEP) introduced in 2002, which provides unskilled or semi-skilled people with temporary jobs at wages exceeding the minimum wage; the Youth Training and Employment Programme Partnership (YTEPP) offered training and counselling for those aged between 18 and 25 years (for a three-month period three times a year); and the Targeted Conditional Cash Transfer Programme (TCCTP), which is designed to be a safety net for transitory unemployed heads of households and/or a temporary food subsidy for those who are undertrained while they utilize training programmes to qualify for gainful employment. However, the two largest of these programmes are the URP and CPEP. Some 16 URP offices have been established throughout the country: three in Port of Spain; one each in San Juan/Laventille, Tunapuna, Arima, Sangre Grande, Couva, San Fernando, Penal, Point Fortin, Princes Town, Fyzabad, Rio Claro, Chaguanas, and Tobago. In FY 2012, beneficiaries of these two programmes alone exceeded the average number of unemployed between 2008 and 2012.[41]

As mentioned, most of the homicides are concentrated in these underserved communities, which are also home to most of the 190-plus 'un-civil' society groups (gangs) in the country, and most studies link violent crime in the Caribbean, and gang-related crime, specifically, to the illicit narcotics trade. Trinidad and Tobago's proximity to Venezuela, and the attendant drug trafficking activities, contribute heavily to the recent upsurge in violent crime, especially homicides (see table 9.3). Therefore, on one level, much of this criminality is the result of groups vying for turf. Equally important, however, is the intersection between illegal drugs, control of turf, and contestation to gain access to the huge sums of money that the government appropriates to fund the various welfare support programmes in these communities. Since it is to the 'community leaders' (gang leaders) that the government turns to implement and oversee work projects designed into these programmes, one aspect of state 'capture' reflects the government's weakness when it franchises out some of its key government responsibilities to these 'un-civil' society groups.

In an effort to manage this violence, the government of Prime Minister Manning agreed to a meeting with gang leaders at the Crowne Plaza Hotel in Port of Spain on September 16, 2006. These gang leaders agreed to a peace pact aimed at reducing the level of gang warfare along the East–West corridor. Among the 'community leaders' at the meeting were Mark Guerra and Sean Francis,[42] both affiliated with the Jamaat al-Muslimeen, the local Islamic group responsible for the 1990 attempted coup d'état. Prior to this event, the Jamaat, under the leadership of the Imam Yasin Abu Bakr, had been involved in a range of community services in the areas of education, health care, buyers' cooperatives, skills development, and spiritual development.

Table 9.3: Homicide Rate 2000–2012

Country	2000	2001	2002	2003	2004	2005	2006	2007	2008	2009	2010	2011	2012
Antigua and Barbuda	6.4	8.9	6.2	6.2	4.9	3.6	13.2	20.1	18.7	18.5	6.9		11.2
Bahamas	24.9	14.2	16.8	15.8	13.6	15.8	18.2	22.8	21.0	24.5	26.1	34.7	29.8
Barbados	7.5	9.3	9.3	12.2	8.1	10.6	12.7	9.8	9.0	6.8	11.1	9.6	7.4
Belize	17.2	26.1	34.6	25.9	29.8	29.8	33.0	33.9	35.1	32.2	41.8	39.2	44.7
Dominica	2.9	1.4	12.9	11.4	11.4	11.3	7.1	9.9	9.9	18.3	21.1		
Grenada	14.8	5.9	13.7	8.8	5.8	10.7	11.6	10.6	15.4	6.7	9.6	3.8	13.3
Guyana	9.9	10.6	18.9	27.3	17.3	18.7	20.0	14.9	20.4	15.0	17.8	16.4	17.0
Jamaica	34.4	43.7	39.8	36.8	55.2	62.4	49.7	58.5	59.5	61.6	52.6	41.1	39.3
St Kitts and Nevis	6.6	13.0	10.7	21.0	22.7	16.3	34.1	31.7	45.0	52.2	40.1	64.2	33.6
St Lucia	14.7	21.4	26.2	22.3	22.6	24.8	25.6	17.0	22.6	22.3	24.8		21.6
St Vincent and the Grenadines	18.5	11.1	18.5	16.6	25.8	21.1	11.9	22.0	14.7	18.3	22.9	19.2	25.6
Trinidad and Tobago	9.5	11.9	13.4	17.8	20.1	29.8	28.5	29.8	41.6	38.3	35.6	26.4	28.3
Average	13.9	14.8	18.4	18.5	19.8	21.2	22.1	23.4	26.1	26.2	25.9	28.3	24.7

Source: Nation Master; UNODC; World Bank

What is instructive here is that this meeting effectively 'legitimized' these gang leaders as 'community leaders' by franchising to them state responsibility for promoting and maintaining stability over certain areas via state-provided and state-sanctioned mechanisms. The incentive offered by the prime minister was the management of public works projects such as CEPEP and URP, with the expectation that the jobs and skills development provided by these programmes would present the young men of these communities with alternatives to crime (*Trinidad Guardian*, August 17, 2008).

While both Guerra and Francis had accumulated considerable amounts of money through illegal drugs activities, the reality is that a great deal of their wealth was obtained as a result of their roles in managing these government programmes. For example, Guerra became a highly paid URP supervisor, earning approximately $150,000 per month, and reputedly owned a number of properties. He was able to attain this role presumably by campaigning for the People's National Movement (PNM) in some of these marginal seats, as photographs show him accompanying former Prime Minister Manning during the 2002 campaign (*Trinidad Guardian*: April 23, 2005).[43] Indeed, in 1995, the Jamaat mobilized its forces in a number of marginalized communities to help swing the general election in favour of Basdeo Panday and the United National Congress (UNC). When that relationship soured sometime thereafter, the Jamaat shifted its support to the PNM in the 2000, 2001, and 2002 general elections.

The nature and extent of state 'capture' is especially reflected in the recently terminated LifeSport Programme, listed in the budget as a Transfer Programme and designed to be implemented in ten centres. Rolled out in 2012 with a budget of $6,647,000, the programme paid $1,500 a month to 'criminal elements' to get them interested in sports as an alternative to crime. However, since several members of Parliament requested that their communities be included, the programme was expanded to a total of 33 centres,[44] and the allocation increased to $29 million in 2013, and dramatically grew $113,502,273 in 2014, making it the largest increase in the ministry's transfer programmes.[45] State 'capture' is clearly demonstrated in this programme in terms of the linkage between the government and the Jamaat, generally, and of the Curapo centre led by the Imam Hassan Ali, which received the bulk of the 2014 allocation of $113,502,273. This programme appears to be one of the ways in which the government has rewarded the Jamaat for getting out the vote in favour of the People's

Partnership coalition led by Prime Minister Kamla Persad. According to the Imam, his assistance to the government was:

> to help bring voters to vote. That kind of thing. I am telling you straight, my position'. 'I, me, prefer the coalition, the Partnership. I know it's not a good example of what that could be but it's a start. I didn't like the one party ruling. I believe in power sharing. You understand what I'm saying?' 'So we decide to help this against orders not to support them. We didn't care. I participated to help the UNC come into power the first time they came into power. We were effective in the streets. We participate in the politics. We help try to bring the voters in and influence the voters and we know we do that well.[46]

The Imam told reporters that 'they gave the program to my son (Rajaee)'; however, he failed to identify the 'they'. Rajaee told the *Trinidad Express* newspaper that he was chosen by the Ministry of Sport to head the Carapo LifeSport Programme, and that he had met with the Minister of Sport and parliamentary representative to that constituency, Anil Roberts, 'about nine to ten times' over the past two years.[47] Many were disconcerted at this outcome because Rajaee is a convicted murderer. Charged with the murder of Amadoo Huggins in 2004 when he was just 18, he was incarcerated for eight years before, he, along with two other prisoners, escaped in 2007. Recaptured and returned to prison, he was released in 2011. Most disconcerting for many is that Ali was allowed to manage the Carapo arm of LifeSport and, according including National Security Minister Gary Griffith, was receiving about $1.5 million monthly and 'about $18 million in the last year'.[48]

Griffith, among others, had been criticizing programmes like LifeSport, CPEP, and URP as being heavily fraudulent, and of being used to fund gang activity. According to Griffith:

> If political parties worked with groups to help them mobilize during election campaigns, that is not my business. It is not an illegal act. My focus is on gangs and specific gang leaders who have access to State contracts and using their profit not to enhance their community and reduce crime, but to use the profit to fuel crime via importation of illegal drugs and weapons and using naïve youths to do their dirty work, upon which they become casualties.[49]

However, justifying the role of the Jamaat, the Imam told the *Express* newspaper that aggrieved citizens have long been turning to the Jamaat rather than the police to seek redress for problems they have encountered:

> You come and see the Imam and he would rectify. The police don't like that, they hate that with a passion...the Jamaat has its own intelligence, is respected among different community leaders, [and] mediates between the warring gangs and runs its own justice system.

Additionally, he noted that the Jamaat actually assists the police by providing them with intelligence, and has assisted them in the retrieval of guns that went missing from various police stations.[50]

From the 'un-civil' society groups' perspective, the realization that such vast sums of money were being made available to 'community leaders' to manage these projects intensified the level of violence as new individuals vied for gang leadership and the mantle of 'community leader'. Part of this mobilization-by-violence stemmed from the increasing realization that vast amounts of money were being made by many well-respected members of society, who had their own transshipment and distribution networks. Some looked with suspicion at the pleasure boat, *Sea Prowler*, owned by the family of then minister of tourism (later minister of national security), which operated as a ferry for pleasure seekers travelling between Trinidad and Venezuela. Upon its return from Venezuela on the evening of January 19, 2005, a Dutch national was arrested for transporting 5.4 kilograms of refined heroin.[51] In a separate search of the vessel, a Venezuelan national was arrested for transporting some 4.7 kilograms of pure cocaine with a street value of $12 million.[52]

On May 8, 2005, the drugs were burnt by the Customs and Excise Marine Interdiction Unit (CEMIU). Surprisingly, the newspapers reported that the Venezuelan national was serving a five-year sentence; however, no mention has been made of the case against the Dutch national. With the docket in the Trinidad and Tobago courts backlogged, two issues arose in citizens' minds: 1) Why was the Venezuelan national's case fast-tracked? 2) Why did he receive such a short sentence for such a large quantity of drugs? 3) What happened to the case against the Dutch national? And 4) if there is still a docket for the Dutch national, why was the evidence burned? These questions arose in light of the fact that a former Minister of National Security, Selwyn Richardson, was reputedly murdered because of his attempts to prosecute members of the political and economic class for their involvement in the illicit drug trade. Some 25 years later, the murder of Dana Seetahal, former senator and prominent prosecutor, is being viewed as another message to anyone who would seek to point a finger at any of the politically connected, who might be involved in the illegal drugs trade. State 'capture' and the suborning of authority is synopsized by Darcus Howe (1999), who noted that Dole Chadee was able to undermine the system of justice with his millions by buying 'judges, juries, political parties, captains, cooks...anybody and everybody. Those whom he could not buy, he murdered...The government has turned a blind eye to the trade because it brings in foreign exchange on a huge scale'. [53] Ironically, Chadee never was convicted on drug charges; instead, he was found guilty and hanged for ordering members of his gang to commit some 30 homicides.[54]

Conclusion

The patterns of violence in Jamaica and Trinidad and Tobago reflect the transnational nature of organized crime that link local organized crime groups, driven largely by the dugs trade. Evidence shows that 'un-civil' society groups are the result of a corruption of the political system and serve as a source of new recruits for TCNs. They are used by TCNs to commit a range of crimes; provide support to TCNs in organizational development; gather useful information for TCNs; can be used by TCNs as security agents; traffic drugs and are essential to related crimes within the structure of TCNs; provide protection in their territories for activities executed by TCNs structure; generate political instability when considered useful to TCNs; terrify the population; and by threatening communities, they further serve the purposes of TCNs. As Luke Dowdney puts it, 'In addition to maintaining "order" and providing "justice" through fear and repression within the communities in which they operate, groups in this category often support community social projects in order to maintain community support'.[55]

The past three decades, therefore, have witnessed these functions increasingly being provided by an emergent 'un-civil society', reflecting gangs, whose leaders and members employ violence as a rational means of exercising their authority over their 'communities'. As a consequence, an almost parallel relationship exists between the emergence of these 'un-civil society' groups and upsurge in crime and violence, which has galvanized in frequency, intensity, and character in recent years. Perhaps no other complex phenomenon, therefore, threatens to undermine the two-generation-old democratic political system in the Caribbean than TNC-related armed violence.

Rival gangs in depressed, inner-city communities fight one another for control over drug turf. Gang leaders also initiate conflict against rival leaders in order to assume the role of 'community leader'. As a 'community leader', the gang leader then is viewed by the government as the individual most able to be the arbiter of violence, agent of stability, and the person most capable of managing public works projects in these communities. The legitimacy acquired by this new role of community leader and power broker provides political cover for expanding drug turfs, which, in turn, expands and escalates the violence as new entrants into the drug trade seek to capitalize on the wealth and opportunity that gang activity presents.

The activities of the TCNs would not be possible without the involvement of powerful and wealthy individuals who have the resources to corrupt state officials. James Mittleman and Robert Johnston note:

> The corruption of political authorities is the crucible in which customs officers, police, and tax inspectors assist in criminal operations or merely look the other way. In this network of criminals, the wealthy, and the politicians, it is the politicians who provide legal protection for their partners. Like global firms, TCN groups operate both above and below the state. Above the state, they capitalize on the globalizing tendencies of borderlessness and deregulation. Embracing the processes of internationalization, these groups create demand for their services, become actors in their own right in the global division of labor and power organized along zonal or regional and subregional lines.[56]

What the incumbents expect in return are the following: 1) maintenance of public order by managing and mitigating the level of crime in the communities such that it does not become widespread and overwhelm the entire society; 2) supervision of various public works projects that reflect government providing resources and benefits to the community. Since these are relatively ungovernable spaces, not many government facilities and services are available in these areas. Consequently, whatever level of services are available are usually provided by members of that community; outsiders will not risk working in these areas and may not be welcome; 3) getting the community to vote for the incumbents at election time. This is the symbiosis of the relationship between gangs and the political structure, which includes corrupt police officers, who are in league with these gang leaders, as well as corrupt politicians and other civil servants, who receive kickbacks to look the other way and/or claim ignorance of any collusion between themselves, their offices and gang-related activity. Nonetheless, there is significant suspicion on the part of the general public that corruption is endemic across the region, and that powerful criminals, including politically connected criminals, manage to avoid and/or evade the law.

As Dani Rodrik notes, there exists a natural tension between national democracy and global markets such that if, for example, policymakers wish to pursue the twin goals of deep globalization and democracy, then they must be prepared to relinquish control of the nation state because the forces of globalization will overwhelm efforts to implement fully the nation state's agenda. If, instead, policymakers wish to keep the nation state while simultaneously deepening globalization, then this must come at the expense of democracy because many of the goals of economic and financial globalization cannot be satisfactorily attained if robust democratic governance measures are followed. If, however, the preference is a combination of democracy and the nation state, then it must come at the cost of deep globalization.[57] In light of the foregoing, it would appear that the real challenge for Anglophone Caribbean states is whether they can act on what should be their preference: pursuing state-based nationalism without being overcome by or succumbing to the economic and financial forces of globalization.

Possessing limited capacity to defend themselves from domestic and international threats, these small and relatively weak states, out of necessity, have had to adapt and adjust to these powerful economic and political forces arrayed against them. Both entities need the same thing: stability. While TCNs need political stability to conduct their criminal activities, the economic and political elite in these countries also need stability to achieve and preserve their economic and political goals. As 'captured' states, therefore, national interests have become suborned to the interests of TCNs. Therefore, as long as there is a market for the goods and services provided by TCNs, citizen security challenges and democratic governance will remain a problem for Anglophone Caribbean countries because their geography provides them with a competitive advantage that is conducive to TCN goals. That is, 'captured' states can function as bases from which smuggling operations can be run, havens where money can be laundered, and launching pads for secure transit zones that permit illicit goods and people to be trafficked. These illicit activities tend to distort local economies and provide outlaws with the wherewithal to establish semi-feudal fiefdoms from which they can exert control on parts of states into which government authorities are often afraid to enter, as in Tivoli Gardens in Kingston, Jamaica, or Morvant/Laventille in Trinidad and Tobago. Moreover, a combination of a lack of meaningful employment opportunities, the prospects of earning vast sums of money, and the power of the criminal bosses who run these areas to extort citizens contribute to suborning of state power and the erosion of democratic governance.[58] Weak states, therefore, create the enabling conditions for TCNs to erode the legitimacy of government institutions through the subornation and extortion of public officials to such an extent that the state is unable to guarantee even the most basic order for citizens.

The central argument here is that these countries have been unable or unsuccessful in pursuing their preferred goals of national interest and democracy due to their own weakness in the face of the overwhelming power of economic and financial globalization. That is, the failure of Anglophone Caribbean countries to strengthen and protect democratic civic order and to enhance citizen security by minimizing or eliminating threats of crime and violence is due in large measure to the globalization paradox. Therefore, regardless of whether the existing, Westminster-derived, institutional structures are kept or are jettisoned and replaced by either modified forms or even new models of governance, such as the American system of checks and balances, citizen security concerns will remain a problem for these countries because they have been 'captured' powerful transnational criminal networks (TCNs). Under these circumstances, Westminster in the Caribbean is, indeed, shackled.

NOTES

1. Samuel P. Huntington, *The Third Wave: Democratization in the Late Twentieth Century*, (Norman, OK: University of Oklahoma Press, 1991).
2. Francis Fukuyama, *State-Building: Governance and World Order in the 21st Century* (Ithaca, NY: Cornell University Press, 2004), ix.
3. Samuel P. Huntington, 'How Countries Democratize'. *Political Science Quarterly* 108, no. 4, (1991–92): 579–616.
4. Robert Muggah and Katherine Aguirre, 'Mapping Citizen Security Interventions in Latin America: Reviewing the Evidence: Report', (Norwegian Peacebuilding Resource Center, 2013). Available at http://igarape.org.br/wp-content/uploads/2013/10/265_91204_NOREF_Report_Muggah-Aguirre_web1.pdf.
5. Cynthia Barrow-Giles, 'Regional Trends in Constitutional Developments in the Commonwealth Caribbean', SSRC Conflict Prevention and Peace Forum, 2010, https://mail.google.com/mail/u/o/#apps/barrowgiles%40gmail.com /1486a79d93308c2e?projector=1; Clifford E. Griffin, *Democracy and Neoliberalism in the Developing World: Lessons from the Anglophone Caribbean* (Aldershot, Hants: Ashgate Publishers, 1997); Clifford E. Griffin, 'Democracy in the Commonwealth Caribbean', *Journal of Democracy* 4, no. 2 (1994):84–94.

6.   Katherine Isbester, *The Paradox of Democracy in Latin America: Ten Country Studies of Division and Resilience* (Toronto: University of Toronto Press, 2011), 1–33.

7.   Dani Rodrik, *The Globalization Paradox: Democracy and the Future of the World Economy* (New York: WW Norton & Company, 2011), ix–xxii.

8.   Ibid.

9.   Ibid.

10. Eisuke Sakakibara, 'The End of Progressivism: A Search For New Goals', *Foreign Affairs* 74, no. 5, (September–October 1995): 8–14.

11. York W. Bradshaw and Zwelakhe Tshandu, 'Foreign Capital Penetration, State Intervention, and Development in Sub-Saharan Africa', *International Studies Quarterly* 34 (1990): 229–51.

12. Fred Rosen, 'The Temperature Rises in the Crucible of Reform', *NACLA Report of the Americas* XXVII, no. 5 (March/April 1994): 23–28; Jorge G. Castaneda, *Utopia Unarmed: The Latin American Left After the Cold War* (New York: Alfred P. Knopf, 1993).

13. Linda Weiss, *The Myth of the Powerless State* (Ithaca, NY: Cornell University Press, 1998).

14. Susan E. Rice and Stewart Patrick, 'Index of State Weakness in the Developing World', (the Brookins Institution, 2008), 23, https://www.brookings.edu/wp-content/uploads/2016/06/02_weak_states_index.pdf.

15. Franklin W. Knight, *The Caribbean: The Genesis of a Fragmented Nationalism*, 2nd ed. (New York: Oxford University Press, 1990); Eric E. Williams, *From Columbus to Castro: The History of the Caribbean 1492–1969* (New York: Harper & Row, 1970).

16. Eric E. Williams, *From Columbus to Castro*, 499–500.

17. Ibid., 500–501.

18. Knight, *The Caribbean*, 278–79.

19. Isbester, *The Paradox of Democracy in Latin America*, 12–13.

20. David Kupferschmidt, 'Illicit Political Finance and State Capture', International Institute for Democracy and International Assistance, 2009, 4–7, http://www.idea.int/resources/analysis/upload/IDEA_Inlaga_low.pdf.

21. Curtis J. Milhaupt and Mark D. West, 'The Dark Side of Private Ordering: An Institutional and Empirical Analysis of Organized Crime', *The University of Chicago Law Review* 67, no. 1 (Winter 2000): 41–98.

22. Clifford E. Griffin and Rajesh Persad, 'Dons, So-called "Community Leaders", and the Emergence of "Un-Civil" Society in the Caribbean'. In *Gangs in the Caribbean*, eds. Randy Seepersad and Ann Marie Bissessar, 80–113 (Cambridge: Cambridge Scholars Publishing, 2013), 107–108. Griffin, *Democracy and Neoliberalism in the Developing World*, 4.

23. Obika Gray, *Demeaned but Empowered: The Social Power of the Urban Poor in Jamaica* (Kingston: University of the West Indies Press, 2004), 23–34.

24. Carl Stone, *Democracy and Clientelism in Jamaica* (New Brunswick, NJ: Transaction Books, 1980); Carlene J. Edie, *Democracy by Default: Dependency and Clientelism in Jamaica* (Boulder, CO and Kingston: Lynne Rienner Publishers and Ian Randle Publishers, 1991), 57–67.

25. Gray, *Demeaned but Empowered*, 178–81.

26. Carl Stone, *Class, State and Democracy in Jamaica* (New York, NY: Praeger, 1986), 54; Mattathias Schwartz, 'A Massacre In Jamaica: After the United States Demanded the Extradition of a Drug Lord, a Bloodletting Ensued', The *New Yorker*, December 12, 2011 http://www.newyorker.com/magazine/2011/12/12/a-massacre-in-jamaica.

27. Mark Figueroa and Amanda Sives, 'Garrison Politics and Criminality in Jamaica: Does the 1997 Election Represent a Turning Point?' In *Understanding Crime in Jamaica: New Challenges for Public Policy*, ed. Anthony D. Harriott, 63–88 (Kingston: University of the West Indies Press, 2003), 65.

28. Lloyd Williams, 'Outsmarting the Criminal Bosses, Crippling Organized Gang Networks', *Jamaica Observer Online*, November 13, 2005, http://www.jamaicaobserver.com/news/92388_Outsmarting-the-criminal-bosses--crippling-organised-gang-networks; 'Tivoli Gardens', *Jamaica Observer Online*, October 23, 2005, http://www.jamaicaobserver.com/news/90901_Tivoli-Gardens---; 'Tivoli Gardens', *Jamaica Observer Online*, October 30, 2005, http://www.jamaicaobserver.com/news/91413_Tivoli-Gardens.

29. Williams, 'Outsmarting the Criminal Bosses', November 13, 2005.

30. James Kerr, 'Behind Jamaica's Garrison, Part 1', Report of the National Committee on Political Tribalism, 1997, http://www.jamaicagleaner.com/pages/politics/kerrful.pdf.

31. Ibid.

32. Kevin Edmonds, 'Guns, Gangs and Garrison Communities in the Politics of Jamaica', *Race & Class* 57, no.4 (2016): 54–74.

33. T.K. Whyte, '1,500 Killings by Cops, No Conviction', *Jamaica Observer*, September 25, 2005.

34. Chris McGreal, 'Christopher "Dudus" Coke tells US Court: "I'm Pleading Guilty Because I Am"', *The Guardian Online*, September 1, 2011, http://www.guardian.co.uk/world/2011/sep/01/christopher-dudus-coke-us-court.

35. US Information Agency, 'Concerns about Sovereignty in the Battle against Drugs', July 31, 1997, https://fas.org/irp/news/1997/97073101_rmr.htm.

36. Alexander Bruzual, 'Cops Make $1.2m Drug Bust', *Express Online*, Port of Spain, November 19, 2014, http://www.trinidadexpress.com/news/Cops-make-12m-drug-bust-283278411.html

37. Geisha Kowlessar and Kamla Georges, '3 T&T Businessmen Linked to Cocaine Haul', Trinidad Express Online, January 22, 2014, http://www.

guardian.co.tt/news/2014-01-22/whistle-blower-helping-dea; Nalinee Seelal, 'Dummy Firm in Drug Cover-up', *Trinidad Newsday Online*, January 22, 2012, http://www.newsday.co.tt/crime_and_court/0,189552.html.

38. Marc Bassant, 'Two-year Hunt for Drug Dealers', *Trinidad Express Online*, January 21, 2014, http://www.trinidadexpress.com/news/TWO-YEAR-HUNT--FOR-DRUG-DEALERS-241396981.html.

39. Kito Johnson, 'Chadee Signs His Death Warrant', *Trinidad and Tobago Guardian*, February 26, 2012, http://www.guardian.co.tt/news/2012-02-26/chadee-signs-his-death-warrant.

40. Dorn Townsend, *No Other Life: Gangs, Guns and Governance in Trinidad and Tobago*, Small Arms Survey, 2009, 23.

41. Unemployment Relief Programme (URP), https://www.ttconnect.gov.tt/gortt/portal/ttconnect/!ut/p/a1/jdDBDoIwDAbgp-FKC8tUvHFARUwMGBV2MWjmwCAjY4KPL3ozKNpbm-9P_hQYxMDKtMlFqnNZpsVzZZ6NDENpIfYfgOkQH7ci3PKQBmY9JB5I3EMInHfCotQh2BBH_y-OXcX_mN7yEPbBBtqQ90K_5AgM9lsBEIY-vnyRueSQTAUzxM1dcmTfVnTOtq3pqoIFt25pCSlFw8ySvBn6KZLLWEL9LqK7b-O5faNGs3AdjOzzp/dl5/d5/L2dBISEvZoFBIS9nQSEh/?WCM_GLOBAL_CONTEXT=/gortt/wcm/connect/gortt+web+content/TTConnect/Citizen/Topic/Employment/National+Employment+Programmes/Unemployment+Relief+Programme+(URP).

42. Yvonne Baboolal, 'Laventille Activist Lennox Smith Testifies: Muslimeen Took Charge of URP', *Trinidad and Tobago Guardian*, December 15, 2011, http://www.guardian.co.tt/news/2011/12/15/laventille-activist-lennox-smith-testifies-muslimeen-took-charge-urp.

43. Ibid.

44. Asha Javeed, 'LifeSport Requests $32m More', *Trinidad Express Online*, June 23, 2014, http://www.trinidadexpress.com/news/LifeSport-requests-32m-more-264190001.html.

45. Asha Javeed, 'Jamaat Raking in Govt $$', *Trinidad Express Online*, May 18, 2014, http://www.trinidadexpress.com/news/Land--from-Govt-259746681.html.

46. Asha Javeed, 'Loans For Criminals', *Trinidad Express Online*, June 21, 2014 http://www.trinidadexpress.com/news/Loans-for-Criminals-264129831.html; Asha Javeed, 'Griffith: LifeSport Fund Financing Criminals,' *Trinidad Express Online*, July 24, 2014, http://www.trinidadexpress.com/news/Inconsistencies-in-certification-of-invoices-260560021.html.

47. Javeed, 'Jamaat Raking in Govt $$'.

48. Javeed, 'Loans For Criminals'; Javeed, 'Griffith: LifeSport Fund Financing Criminals'.

49. Javeed, 'Griffith: LifeSport Fund Financing Criminals'.

50. Asha Javeed, 'Cops Seek Jamaat Help', *Trinidad Express Online*, May 19, 2014, http://www.trinidadexpress.com/news/COPS--SEEK--JAMAAT-HELP-259880071.html.
51. Darryl Heerlal, '$3.5m Heroin Bust at Chag', *Trinidad and Tobago Express*, January 21, 2005.
52. Anna-Lisa Paul, 'Customs, Cops Burn $12m Drugs', *Trinidad and Tobago Express*, May 28, 2005.
53. Darcus Howe, 'Life and Death of a Caribbean Drugs Baron', The *Independent Online*, June 6, 1999. http://www.independent.co.uk/life-style/life-and-death-of-a-caribbean-drugs-baron-1098548.html#.
54. Mark Fineman, 'Triple Hanging Returns Death Penalty to Trinidad', *Los Angeles Times Online*, June 5, 1999, http://articles.latimes.com/1999/jun/05/news/mn-44346.
55. Luke Dowdney, *Neither war nor peace: International comparisons of Children and Youth in Organised Armed Violence*. (Rio de Janeiro, Brazil: 7Letras, 2005), 41.
56. James H, Mittleman and Robert Johnston, 'The Globalization of Organized Crime, the Courtesan State, and the Corruption of Civil Society', *Global Governance* 5, no. 1 (January–March 1999): 103–26, at 110.
57. Rodrik, *The Globalization Paradox*, 200–205.
58. Kimberly L. Thachuk, ed., *Transnational Threats: Smuggling and Trafficking in Arms, Drugs, and Human Life* (Westport, CT: Praeger Security International, 2007), 10.

FURTHER READING

Bailey, J., and R. Godson, eds. 2000. *Organized Crime & Democratic Governability: Mexico and the US-Mexican Borderlands*. Pittsburgh, PA: University of Pittsburgh Press.

Bailey, J., and Sergio Aguayo, eds. 1996. *Strategy and Security in US–Mexican Relations: Beyond the Cold War*. San Diego, CA: University of San Diego, Center for US-Mexican Studies.

Downes, Andrew S. 2010. Poverty and its Reduction in the Small Developing Countries of the Caribbean. Paper presented at the conference on 'Ten Years of War Against Poverty'. Chronic Poverty Research Center, University of Manchester, UK, September 8–10. http://www.chronicpoverty.org/uploads/publication_files/downes_caribbean.pdf.

Gray, Obika. 1991. *Radicalism and Social Change in Jamaica, 1960–1972*. Knoxville, TN: University of Tennessee Press.

Gleaner. 2010. A Convenient Affair: Bruce & Dudus – the Constituency Power-Share'. http://jamaica-gleaner.com/gleaner/20100523/news/news1.html.

International Monetary Fund. 2013. Caribbean Small States: Challenges of High Debt and Low Growth. February 20. https://www.imf.org/external/np/pp/eng/2013/022013b.pdf.

Jamaica Observer. 2011. We Hope That Mr Christopher "Dudus" Coke Will Sing His Heart Out, September 1. http://www.jamaicaobserver.com/editorial/We-hope-that-Mr-Christopher--Dudus--Coke-will-sing-his-heart-out_9579010.

Javeed, Asha. 2014. I Did Not Kill Dana. *Trinidad Express* online, May 17. http://www.trinidadexpress.com/news/I-DID-NOT--KILL-DANA-259682291.html.

———. 2014. LifeSport Spending Spree. *Trinidad Express* online, July 26. http://www.trinidadexpress.com/news/Report-in-DPPs-hands-268753641.html.

Khan, Vikaas. 2011. Drug Gangs Force Curfew on Trinidad. *Allvoices* online, Puerto Rico, August 27. http://www.allvoices.com/contributed-news/10171907-drug-gangs-force-curfew-on-trinidad.

Tanzi, Vito. 2000. *Policies, Institutions and the Dark Side of Economics*. UK: Cheltenham, Edward Elgar.

Thomas, McDonald and Eleanor Wint. 2002. Inequality and Poverty in the Eastern Caribbean. Paper presented at the ECCB Seventh Annual Development Conference November 21–22, Basseterre, St Kitts and Nevis. http://www.caribank.org/uploads/publications-reports/staff papers/inequalityandpoverty%5B1%5D.pdf.

United Nations. 2009. Caribbean Development Report, vol. 2. CEPAL. http://www.cepal.org/publicaciones/xml/3/38253/lcarl.245part1.pdf.

United Nations Office on Drugs and Crime. 2012. *World Drug Report 2012*. http://www.unodc.org/unodc/data-and-analysis/WDR-2012.html.

10 Towards a New Democracy in the Caribbean: *Local Empowerment and the New Global Order*

Percy C. Hintzen

Introduction

Governance, whether democratic or not, is exercised as an entangled set of institutional and bureaucratic practices aimed at ordering and directing people and their relationships to other people and to things. It must be judged by its 'far-reaching effects' on the governed – what I choose to call its 'instrument effects'.[1] It is in these effects that the intent of sovereign power is both revealed and realized. And intent is closely aligned with the constitutive interests of its *effective* participants.

The West Indies is inscribed in global entanglements effectuated in 'interlinked transnational formations' through which the local, the national, and the global coalesce.[2] The role of postcolonial West Indian governance has been confined almost exclusively to establishing and guaranteeing contractual legal authority to legitimate the extractive work of transnational firms, to fashioning institutional practice consistent with the needs of the market in the formal economy, to the establishment and running of legal order (from which many are exempted), to the organization of political parties, to the co-optation and control of public interest groups, and to the disciplining of public discussion and opinion. All of these respond to demands placed upon national governing authorities by powerful international interests. This chapter addresses the manner in which these inter-linkages, both historically and currently, explain the region's practices of governance, irrespective of form. Our focus on the 'Westminster' model, universally adopted by all of the former colonies of Britain in the Caribbean region, makes analytical sense because it allows for the disentanglement of form and practice through a focus on democracy. However closely it does or does not adhere to its British provenance, there is considerable convergence in the practices of governance throughout the region.

Democracy, according to the Nobel Prize-winning economist Amartya Sen, must be understood as an 'institutional arrangement' organized for 'the exercise of people's freedoms through the liberty to participate in social choice and in the making of public decisions.' Ideally, the result of its practice must be the achievement and expansion of 'economic opportunities, political liberties, social powers, and the enabling conditions of good health, basic education, and the encouragement and cultivation of initiatives'.[3] It is effectuated through the expansion of human capabilities. I employ this as the benchmark of political freedom.

Representative democracy in the West Indies does not meet this benchmark. The networks of neocolonial and imperialist relations through which representative democracy in the West Indies is practised, have constrained attempts at the expansion of human capabilities necessary for the guarantee of rights and freedoms. In protecting powerful global interests and meeting their demands, and in ensuring conditions for their own survival, regimes may be forced to constrict, coerce, and control political expression and dissent. In this context, attempts to incorporate subaltern interests in governing practice can result in political crises, because such incorporation can threaten regime survival by rendering it vulnerable to punitive retaliation by global actors and their local supporters. There is, therefore, a disjuncture between representative practice and the ability of national apparatuses of governance to expand substantive freedoms. As a result, when demands for freedom impose themselves upon governance, there is no hesitation in their curtailment.

This chapter focuses on the manner in which the interests of global actors, including nationals acting on the global stage, affect governing practices. I do this through examination of consequences, positive or negative, of these imposed interests on the stated goals of governance, particularly as these relate to the interests of local communities and constituencies. In the final analysis, the compatibility between governing practices and the conditions for genuine development are explored. Such an examination is not inconsistent with the declared assertions of West Indian postcolonial governments, whose demands for democratic transformation were closely linked to goals of 'development'. Postcolonial governance implied the expansion of freedom to the colonized subjects, not as an end in itself, but as the principal means by which to achieve development: the singular and universal goal of West Indian governance. Indeed, 'development' has been the goal for all forms of postcolonial governance, legitimizing all forms of governing practice.[4]

This point brings into question the constitution of the state and its relationship to national governance. Michel-Rolph Trouillot has pointed out the fallacy in claims of an integral connection between the two in assertions of a 'nation-state homology'. He insists upon an understanding of the state as 'a set of practices and processes and their effects...whether or not they coalesce around central sites of governments.'⁵ The point of such a departure from convention is to direct our attention away from forms of governance in order to explain the manner in which 'state effects' are imposed on its practice. By state effects, I refer to the actual effects of the processes and practices of power on the material lives of people and on their subjectivities, exercised either directly in the deployment of the technologies of global power or indirectly through the authority of the national apparatus of governance. My concern is that the true conditions of development, as freedom, rest with 'novel articulations of social power' as counter forces to these effects.⁶

Westminster, Democracy, and Development

By the Westminster model, the reference here, most fundamentally, is to a codified system of laws and governance contained in a written constitution, a sovereign Head of State, a cabinet led by the head of government, a bicameral or unicameral Parliament with one branch comprising members elected by local constituencies in a general election, a parliamentary opposition, an independent judiciary, and an independent civil service. Postcolonial adoption of the formalities of the Westminster model has been the instrumentality through which nationalist concentration was consolidated in the British West Indies. As the legitimizing practice of postcolonial formation in the West Indies, it provided the necessary condition for continued participation in global topographies of neocolonial and imperialist power.

Democracy is presented universally as a particular and desirable ideal form of governance. Almost universally in postcolonial formation, it has been portrayed as the instrumental link between (political) freedom and development. But when judged by Sen's criteria of its role in creating and expanding the capabilities for the exercise of freedom, in varying degrees and under different registers, democratic practice has failed in the West Indies. Indeed, there has been no necessary connection between 'democracy' and 'development'. For most of the former British colonies in the West Indies, notwithstanding their impressive scores on various democracy indexes and rankings (to which they point with pride), their populations have not escaped the maladies of recurring, even perpetual, universal global crises that have intensified with the shift in emphasis from 'national development' to neoliberal induced forms of globalization. The explanation for such failure rests with the manner in which development has been specified, universally, and for West Indian governments, as 'convergence' with the modern industrialized global North. This has become inscribed upon the practice of governance, converting its goals almost exclusively to the pursuit of growth in production, consumption, and accumulation, producing the postcolonial dilemma of failure of both development and democracy.

The quest for development convergence has imposed in the space of postcolonial governance a form of decomposition where rights that are integral to democratic practice are understood to exist independently of conditions for development transformation. The two have become sequentially rather than integrally linked.[7] But neither is an immediate imperative because each can be realized only through forms of modernity not yet achieved in 'developing' societies. This explains the ability to curtail democratic practice in 'underdeveloped societies' with impunity because it can hinder the progress of development. As such, the right to participate in public decision-making must be placed in a lock box for the future. Modernity, and therefore the freedom to participate, comes at the end of the process of development. This legitimizes forms of exclusion from democratic practice through the denial of the rights of participation to those seen as impediments to progress. In the West Indies, as a result, there is a disjuncture between form and practice of democratic governance. Regime legitimacy rests on the claim to representation of the popular will. Such a claim legitimizes the divergences between formalized processes of democratic elections, institutionalized in the West Indies, for example through the Westminster model, and the actual practice of governance. Elections become transformed into a mere legitimizing discourse as postcolonial regimes renege on the promise of political freedoms denied by colonial governance. This very denial, ironically and in a fundamental way, was the charge made against colonization. It became the issue that drove nationalist demands for independence. But once development, specified as convergence with Western industrialized modernity, became integral to nationalist objectives and to the goals of postcolonial governance, rights and freedom became dismissed or sidelined as impediments.

Governance, Rights, and Exception

As is currently practised, there is an ideological distortion that ties development and democratic discourse together. As ideologies, both 'development' and 'democracy' are imposed by global conditions and global interests in ways that explain their failure. This brings into focus the inevitable connection between the local and the global (known as 'glocalization'),[8] as an essential characteristic of colonial and postcolonial formation in the Caribbean. Here, I refer to the manner in which local communities become inserted into global spaces. What is at stake is whether or not (and how) such insertion can provide opportunities to enhance individual and collective rights to freedom and development.

Governance, then, must be judged on the basis of the link it creates among conditions of freedom, rights, and development. Their contemporaneous interlinking, according to Sen's formulation, provides the necessary condition for guarantees of 'a standard of living adequate for health and wellbeing including food, clothing, housing and medical care and necessary social services, and the right to security in the event of unemployment.'[9] By this criterion, governance in the West Indies has failed to meet its 'desired' objectives. Such failure has forced subaltern social groups[10] to depend on the harnessing of opportunities existing outside of and in opposition to the official and formal system of 'democratic' governance to guarantee their sustenance, security, and survival. They have become exceptions to the provision of the rights and benefits of citizenship. While engaged with the established structures of political representation, they are excluded from effective participation. This is one form of exception.[11] The other references the privileges exercised by the governing elite and the interest groups that it represents that exempt both from compliance with constitutionality and the rule of law.

The problem exists on two levels. The first has to do with the incongruence between participation and representation built into the Westminster model (and its modifications and deviations). As liberal practice, Westminster democracy relies on mobilization for support through diffuse claims of representation that do not come with the guarantee of rights, even when there is strict adherence to the principle of 'one person one vote'.[12] The limitations placed on *effective* participation in governance by the subaltern have allowed members of the middle and upper strata of West Indian society to use conditions of exception, understood here as their ability to depart from legality and constitutionality, 'to intervene in the logics of ruling and being ruled' in order to gain access to state resources – in other words, to function 'outside of the law'.[13] They engage in pervasive practices of corruption, cronyism, and nepotism that have become normalized in the region. The lower strata, as the overwhelming majority, by and large are without these opportunities, except indirectly through forms of patronage and clientelism.[14] They are forced to create their own conditions for economic opportunity, their own extrajudicial forms of political practice (including riots), and their own forms of social welfare and protective security. For them, the 'societal arrangements', formed and fashioned to satisfy social needs through the guarantee of economic and political rights occur outside of governing practice. At the same time, members of the upper and middle strata use access to the state (i.e., to processes and practices of global power whether exercised through the apparatuses of national governance or through global presences) to establish and maintain participation in international and national networks through which their need for economic, social, and political capital is satisfied and their freedoms to pursue them are maintained and expanded.

Postcolonial development in the West Indies has been disconnected, piecemeal, uneven (as it relates to the various sectors of society), ad hoc and reversible. Development is practised as a problem of technicality and efficiency consistent with understandings derived through the regime's engagements with 'transnational topographies of power.'[15] Rather than a mechanism for bringing the grounded realities of diverse social groups, families, and individuals into effective representation in governing practice, governance is directed towards the coordination of 'societal arrangements and institutional practices' in keeping with the imperatives of such engagements.[16] This has imposed a universalized uniformity in governing practices throughout the region, legitimized as it is in discourses of the pursuit of political freedom and economic development not immediately realizable. As the object of statist intervention, governing practice is directed toward ensuring that 'societal arrangements and institutional practices' accord with goals imposed through participation in international topographies of power necessary for such realization. The role of government is reduced to one of harnessing, in one form or another, what is 'usable' for global interests in its pursuit of development and as a condition of freedom. As pointed out by Suzanne Bergeron, following James Scott, 'people and activities' that do not fit into the model are 'left out of the frame' and turned into 'anomalies or pathologies' that need to be transformed. They are either 'ignored or eliminated', resulting in 'the loss of freedom, social dislocation, alienation, (and) environmental degradation'.[17]

The struggle for national independence occurred in the West Indies through the formation of political parties, labour unions, clientelistic networks, ethnic and communal organizations, etc. that were fashioned into 'civil society'. In the process of structural reformulation to satisfy the legitimizing legalities of liberal democratic practice, civil society was rendered incapable of articulating to the structures of governance, on its own terms, the interests and demands of the diverse constituencies out of which it was fashioned.[18] As a result, in the West Indies the instrumentality of 'democratic governance' has systematically limited, constrained, and/or foreclosed the imperatives of freedom and conditions for the realization of true development. From its inception, formalized 'independence' gave the postcolonial state constitutional and legal contractual authority to receive foreign assistance and foreign loans, to provide legal frameworks and the legal bases for foreign investments, and to receive formal recognition as a sovereign unit in international relations as conditions of developmental convergence.[19] In other words, the postcolonial Caribbean was *internationally* inscribed in a transnational apparatus of governmentality. Its governments became incapable of exercising 'the range of powers we usually associate with a sovereign nation-state.'[20] Thus, 'good government' became the exercise of effective means of meeting the demands of powerful global actors. All the diverse segments of the population had to become conscripted into such an exercise. When the interests of powerful global actors conflicted with the rights of segments of the national population, good government came into conflict with 'government that is good'. Governing practice came to be organized in and through 'efficient and technically functional institutions' (including elections) aimed at meeting demands imposed by global forces rather than at guaranteeing rights that are 'benevolent and protective' of a diverse citizenry.[21] Segments of the national population have become differentially constrained and contained by the demands of global interests. Given the nature and character of the formation of Caribbean (and postcolonial) political economies, domestic social groups, families, and individuals have come to rely on accessing both local and global resources that the government is not in a position to fully guarantee. Those excluded by the governing apparatus, through forms of exception, are left to develop their own strategies for securing such access.

The Struggle for Meaningful Rights and Recognition

It is certainly not the case that 'development', understood here as guarantees of economic rights, has not occurred in the Caribbean, quite the opposite. But access to its conditions is class differentiated due to the state effects of exclusion and privilege. For freedom, rights, and development to become aligned, the strategies adopted by subaltern groups to secure, guarantee, and produce development change *on their own terms* need to become integral to governing practice. The instantiation of the middle and upper strata in neocolonial networks of global capital to which their interests are integrally tied have stymied possibilities that they can be the sources of development transformation.[22] The exercise of their privilege, through exception, has become the major impediment to such transformation because their interests are fashioned and formulated by the demands of the system of global capital.

There have been periods in the early phases of postcolonial practice where technical and social conditions at the global and local levels have combined with the interests of global actors to open up possibilities for the pursuit of subaltern rights. During the 'national development' phase of pre-independence, popular mobilization of workers and peasants and party organization combined with the needs of foreign investors for labour and with Cold War contestation to produce 'thick social investments' in the former colonies. This created a space for accommodation by the region's political elite of demands for economic, political, and civil rights by its working classes and peasantry. 'Far reaching investments' in social welfare, education, health, housing, etc., became conditions for popular support in the immediate pre and post-independence period.[23] But such accommodation came with considerable inefficiencies and high remuneration and transaction costs for global and local capital that negatively affected surplus accumulation in ways that made them unsustainable. As these became excessive, their accommodations had to be curtailed through pre-emption or prevention by the governing regime. In the West Indies, this necessitated modifications in the formal arrangements of the Westminster model and liberal democratic practice.

Subaltern Struggles and Curtailments in Democratic Practice

Working-class agency that was expanded through capabilities derived from insertion into global networks of anti-capitalism was integral to the success of the nationalist movement in expanding political freedoms and economic rights. Anti-colonial mobilization for independence in the former British colonies was inserted into and supported by these transnational anti-capitalist networks. These included the radical wing of the British Labour Party; the World Federation of Trade Unions (WFTU); the Red International of Labour Unions (through which the Soviet Union, via the Comintern, channelled organizational and ideological support); the Negro Bureau of the Communist International of Labour Unions; and the International Trade Union Committee of Negro Workers (an offshoot of the Red International of Labour Unions). The West Indian working class and peasantry, by providing the mass base for such mobilization, became inserted into international anti-capitalist movements, which through their socialist ideology made explicit the links between capitalism, class exploitation, and colonialism. As a result, anti-capitalism became the crucible in which the struggle for political and economic rights by the subaltern was forged. The Caribbean Labour Congress (CLC), formed by middle-class leaders who had cultivated ties with the British Labour Party, became an instrumental conduit for such insertion.[24] Labour mobilization escalated into violence throughout the West Indies during the 1930s in protests against low wages, colonial neglect of the welfare of workers, substandard housing, subhuman working and sanitary conditions, and the denial of worker-participation in decision-making on the terms and conditions of their labour through collective bargaining.[25]

The British colonial response was the introduction of 'representative government' with the promise of full independence. In exchange for governance and participation in the global system of sovereign nations, middle-class creole leaders of the nationalist movement used their control of organizations of mass mobilization, now converted into political parties and trade unions, to co-opt, regulate, and control the subaltern and to harness their members to the interests of global capital.[26] The institutionalization of formal democratic practice allowed this elite to legitimize their claims as representatives of the 'will of the people'. In representing this 'will' as popular universal demands for development, the governing elite was able to fashion new forms of neocolonial domination and dependency that were rendered invisible under the symbolic camouflage of the exercise of the sovereign right of international association. The idea of sovereignty, with its connotation of free unencumbered association in the community of nations and of the statutory imperative, documented in regimes of international law, became the instrumentality of such camouflage.[27]

But what was being represented was neither the 'general will' nor the economic interests of the mass supporters of the political elite. In the process of 'democratic transition', sectarian interests, organized through the forging of ties of race and clientelism, became pitted against each other in political competition. Insertion into emerging neocolonial capitalist networks, increasingly centred on the United States, came to be justified as the sole means of development, which in its statist narration, could be realized only through convergence with the industrialized North.

The case of Guyana is exemplary of the turn to sectarianism, under the guise of democracy, in the face of popular challenges to policies and practices of convergence. There, racial fracturing orchestrated by the colonial state just before independence produced a split in the radical nationalist party into politically organized racial segments. This significantly compromised and weakened working-class mobilization that had managed, quite successfully, to secure the expansion of their political, social, and cultural rights denied by colonial governance. Under the guise of 'democracy', and exploiting the racial fissure, effective power was handed to political leaders of the country's white and 'near-white' merchant class, representing less than five per cent of the country's population. With the goal of ensuring capitalist control of postcolonial formation, the Colonial Office in Britain orchestrated a fundamental shift away from locally elected constituency representation (one of the central pillars of the Westminster model) to proportional representation based on percentages of the national vote received by competing political parties. This forced an alliance between leaders of the black racial faction and political representatives of the minority white and near-white local capitalists under conditions that gave the latter absolute control of economic and development policy.[28] With their struggle for economic rights compromised by 'democratic' representation, members of the black lower strata rejected democratic legitimacy in order to support their political leaders' successful efforts to gain exclusive control of the national apparatus of governance. To do so, their leaders resorted to 'undemocratic' and 'fraudulent' practices. Elections, however rigged, became transformed into a legitimizing ritual by the regime. For the black working class, support for their political leaders became the only way to escape the clutches of global capital, instantiated through the practice of proportional representation.[29] It was also the only way to secure the patronage benefits derived from black middle-class control of the state against similar racialized claims by the racially mobilized Asian Indian population. Given the racialization of politics, support for electoral fraud practised by their political representatives became the only available choice if they were to escape from the consequences of control of the apparatus of governance by representatives of the domestic capitalist class.

The critical assertion here is that conditions for development cannot be separated from global processes and international entanglements that both constrain and support their realization. In Guyana in the 1970s, working-class radicalism, out of which the nationalist movement was forged, gained more agentive power in the wake of an internal political crisis in the United States that culminated in the resignation of President Richard Nixon and in a weakening of its global power following the debacle of the Vietnam War. The defeat and withdrawal of US military forces from Indochina, by 1975, compromised American global influence. To this was added the consolidation of the Organization of the Petroleum Exporting Countries (OPEC) and its willingness to use oil as an economic weapon in response to the Yom Kippur War between Israel and its Arab neighbours in 1973. These came in the wake of growing radical anti-capitalist popular challenges to Western democracies and to US global hegemony, signalled in a global explosion of militancy that came to a head in 1968. All these contributed to a 'shift in global sentiment' away from the capitalist status quo.[30] The changes in the global topographies of power wrought by these forces contributed to an expansion of the agentive power of radical and working-class forces in the Caribbean, as elsewhere. The subaltern began to use their agency to force transformations in the practices of governance in the Caribbean. In Guyana, it opened the space for a realignment of the country's international relations and for radicalization of the regime's economic policy. These were publicized in 1975 in official announcements of decisions to reorient the country's global alliances toward Cuba, Eastern Europe, China and the tri-continental 'Third World' and of the regime's commitment to a Marxist-Leninist orientation.

In Trinidad and Tobago, the influence of black radical assertions in North America and Europe combined with mass dissatisfaction over rights in the 1960s fuelled a widespread 'Black Power' rebellion against the extant form of Westminster governance in 1970. The rebellion was sparked by 'exceptions' granted to a group of powerful elites tied to international capital and by the exclusion of the black working class from effective participation in governance. In its successful efforts to retain power, the ruling party was forced to institutionalize massive expansions of clientelistic transfers. Like the Guyanese case, the stage for racially mounted challenge had been set in earlier colonial attempts to resolve fundamental problems that inhered in the practice of Westminster liberal democracy by gerrymandering constituency boundaries to favour the ruling party. These concessions were made after declarations by its leaders of commitments to pro-capitalist and pro-Western policies just prior to the granting of independence in 1962.

The Trinidad regime was able to satisfy demands for economic rights by its rebelling black working-class erstwhile supporters and their middle-class allies by exploiting opportunities provided by OPEC's de facto deployment of the power of cartelization. This led to dramatic increases in global oil prices and gave oil-producing countries enormous leverage that they used to dictate the terms of trade for their petroleum products. By introducing fundamental changes to the tax structure, the Trinidad regime was able to reallocate portions of its phenomenally expanded oil revenues into its patronage agenda, thus satisfying the demand for expanded economic rights by its strategic support base.[31] This allowed it to maintain its commitment to development convergence while guaranteeing transfers to its strategic base and marginalizing an equally vocal East Indian challenge to its authority. Its 'democratic' bona fides were retained through patronage transfers that marshalled the support of its racial base, allowing it to maintain the mantle of democratic legitimacy. But while the challenge to the regime by a coalition of students, workers, the unemployed, and radical intellectuals effectuated considerable changes in the pattern of ethnic representation in governance, it failed to resolve the crisis of effective participation that continues to haunt the society to this day. The reason for the failure rested upon the conditioning of the regime's clientelistic response by intensification of its participation in global capitalist networks.[32] It was able to meet the demands of its racial supporters only through transfers of significantly increased oil revenues from newly discovered reserves during a period of escalating prices in global markets. Profound changes in the capacities of oil-producing states to dictate their terms of trade allowed the regime to refashion the tax structure under terms that were much more conducive to securing a much larger portion of oil revenues. The country's subaltern black population was able to barter support for the ruling regime in exchange for considerable access to these revenues. This became the basis for significant expansion of their economic capabilities. But these transfers were tied to the vagaries of the international oil market. For the lowest strata of society, they proved inadequate, even in the best of circumstances. Their members continue to be subjected to perpetual crises that ebb and flow with the rise and fall of global oil prices.

Regimes become vulnerable to international retaliation when global economic transfers cannot be guaranteed. In the Guyana case, the turn to the Soviet bloc produced an intense political and economic crisis in the wake of punitive retaliation by Western capital. The result was dramatically reduced access to global transfers upon which the Guyanese political economy depended. This sparked new radical challenges and a resort by the regime to repressive violence. To maintain its authority, it jettisoned the formalities of the Westminster model in favour of an executive presidency in which power was concentrated and coercively deployed. This undermined its legitimacy, both globally and domestically. In the final analysis, the crisis was resolved only through re-insertion into the network of global capital, conditioned by a renunciation of the country's socialist aspirations by its ruling elite.[33] The dilemma facing the regime was that, in its effort to meet radical demands, it had to face the consequences of Western capitalist retaliatory response. This came with the loss of its ability to secure global transfers upon which its survival rested. With no alternative, it was forced to agree to restoration of the formalities of democratic legitimacy that led to its loss of control of the governing apparatus in 'free and fair' elections conducted in 1992. Democratic legitimacy became the justifying mantra for international intervention. Such intervention was conditioned by declarations of commitment to global capitalism and renunciations of anti-Western hostility. But the claim to legitimacy by the opposition party that came to power continued to rest with its ability to win elections through its racial appeal to the more numerous East Indian population. The perseverance of the racial fissures that existed between the black and Asian Indian working class were exploited to the benefit of the new ruling party. International intervention to underwrite the conditions for the exercise of free and fair elections came only when the necessary declarations and renunciations were made.

The return to the formalities of democratic practice was framed by considerable transformations in the global topographies of power in the wake of the collapse of Euro-Communism, the dismantling of the Warsaw Pact group of countries and their turn to capitalism, and the increasing insertion of China into global capitalist networks. There was no alternative but capitulation to neoliberal capitalism, now imposed by international financial institutions (IFIs) through the conditionalities of structural adjustment. Regime legitimacy, tied to the formalities of democracy and declarative guarantees of such capitulation, provided the terms under which the formerly Marxist-Leninist opposition People's Progressive Party came to power.[34]

In Jamaica, subaltern assertions of rights were meliorated, accommodated, and regulated through patronage networks in which transfers to the urban and rural poor were made.[35] Like Trinidad and Tobago and Guyana, the Jamaican regime was able to exploit new possibilities for effective development in the currents that were transforming the global topographies of power during the late 1960s and 1970s. These allowed for a shift in the regime's patterns of global alliances to Cuba, Eastern Europe and the tri-continental 'Third World', beginning in 1972 when support from a radicalized working class swept into power the People's National Party (PNP) under the leadership of democratic socialist Michael Manley. The Manley regime exploited the space provided by the favourable international environment to make far-reaching social investments in poor communities while placing new conditions on foreign investors and national capitalists to underwrite domestic retention of a larger share of the economic surplus. But the regime soon found itself dealing with the identical realities that stymied similar efforts in Guyana, namely, its dependence on transfers from the system of global capital in which the governing apparatus was inextricably entangled. Retaliatory withdrawals of investments, reductions in bilateral and multilateral transfers, and capital flight soon produced a severe economic crisis that prevented the realization of the promise of reallocation. The ensuing and inevitable international economic retaliation came with the constriction of access to global resource transfers that undermined the material base of society, forcing an uncritical and even deeper insertion into the postcolonial imperialist networks of the globalized capitalist system. The progressive anti-capitalist ruling party lost support in the wake of the crisis and in 1980, lost power to its pro-American, pro-capitalist, and pro-Western counterpart.[36] This was followed by constriction of the economic rights of the poor and an intensification of its hardships.

The discussion of Guyana, Trinidad and Tobago, and Jamaica highlights the inability of formal democracy to create the conditions for access to economic rights and political freedom in postcolonial practice because of the inscription of the postcolony in global topographies of capitalist power and in global forms of capitalist transfers. Under such inscription, demands for economic rights become circumscribed. Inevitably, efforts to satisfy subaltern demands produce even more strictly enforced curtailment of their access to political and economic rights because they come into inevitable conflict with the perpetual and endless need by both global and national capital for surplus accumulation.

Prospects for a New Democracy

The question becomes, then, whether opportunities exist for the conjoining of development, rights, and freedom. Such opportunities may rest in changes in the structure of global relations that might support a reconstitution of forms of governance to accommodate the different and diverse demands of those excluded by exception from the ambit of national authority. The need is for escape from the state effects of global capital, that is, from its power to shape life conditions. The following section assesses prospects for such escape that might exist in the current global geopolitical environment. I explore whether historical or extant practices, realignments of global power, and/or the emergence of counter-hegemonic transnational networks can offer a space through which more meaningful realizations of democracy and development in the Caribbean might be achieved.

Exception, Development, and Systemic Changes in Global Capital

There are systemic changes occurring in global capitalism. These are becoming evident in the strategic positioning of newly emerging powers in the global South. At the same time, they are leading to the abandonment of localities and people deemed 'unusable' to capitalist accumulation.[37] The changes are emerging in the face of what David Harvey identifies as a 'crisis' of 'overaccumulation'[38] in the global North that can be resolved only by seeking out new markets, new investment opportunities, and new sources of raw materials in the global South.[39] To do so, global capital has been developing new efficiencies and new strategies for reining in remuneration and transaction costs while, relatedly, reducing its dependence on national governmental authority. This has produced a new pattern of direct engagement by capitalist investors in the governing of 'usable' localized areas and workers in the global South.[40] They 'hop over' unusable areas while reducing their commitment to the agendas of governing regimes. This has reduced access by these regimes to transfers from the global system and has compromised and diminished their capacities to exercise control over 'unusable' areas and people, leading to their relative abandonment.[41]

This shift in production and investment functions to the global South has engendered new challenges to Euro-American global capitalist interests. New patterns of global allocation have created opportunities for the emergence of new blocs of countries that are growing in power. They are known by acronyms such as BRICS (referring to the growing alliance of Brazil, Russia, India, China, and South Africa), MIST (the newest emerging market club of Mexico, Indonesia, South Korea, and Turkey), and CIVETS (the market alliance of Colombia, Indonesia, Vietnam, Egypt, Turkey, and South Africa). Their emergence portends a 'reversal of fortune' of the 'aging industrial powers of North America (and) Europe.'[42] The shift comes with the potential to destabilize typical and entrenched forms of neocolonial statist power. It represents, according to Jack Goldstone, a 'megatrend that will change the world.'[43] In its wake, we are beginning to see the development of new global networks of connections organized around new patterns of 'South–South' relations. The question is whether the ensuing freedom from neocolonial and imperial topographies of power comes with new opportunities for genuine development in the global South. Can it create conditions for new forms of governing practice that are freed from colonial and imperialist impositions?[44] The point here is not that the interests of these emerging multipolar centres of global and economic power predispose them to support conditions of development consistent with the expansion of rights and freedom. Their interests are inextricably tied to a newly reconstituted global capitalist economy characterized by increasing intensities in capital formation and transnational flows. But their relative weakness does restrict their capacities to impose conditions of governance on national apparatuses of authority. When this is combined with declining neocolonial power, it can open up spaces for genuine development, democracy, and freedom in the global South. There is the real possibility for these spaces to emerge in the confluences of a trifecta of the relative weakness of these emerging powers, Western relative decline, and the growing incapacity of national apparatuses of governance to exercise authority over segments of its people and swathes of its territory. If Goldstone is correct, then this 'megatrend' might offer up new opportunities for refashioning governing practice in ways that enhance the effective participation of the subaltern. It might provide unique opportunities for bringing into governing practice effective strategies for genuine development that are occurring outside of both state practices and processes and the authority of national governance. And it might allow for the expansion of capabilities that are instrumental for guarantees of political and economic rights.

Glocalization and Counter-Hegemonic Transnational Networks

My argument thus far is that opportunities for effective development and genuine democracy can be opened up by global processes and practices occurring outside of the space of governance, or by possibilities provided by global actors who are relatively free from the state effects of global capitalist power and from their capacity to impose their will on national apparatuses of governance. Such processes and practices are organized around counter-hegemonic transnational actors.

Transnational Social Movements

There are transnational social movements currently engaged in forms of 'counterhegemonic globalization.'[45] Their goal is the 'complex deterritorialization and reterritorializaton of political authority'. They provide examples where disengagement with global capital made possible by the 'megatrend' identified by Goldstone might allow spaces of possibilities for development transformation.[46] These movements are challenging the very hegemonic forces of transnational domination in which forms of representative democracy in the Caribbean are inscribed. Possibilities for democratic and development transformation at the local level may, in part, emerge through global alliances with these anti-capitalist forces.

Andreas Hernandez documents the emergence of the World Social Forum (WSF) as one such movement. Organized around an 'alternative vision' of social organization, the WSF serves as a counterweight to the World Economic Forum, the organization through which the global and national conditions of capital are coordinated.[47] As a 'global counter movement to neoliberalism' it sees one of its roles as connecting 'many of the most vital popular movements struggling against the neoliberal project.'[48] Many of these movements are mounting fundamental challenges to the materialist assumptions of capitalist production and consumption that undergird the logic of convergence with the North Atlantic adopted by the global South as the sole condition of development. Three of the most significant global movements with particular relevance for Caribbean freedom and development have been labour movements, women's movements, and environmental/indigenous movements.

Transnational Labour

Global labour movements are important to this analysis, not because of their currency in challenging global capital but because they provide a historical example of the possibilities to do so. The historical impact of global labour on the expansion of political and economic rights and capabilities for the Caribbean subaltern has been well documented and already discussed. Almost all of the leaders emerging during the first phase of West Indian nationalism successfully employed links to radical movements in Britain to support labour agitation in their respective territories. They successfully employed the class appeal of radical socialism to gain traction with the urban and rural colonized proletariat and peasantry. The liberatory potential of labour rested with its demonstrated and extant capacity for the global organization of workers as a counterforce to global capital. But its counter-hegemonic potential has been nearly eviscerated in the Caribbean through conscription into the project of global capital as an arm of party mobilization or by the state effects of technologies of discipline and control.

Transnational Women's Movements

Transnational women's movements have played significant roles in the expansion of political and economic rights in the Caribbean. Universally, networks organized around transnational feminism and employing 'class and gender struggles' have demonstrated their 'creative ability to transform and reinterpret (gender concepts) to fit local circumstances.'[49] Successful participation in these global networks by women in the region is evident in the growth in the number of women's organizations that are challenging the neocolonial script. They include the influential Red Thread Women in Guyana, engaged in mounting persistent challenges to statist forms of exception and exclusion. Quite important has been the penetration of feminist and gender struggles into the scholarship of the region. The establishment of the multi-campus Institute for Gender and Development Studies at The University of the West Indies is one particular outcome of these struggles. At the time of writing, a former director of this institute was the principal of the university's Cave Hill Campus. Another was deputy principal of its St Augustine Campus. And a third was the principal of the university's fourth campus that caters to students in countries of the region without a main campus. The female to male ratio of students enrolled in the university was 80:20 at the university's Mona Campus and 60:40 at its St Augustine Campus, attesting to the significant strides made in women's access to higher education. Women's access to rights have paid dividends in their increased representation in governance, including, at the time of writing, two prime ministers, one leader of the opposition, one former prime minister, one former executive president, and one former governor.[50] Notwithstanding these successes, the mere replacement of men by women does not necessarily signal economic or political transformation. As both Chandra Mohanty and Aihwah Ong have pointed out, global liberal feminist networks have done much to conscript women positioned in the upper and middle strata of the global South into the project of capitalist modernity.[51] It is only through women's engagement in counter-hegemonic global networks that new horizons of possibility for such transformation can emerge.

The Global Indigenous Movement

The global indigenous movement has also created new possibilities for expansion of rights to subaltern populations in Guyana, Dominica, and St Vincent and the Grenadines. Indigeneity, with its moral claim to territory, continues to act as a bulwark against the national apparatus of liberal representative democracy. In Dominica, Karifuna descendants of the indigenous Caribs inserted in regional networks of indigenous peoples in Latin America and the Caribbean have successfully challenged statist practices of exclusion, marginalization, and displacement in ongoing struggles for autonomy. They forced the country's courts to grant them exclusive occupation of a 'Carib Territory'.[52] Parallel movements have emerged among Carib-descended populations in St Vincent and the Grenadines. In 1999, nine indigenous groups in Guyana came together to formulate a comprehensive strategy to 'redefine prevailing political, legal, economic, and cultural relations with the state and thereby to transcend four centuries of colonial domination and institutionalized racism that *remain firmly entrenched in Guyanese law, policy, and practice'.*[53]

What these examples suggest is the possibility in the West Indies for 'a reinvigoration of the conditions by which local communities regain the power to determine and control their preferred economic and political paths.' It demands changes in governing democratic practice that allow people to 'control the conditions of their life'.[54] There are examples of these changes occurring everywhere through which those who are excluded by exception are creating opportunities for their democratic and developmental transformation. Journalist Dayo Olopade has identified new forms of social organization in Africa located outside of the forces of the state, nation, and capital.[55] People abandoned by national governments are becoming organized around family, innovative technology, sustainable use of the natural environment, alternative forms of commerce, and youth formations to 'map' new identities and communities consistent with the imperatives of development, rights, and freedom. Case studies in an edited volume by Philip McMichael document the struggles of local communities in Asia, Africa, and Latin America by people who are challenging national authorities and state processes and practices fashioned out of the forces of global capitalism.[56]

Informality, Entrepreneurship, and Development

These local struggles are ever-present in the Caribbean in the responses of the subaltern to crises. One almost universal example is the turn to informal entrepreneurship by members of the lower strata. This has been particularly evident when governing authority and the presences of global and national capital in the domestic economy have become constricted. Such constriction has opened up opportunities for the exercise of political and economic freedom formerly foreclosed by the legalities and practices of governance and by opposition from international and domestic capital.

In both Guyana and Jamaica beginning in the 1970s, excruciating foreign exchange shortages, the burden of foreign debt, and punitive measures imposed by bilateral and multilateral agencies placed severe constraints and restrictions on the capacity of the institutions of national governance to function effectively. The vacuum was filled, partly but significantly, by subaltern petty-traders organized in the informal sector through the use of networks of family ties and informal communication systems. Freed by social stigma from constraints of 'respectability', these traders effectively overcame the limitations of 'dispersed and unpredictable demand' and 'limited capital reserves' to meet pressing national needs. They were able to do so because of their 'political remoteness' from dependence on the state and their freedom from 'ethical constraints' imposed by middle and upper class morality that prevented the latter's participation in the informal (and illegal) sector. They were able to meet the demands of their countries' populations for essential products and foreign currency, both in short supply in the formal economy. The transnational networks in which these petty-traders are involved have become even stronger today with the enormous increases in the numbers of the overseas diaspora populations as the source of significant material transfers. These transfers are occurring outside of statist practice. The development of small-scale informal entrepreneurship has been much more significant for the enhancement of economic capabilities of the subaltern than efforts to do the same undertaken by the state. They have persisted and grown over the years. Petty trading has been much more successful than the state-dependent formal commercial sector in creating opportunities for 'effective development' of the lower strata. The informal economy has also provided means for assertions of the economic rights of subaltern women.[57]

While existing outside of the space of governing practice, petty traders and diaspora populations living abroad bring the concerns of those who are excluded and of those in the networks in which they participate into the arena of state decision-making.[58] This can offer significant opportunities for the reconstitution of governing practice when there is increasing dependence by the national governing apparatus and the local private sector on the global transfers in which they are engaged. In Guyana, for example, the trading practices of the subaltern and the transfers of financial and 'in kind' remittances from abroad through family and other effective networks have become critical to the country's economic functioning. They were directly responsible for the formation in 1983 of the Laparkan Group of companies, one of the few locally owned multi-national enterprises in the country. It is now the regional leader in freight and cargo services.[59]

Conclusion

Conditions of effective development can occur outside the framework of forms of liberal governance. These conditions are foreclosed when governance is instantiated in representative democratic practice. They are enhanced when and where the state effects of the entangled relationships with global topographies of power are minimal. Western liberal democracy and its Westminster version distort and render invisible the true conditions of global capitalist power by giving credence to the false notion of national sovereignty. This notion of national sovereignty serves as mere justification and legitimization for the entanglement of national authority in the network of global capital. Formed and fashioned in the crucible of the demand imposed by capitalist and pre-capitalist forms of global accumulation,[60] it renders invisible the very effects of state processes and practices on territories under national jurisdiction. It inscribes national forms of institutional authority, 'civil society', and localized social formations in the entangled relations of global state forces.

Genuine democracy and development rest with the possibilities for disentanglement and disarticulation from these global relationships. Political philosopher Thomas Pogge points to the injustice of 'the territorial state as the preeminent mode of political organization' because of its absolute power to 'check and dominate the decision-making of political subunits.'[61] For the purpose of this analysis, we need to emphasize the entangled relationships among the state, national authority, and local social formations and the absolute dependence of national governance upon global transfers. When such transfers are curtailed or diminished, it weakens the power of national authority to 'dominate decision making'. This is where spaces of possibility can open up for alternative visions of sovereignty. As centralized forms of national authority begin to lose their capacities to dominate decision-making, possibilities for transformation can emerge from the 'manifold and multiple selves' of the 'underdeveloped' through organization in 'localized, pluralistic grassroots movements' using 'local knowledge' and deploying 'popular power' in developing 'alternatives to development' that constitute a 'rejection of the entire paradigm itself.'[62] These movements may produce conditions, where, according to Pogge, people are able 'to govern themselves through a number of political units of various sizes without any one....occupying the traditional role of the state.' As such, 'political allegiance and loyalties [would] be widely dispersed over these units: neighborhood, town, country, province, state, region, and the world at large, without converging on any one of them as the lodestar of political identity.'[63] Pogge advances this as a means of accommodating the diversity of human reality and as a check on the global deployment of power in ways that can provide people with the right to participate equally in decision-making that affects their lives at any level. This is but one proposal to accommodate the form of democratic and developmental transformation consistent with the right to self-determination and to genuine 'development as freedom'. The goal here is to remove the constraints and limitations imposed by forms of statist processes and practice inscribed in neocolonial and imperialist cartographies of power. Changes in the global architecture of international relations discussed previously might offer up possibilities for such removal. Examples in the exercise of freedom as the condition of the right to development are opening up in spaces where the state effects of global capitalism are diminishing.

NOTES

1. A. Escobar, *Encountering Development: The Making and Unmaking of the Third World* (Princeton, NJ: Princeton University Press, 2011), 107–109.
2. J. Ferguson, *Global Shadows: Africa in the Neoliberal World Order* (Durham, NC: Duke University Press, 2006), 103–12.
3. A. Sen, *Development as Freedom* (New York: Anchor, 2000), xii, 4–5.
4. See, for example, the discussion of postcolonial practice and its relationship to economic development in N. Harris, *The End of the Third World: Newly Industrializing Countries and the Decline of an Ideology* (London: I.B. Tauris, 1986), chapter one.
5. Michel-Rolph Trouillot, 'The Anthropology of the State in the Age of Globalization', *Current Anthropology* 42, no. 1 (2001): 125–38 at 137.
6. W. Robinson, *Global Capitalism and the Crisis of Humanity* (New York: Cambridge University Press, 2014), 2.
7. See Ferguson's discussion of the relationship between time and status in development discourse in his *Global Shadows*, 176–82.
8. 'Glocalization' refers to the complex interaction of the local and the global and the fact that global processes always take place in specific contexts. See M. Steger, *Globalisms: The Great Ideological Struggle of the Twenty-First Century* (Lanham: Rowman and Littlefield, 2009), 42 and R. Robinson, 'Glocalization: Time-Space and Homogeneity-Hetereogeneity' in *Global Modernities*, ed. M. Featherstone et al., 25–44 (London: Sage, 1995).
9. Sen, *Development as Freedom*, 5.
10. By subaltern, I refer to social groups who are excluded from a society's established structures for political representation, the means by which people have a voice in their society.
11. I have taken the term 'exception' from Aihwa Ong, *Neoliberalism as Exception: Mutations in Citizenship and Sovereignty* (Durham, NC: Duke University Press, 2006). It refers to the practice of governing authorities to deny segments of the population access to the rights and benefits that they deserve as citizens. It also refers to the exemption of the privileged from legality and the rule of law.
12. In the Caribbean, politics are characterized by pervasive practices of vote-buying and clientelism, and in some cases even voter fraud (the latter most notably in Guyana). Prior to independence, constituencies in Guyana and Trinidad and Tobago were manipulated to ensure that representatives of the Creole middle and upper strata inherited colonial power. See P. Hintzen, *The Costs of Regime Survival: Racial Mobilization, Elite Domination, and Control of the State in Guyana and Trinidad* (Cambridge, MA: Cambridge University Press, 1989).
13. Ong, *Neoliberalism as Exception*, 5.

14. See, for example, C. Stone, *Class, Race, and Political Behaviour in Urban Jamaica* (Mona: ISER, 1973). For a modification of Stone's thesis see C. Edie, *Democracy by Default: Dependency and Clientelism in Jamaica* (Boulder, CO and Kingston: Lynn Rienner Publishers and Ian Randle Publishers, 1991).

15. Ferguson, *Global Shadows*, 89–99.

16. Ibid., 95–99.

17. S. Bergeron, *Fragments of Development: Nation, Gender and the Space of Modernity* (Ann Arbor, MI: University of Michigan Press, 2006), 31. See also J. Scott, *Seeing Like a State: How Certain Schemes to Improve the Human Condition Have Failed* (New Haven, CT: Yale University Press, 1998), 88.

18. This critique is reflected in Immanuel Wallerstein's assessment of the emergence of liberalism in chapter one of his *World-Systems Analysis: An Introduction* (Durham, NC: Duke University Press, 2004).

19. This is the fundamental point made in Ferguson, *Global Shadows*, 50–88.

20. Ibid., 93.

21. Ibid., 86.

22. Global feminists, for example, use universal forms of 'sister solidarity' to impose forms of feminism on the global South that legitimize and strengthen imperialist interventions. Diasporic populations in the global North use claims of 'ethnicity' to intervene in countries with which they have absolutely no connection, in ways that can jeopardize efforts at national reconciliation and accommodation (See Ong, *Neoliberalism as Exception*, 53–72). 'Human rights' groups can intervene in national conflicts as 'saviors' in ways that are totally inappropriate to the situation, violating rights of segments of populations, intensifying conflicts and creating conditions for the violation of state sovereignty. See M. Mamdani, *Saviors and Survivors: Darfur, Politics and the War on Terror* (New York: Random House, 2010).

23. For the general case, see *Contesting Development: Critical Struggles for Social Change*, ed. P. McMichael (New York: Routledge, 2010).

24. S. Howe, *Anticolonialism in British Politics: The Left and The End of Empire 1918–1964* (Oxford: Clarendon, 1993), 84–89.

25. See N. Bolland, *On the March: Labour Rebellions in the British Caribbean, 1934–39* (Kingston: Ian Randle Publishers, 1995) and C. Fraser, *Ambivalent Anticolonialism: The United States and the Genesis of West Indian Independence, 1940–1964* (Westport: Greenwood Press, 1994), 37–50.

26. P. Hintzen, 'Democratic Processes and Middle Class Domination in the West Indies', in *Democracy in the Caribbean: Myths and Realities*, ed. C. Edie (New York: Praeger 1994).

27. P. Hintzen, 'Reproducing Domination: Identity and Legitimacy Constructs in the West Indies', *Social Identities* 3, no. 1 (1997): 47–76.

28. See Hintzen, *The Costs of Regime Survival* and P. Hintzen and R. Premdas, 'Race, Ideology and Power in Guyana', *Journal of Commonwealth and Comparative Politics*, 21, no.2 (1983): 175–94.

29. Ibid.
30. Wallerstein, *World-Systems Analysis*, 84–88. See also A. Amsden, *Escape from Empire: The Developing World's Journey through Heaven and Hell* (Cambridge, MA: MIT Press, 2007), 103–114.
31. Hintzen, *The Costs of Regime Survival*, 142–50.
32. See ibid.; S. Ryan, *The Muslimeen Grab for Power* (Port of Spain: Inprint Caribbean, 1991); and S. Ryan, *Pathways to Power: Indians and the Politics of National Unity in Trinidad and Tobago* (St Augustine: ISER, 1996).
33. See P. Hintzen, 'Cheddi Jagan (1918–97): Charisma and Guyana's Response to Western Capitalism', in *Caribbean Charisma: Reflections on Leadership, Legitimacy, and Populist Politics*, ed. A. Allahar, 121–54 (Boulder, CO and Kingston: Lynn Rienner Publishers and Ian Randle Publishers, 2001).
34. Hintzen, 'Cheddi Jagan', 121–54.
35. See Stone, *Class, Race and Political Behaviour* and Edie, *Democracy by Default*.
36. See M. Manley, *Jamaica: Struggle in the Periphery* (London: Third World Media, 1983); M. Manley, *Up the Down Escalator: Development and the International Economy: A Jamaican Case* (Washington, DC: Howard University Press, 1987); and E. Stephens and J. Stephens, *Democratic Socialism in Jamaica* (Princeton, NJ: Princeton University Press, 1987).
37. See Ferguson, *Global Shadows*.
38. D. Harvey, *The Limits to Capital* (London: Verso, 2006), 411–51.
39. Ibid., 413–45.
40. Ferguson, *Global Shadows*, 38–42.
41. Ibid.
42. J. Goldstone, 'The New Population Bomb: The Four Megatrends that Will Change the World', *Foreign Affairs* 89, no. 1 (2010): 31–43.
43. Ibid., 31.
44. Ibid., 31–43.
45. P. Evans, 'Counterhegemonic Globalization: Transnational Social Movements in the Contemporary Global Political Economy', in *The Globalization and Development Reader: Perspectives on Development and Global Change*, ed. J. Timmons Roberts et al. 420–42 (Malden: Blackwell, 2007).
46. D. Held and A. McGrew, 'Towards Cosmopolitan Social Democracy', in *The Globalization and Development Reader, Perspectives on Development and Global Change*, ed. J. Timmons Roberts et al., 360–69 at 363 (Malden: Blackwell, 2007).
47. A. Hernandez, 'Challenging Market and Religious Fundamentalisms: The Emergence of Ethics, Cosmovisions, and Spiritualties in the World Social Forum', in *Contesting Development: Critical Struggles for Social Change*, ed. P. McMichael, 215–29 (New York: Routledge, 2010).
48. Ibid., 215–16.
49. Evans, 'Counterhegemonic Globalization', 431.

50. These figures apply at the time of writing in November 2014.

51. See C. Mohanty, '"Under Western Eyes" Revisited: Feminist Solidarity through Anticapitalist Struggles', in *Feminism without Borders: Decolonizing Theory, Practicing Solidarity*, ed. C. Mohanty, 331–51 (Durham, NC: Duke University Press, 2004), and Ong, *Neoliberalism as Exception*, 31–52.

52. C. Gregoire et al., 'Karifuna: The Caribs of Dominica', in *Ethnic Minorities in Caribbean Society*, ed. R. Reddock, 107–171 (St Augustine: ISER, 1996).

53. See J. La Rose and F. Mackay, 'Our Land, Our Life, Our Culture, The Indigenous Movement in Guyana', *Cultural Survival Quarterly* 23, vol. 4 (1999): 29–34. My italics.

54. J. Cavanagh and J. Mander, *Alternatives to Economic Globalization: A Better World is Possible* (San Francisco, CA: Berrett-Koehler, 2004), 146–63.

55. D. Olopade, *The Bright Continent: Breaking Rules and Making Change in Modern Africa* (Boston, MA: Houghton Mifflin Harcourt, 2014).

56. See the contributions to McMichael, *Contesting Development*.

57. From M. Edwards, *Jamaican Higglers: Their Significance and Potential* (Swansea: Centre for Development Studies, 1980), 58.

58. The real possibilities for transformation were observed by Deborah Thomas, *Modern Blackness: Nationalism, Globalization, and the Politics of Culture in Jamaica* (Durham, NC: Duke University Press, 2004). The manner in which statist discourse can conscript the diaspora into its agenda is discussed by P. Hintzen, 'Commentary on Berg's article "Homeland and Belonging among Cubans in Spain"', *The Journal of Latin American Anthropology* 14, no. 2 (2009): 293–96.

59. Taken from 'Laparkan' in West Indian Encyclopedia, westindianencyclopedia. com/wiki/Laparkan. Accessed 09/09/2014.

60. P. Lauren, *Power and Prejudice: The Politics and Diplomacy of Racial Discrimination* (Boulder, CO: Westview Press, 1996).

61. T. Pogge, *World Poverty and Human Rights* (Malden: Polity Press, 2008), 184.

62. Escobar, *Encountering Development*, 215.

63. Pogge, *World Poverty and Human Rights*, 184.

Contributors

Cynthia Barrow-Giles is Senior Lecturer in Political Science at the University of the West Indies, Cave Hill. Her most recent book, *Women in Caribbean Politics*, was published in 2010.

Bruce Golding served as the eigth Prime Minister of Jamaica from 2007–2011. A former Chairman of the Jamaica Labour Party (JLP), he left it in 1995 to lead the National Democratic Movement (NDM) until his return to the JLP in 2002.

Ralph Gonsalves has been the Prime Minister of St. Vincent and the Grenadines since March 29, 2001. He obtained undergraduate and postgraduate degrees from the University of the West Indies, Mona, and a PhD in Government from the University of Manchester, United Kingdom. He was a university lecturer and a practising lawyer in the Caribbean before becoming Prime Minister.

Clifford E. Griffin is Associate Professor of Political Science at North Carolina State University, who has published widely on democracy, political economy and security in the Caribbean. He is the co-author of the forthcoming *Historical Dictionary of US-Caribbean Relations*, 1st ed. (Rowman & Littlefield, 2017).

Percy C. Hintzen is Professor in the Department of Global and Sociocultural Studies and Director of the Africa and African Diaspora Studies Program at Florida International University, and Professor Emeritus at the University of California, Berkeley. He earned his PhD in Comparative Political Sociology from Yale University. His research and publications examine relationships among modernity, political economy, and the production of difference. His primary fields of enquiry are postcolonial studies, globalization, and development.

Derek O'Brien is Reader in Public Law at Oxford Brookes University. His most recent book is *The Constitutional Systems of the Caribbean* (2014).

Tennyson S.D. Joseph is a Senior Lecturer in Political Science and Head of the Department of Government, Sociology, Social Work and Psychology at the Cave Hill campus of the University of the West Indies. He is the author of *Decolonization in St. Lucia: Politics and Global Neo-Liberalism 1945–2010* (2011).

Patsy Lewis is Professor, Regional Integration and Small States Studies, at the University of the West Indies, Mona, and Visiting Professor of International and Public Affairs and Faculty Fellow, Watson Institute for International and Public Affairs, Brown University. Her latest book, co-edited with Gary Williams and Peter Clegg, is *Grenada: Revolution and Invasion*, (University of the West Indies Press, 2015).

Brian Meeks is Professor and Chair of Africana Studies at Brown University. He has published 11 books and edited collections. His most recent is *Critical Intervention in Caribbean Politics and Theory* (University of Mississippi Press, 2014).

Peter Phillips is Leader of the Opposition in Jamaica since April 2017. A Political Economist by training, he has served extensively in Parliament and Government – most recently as Minister of Finance. He is Member of Parliament for East Central St Andrew. Formerly, he was a member of the Faculty of Social Sciences, University of the West Indies, Mona and has published extensively on a wide range of Caribbean development issues.

Kate Quinn is Senior Lecturer in Caribbean History at the Institute of the Americas, University College London. Her most recent book is the edited volume *Black Power in the Caribbean* (University Press of Florida, 2014).

Index

Index

203

www.ingramcontent.com/pod-product-compliance
Lightning Source LLC
Chambersburg PA
CBHW071117280326

41935CB00010B/1042

9789766379568